WANNABE U

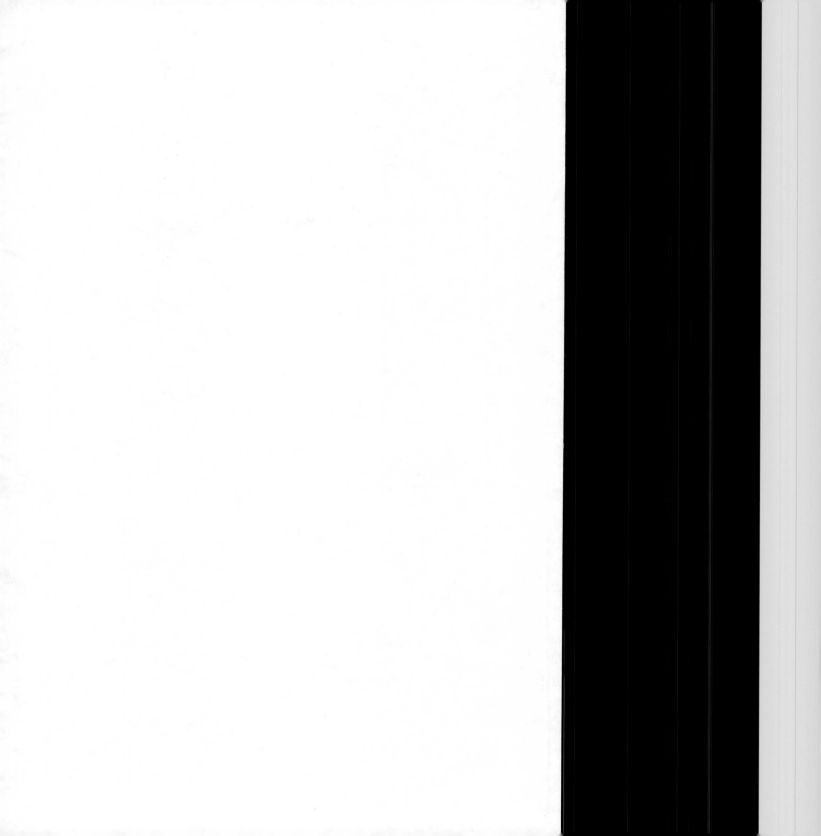

Wannabe U

INSIDE THE CORPORATE UNIVERSITY

Gaye Tuchman

THE UNIVERSITY OF CHICAGO PRESS

Chicago and London

GAYE TUCHMAN is professor of sociology at the University of
Connecticut. She is the author of *Making News: A Study in the
Construction of Reality* and *Edging Women Out: Victorian Novelists,
Publishers, and Social Change*; coeditor of *Hearth and Home: Images
of Women in the Mass Media*; and editor of *The TV Establishment:
Programming for Power and Profit*.

The University of Chicago Press, Chicago 60637
The University of Chicago Press, Ltd., London
© 2009 by The University of Chicago
All rights reserved. Published 2009
Printed in the United States of America

19 18 17 16 15 14 13 12 11 10 09   1 2 3 4 5

ISBN-13: 978-0-226-81529-9 (cloth)
ISBN-10: 0-226-81529-3 (cloth)

Library of Congress Cataloging-in-Publication Data

Tuchman, Gaye.
  Wannabe u: inside the corporate university / Gaye Tuchman.
      p.   cm.
  Includes bibliographical references and index.
  ISBN-13: 978-0-226-81529-9 (cloth: alk. paper)
  ISBN-10: 0-226-81529-3 (cloth: alk. paper)
  1. Universities and colleges—United States—Administration.
2. Universities and colleges—United States—Accounting.
3. Universities and colleges—United States—Business
management. 4. Universities and colleges—United States—
Faculty. 5. Universities and colleges—United States—Evaluation.
I. Title.
  LB2341.T774   2009
  378.1'010973—dc22

                    2009005076

♾ The paper used in this publication meets the minimum
requirements of the American National Standard for Information
Sciences—Permanence of Paper for Printed Library Materials,
ANSI Z39.48-1992.

In memory of Evelyn and Jack Tuchman,
who loved art, learning, and the beauty of ideas

Caught in the limited milieux of their everyday lives, ordinary men often cannot reason about the great social structures—rational and irrational—of which their milieux are subordinate parts. Accordingly, they often carry out series of apparently rational actions without any idea of the ends they serve. . . .

C. WRIGHT MILLS

. . . an educational philosopher might claim that those things of greatest value are precisely those things that cannot be measured. . . . If we cannot measure what is valuable, we will come to value what is measurable.

ROBERT BIRNBAUM

Contents

1: Wannabe University Is Transformed 1

2: Situating Wannabe U 25

3: Conforming, Branding, and Research 48

4: Outsiders and the New Managerialism 69

5: The Politics of Centralization 88

6: Teaching, Learning, and Rating 112

7: Carrots, Sticks, and Accountability 131

8: Plans and Priorities 152

9: Making Professors Accountable 173

10: The Logic of Compliance 192

Acknowledgments 211
Notes 213
References 235
Index 247

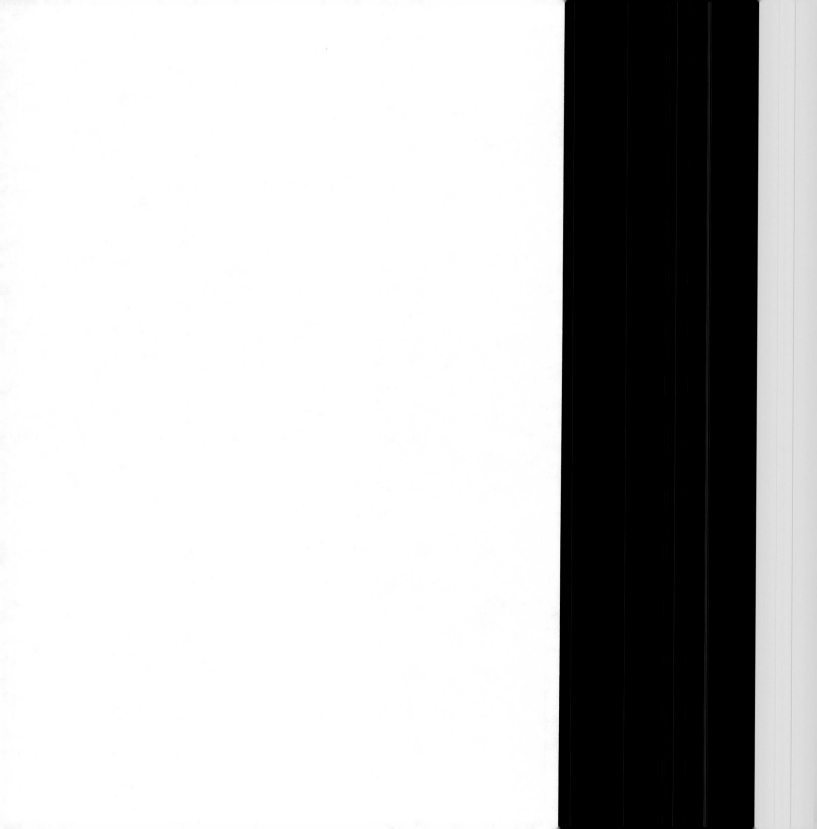

1

Wannabe University Is Transformed

"Make no mistake about it," James Whitmore, president of Wannabe University, announced to the two hundred people attending the retirement party for one of the university's lawyers. "This is a university in transformation." A few people smiled. Some clapped. For the past few years, the president had informed legislators, donors, trustees, members of the University Senate, parents—almost anyone whom he was invited to address—"This is a university in transformation."

Everyone at the reception had often heard the term "a university in transformation," but they probably shared little, if any, consensus about what that term meant. No one ever had the audacity to ask publicly, "Just what do you mean, President Whitmore?" Nor did or could anyone challenge that "it" was occurring, whatever it might be. When the president of Wannabe University said what the university was doing, one listened.

Now in the seventh year of his presidency, James Whitmore stood tall in the classic business wear favored by university administrators: a dark suit, well cut but not too fashionable, white shirt, conservative tie, more Brooks Brothers than Barneys. His hair was also conservatively cut, a few wisps of the gray-brown falling gently on his forehead. Handsome enough to be a United States senator, President Whitmore had arrived at the reception relatively late and had stood on line, waiting his turn to wish the retiring lawyer well. He had already served longer than the average term of the president of a public research university.

The crowd, almost as lily-white as Ashton, the home of Wannabe University, had arrived slowly and milled around the ballroom, named for a former chairperson of the university's board of trustees. The ballroom was large enough to hold twenty round tables, each seating ten people; several twenty-foot-long tables burdened with hors d'oeuvres; and a mingling crowd

smiling and unobtrusively reading one another's name tags—all punctu-
ated by student servers carrying trays of stuffed mushrooms and teeny en-
crusted hot dogs. Today, though, no one sat except a vice president in his
wheelchair. The long tables held trays of grapes, strawberries, and melon
balls; carrots and celery strips, some olives; slices of American and Swiss
cheese, crackers. The French doors to the twenty-by-twenty-foot alcove,
which sometimes served as a bar, were closed. Instead, the refreshment
tables also held glass pitchers of iced water and two large punch bowls filled
with a pinkish liquid that begged for lemon to diminish its sweetness.

The retiree had arrived early to greet his invited guests as they filtered
off the foyer elevator and stopped to pick up their name tags at the portable
institutional table hidden by a white institutional tablecloth. Almost all of
the guests knew the routine. Mainly administrators—some from the central administration, others from the schools and colleges, a few from the retiree's church—they had visited this hall for other receptions: retirements,
dinners for student athletes receiving academic awards, even the Sunday
brunch auction of the local chapter of a national women's service group.
Most had attended so many university receptions that they could glance at
the refreshments and calibrate the retiree's status at the university, just as
they could count the deans, associate provosts, department heads, and vice
presidents attending this party to gauge how much the lawyer mattered.

When a provost left the university and the central administration threw
a party, they knew, the refreshments were fancier. Those same student servers, but more of them, circulated with trays of scallops wrapped in bacon
or miniature Chinese scallion pancakes; tables were burdened with shrimp
and an assortment of soft cheeses; a silver-colored fountain spewed melted
chocolate, its base surrounded by trays of strawberries; and if the provost
had served the university for many years, the guests might even include
trustees, who would be formally welcomed by the president when he spoke.
(One never ignores the presence of the twenty-one members of the board
of trustees, twelve of whom were appointed by the governor. Students and
alumni elected their representatives to the board, and several state commis-
sioners held automatic seats on the board.)

There were no trustees today. But when the president had stood on the
snaking reception line, his mere presence had created a bit of a lump as
though the snake had ingested a meaningful meal, for many guests were as
dutiful about greeting President Whitmore as they were about greeting the
retiree. Some of his staff surrounded him on the line. Not the provost and
the vice provosts; they came and went independently, just as their offices
were on the ground floor and so separate from the (symbolically higher)
second-floor offices of the president, his "personal" assistants, the chief

financial officer, and the chief operating officer in Top Hall, the small building shared by the central administrators who mattered.

The most powerful of the president's staff—a man in his fifties, pale, suited but jacket unbuttoned, his hair blond-brown with the beginnings of a tonsure—shook hands with the social science professor immediately in front of him. "I'm Peter Lynch. I work with the president," he informed her. There would be no need to announce his identity and rank to administrators, not even department heads. They all knew who Peter Lynch was, but faculty members might not. For them, the transformation of the university meant less familiarity with central administrators, less of a say in university affairs, larger classes, more pressure to publish and get grants. Nonetheless, even the social science professor understood that Lynch's presence and the attendance of so many central administrators from Wannabe University's "non-academic" sector contradicted the budget for refreshments. The lawyer had apparently done his job well, devoting his last years at Wan U to assisting the push to improve the university or at least to increase its prestige. When he took the podium to address the guests, he spoke with sincerity: "I have no doubt that if I come back in ten years, Wan U will have risen in the rankings to be one of the great American universities."

The lawyer would not have to wait that long. In the tenth year of his presidency, at a reception honoring the founding of Wan U, President Whitmore announced: "This university has been transformed." Now the guests were seated in a long rectangular room in one of the older buildings on campus, the white gold-domed ex-library that currently housed such administrative officers as the vice provost for enrollment management and the vice president for student affairs, and offices that "processed students," such as the Office of the Registrar, the Office of Student Financial Aid Services, and the Office of the Dean of Students. On this occasion, the audience included people from more of the university's constituency, several specially invited students, some administrators, some faculty (mainly those active in the University Senate and a few department heads), a few alumni, two trustees, and the families of speakers. When the town's mayor, the state historian, and a black alumnus delivered their addresses, they too affirmed that this "transformed" university is a special place.

Unfortunately, neither the president nor the other speakers fully explained what they meant by "transformation." Rather they cited a series of "measurements," what the university website and a provost's presentation to the board of trustees were eventually to call "Points of Pride": Students included more valedictorians and salutatorians than ever before; the freshman class had higher scores on the Scholastic Aptitude Test than previous classes; more underrepresented minorities were enrolled; student retention had increased. Some faculty had received million-dollar research grants. The university had achieved a higher ranking in the annual college edition of *U.S. News & World Report*. (Although those rankings have neither a solid theoretical or methodological basis, administrators care about those rankings, because potential students and their parents consult them to plan college applications. Improvement in those rankings influences the flow of applications [Monks and Ehrenberg 1999; Stevens 2007].)[1]

At least one faculty member wondered about this litany of accomplishment. What about how the basic processes associated with education had changed? Was the focus on education or more efficient management? What about the presence of more and more managerial personnel and the increased centralization of administration, the interminable forms, the emergence of the university as an explicitly capitalist institution weighing revenue streams and seemingly paying more attention to the components of the university that brought revenue, such as the dining halls and cafeterias, rather than those that did not support themselves, such as the counseling services for students with "personal problems"?[2] What about the ever-larger classes and the increased pressure on faculty to engage in funded research?

These processes of centralization, bureaucratization, and commodification seemed as crucial to the transformation of Wannabe University as the "Points of Pride" proclaimed by President Whitmore, perhaps even more so, for they had a direct impact on the work environment, particularly its atmosphere. But even though a fundamental change in institutional processes is central to the transformation of a university, President Whitmore stuck to the sorts of quantified accomplishments that seemed to express such basic American ideological themes as "With hard work, anyone can join the ranks of the elite" and "We can achieve prosperity through education." I will consider these themes later in this chapter and the processes of centralization, bureaucratization, and commodification in later chapters. For now, I note that President Whitmore was using the language of the managerial literature about higher education and that he was bold to declare that Wan U was participating in "institutional transformation."

INSTITUTIONAL TRANSFORMATION

In the literature about higher education that seems designed for college administrators, such terms as "institutional transformation" and "university in transformation" have a specific meaning. They refer to profound change, as defined by Eckel and his colleagues, who studied twenty-six colleges or universities seeking to transform themselves (Eckel, Hill, and Green 1998: 3;

cf. Eckel and Kezar 2003: 17; Keup et al. 2001). That definition asserts that "institutional transformation"

1 alters the culture of the institution by changing select underlying assumptions and institutional behaviors, processes, and products;
2 is deep and pervasive, affecting the whole institution;
3 is intentional; and
4 occurs over time.[3]

Thus, when President James Whitmore first declared Wannabe University to be a university in transformation and then proclaimed it to be a university that had transformed itself, he had implicitly asserted that the administration had purposively altered the university's culture, assumptions, behaviors, processes, and products. That is indeed a bold claim, especially because it is so difficult to define the culture of a large American university and to streamline its often cumbersome processes.

To understand the problem of change, one must understand something of how American universities work. As Clark (2004: 133) explains:

> The American system of higher education . . . combines very large size, extreme decentralized control, great institutional diversity, sharp institutional competition and substantial status hierarchy. Its most important feature is the radical disbursement of authority. It is a system composed both of major private sectors, in which over 2,000 private universities and colleges of all sizes operate under individual boards of control, devising their own viable niches, and of numerous public sectors in which another 1,600 institutions fall primarily under the 50 states rather than under the national government.

They all must respond to national policies, such as those governing student loans, research grants, and minority admissions. But, Clark (1983) says, they develop their own responses.

The structure of nonprofit institutions of higher education is also decentralized.[4] To be sure, there is a central administration that reports to some sort of board of trustees, managers, or overseers. At some institutions, the central administration has much authority, at others less. The kind and amount of authority exerted by that central administration expresses itself in such crucial matters as appointing and tenuring staff and planning and executing budgets, although it affects less controversial matters as well. Conflicts between the central administration and the faculty are endemic to American universities, as discussed by Thorstein Veblen (1918), almost a hundred years ago.

On the whole, whether they are organized into academic departments or colleges, professors tend to be oriented toward their discipline. Mostly, members of disciplinary departments and colleges are oriented toward their professional colleagues and professional associations, as well as the logic implicit in their area of expertise. Many of them see administrators as "mere" managers, whose activities should serve such "core academic values" as advancing knowledge for its own sake. (Many managers perceive this disdain and resent it.) To be sure, many scientists do not understand the concerns of professors in the humanities or social sciences and vice versa; their last exposure to one another's areas of expertise and concern may have been the general-education courses required of undergraduates. Conflicts may also arise between professors working in professional schools, such as business and law schools, and those in the liberal arts and sciences. However, as different as their disciplines may be, professors tend to believe that their activities are the crux of higher education.

Conversely, administrators tend to believe that their own activities define the essence of the university. They see the world in radically different terms than faculty do. Where a professor may define a grant as the funds that enable research and support graduate students, an administrator may see a revenue stream. "Instead of being arms of the state, or representatives of the professors, [administrators] are, in pure form, the leaders—'captains'—of autonomous enterprises" (Clark 1983: 209). Instead of engaging in the competition of discovery, "their efforts on behalf of the welfare of individual institutions leads toward market-like interactions in which competition is the catalyst for change" (209). They may disdain individual professors or even the professoriate as unrealistic or unworldly. For instance, when administrators "decided to grow the undergraduate enrollment"—to invoke the business language that one provost customarily used when speaking to the board of trustees—professors created a hew and cry for additional faculty appointments. However, central administrators may find such desires naive. From their point of view, one can always squeeze another student in a lecture hall (if one has enough large lecture halls and the additional students are not seriously inflating the faculty-student ratio and so affecting a school's competitive edge over other colleges and universities). However, every additional hundred students may mean one has to hire another librarian, additional servers in the dining halls, and additional janitors, as well as to find additional spaces for beds.[5] At Wannabe University, the chief financial officer has calculated such formulas innumerable times. As an administrator experienced with budgets explained, professors "have no appreciation for the mechanics" of running a university.

The central administration is oriented toward its competition with other institutions for students and for potentially profitable inventions (intellectual property) that may become technology transfers (an invention that moves from the university to the corporate sector ideally bringing profit to all; see Powell and Grodal 2005; Slaughter and Leslie 1999; Slaughter and Rhoades 2004; Etzkowitz, Webster, and Healey, 1998). It may also be oriented toward such auxiliary revenue streams as athletics, theatrical performances, and even the economics of managing the university as a city (such as its police and fire departments, its "town green" or student union, and even its restaurants and hotels, more properly identified as student cafeterias and dormitories).[6]

In essence, conflict is built into the university system, and that profound conflict affects the ability of a university to make profound changes. In the post–World War II environment, change within universities was generally "incremental, disjointed, contradictory and opaque" (Clark 1983: 8, 9). In the present environment, conflicts between administrators and professors may be more acute, for many who study higher education believe that now central administrators can only achieve meaningful change if the faculty cede some power (see, e.g., Clark 1998, 2004)—or, as others imply (Rhoades and Sporn 2002a, 2002b), if administrators simply centralize power. To attempt the transformation of a university is thus a complex and daring endeavor.

WANNABES, RANKINGS, AND THE MARKET ETHOS

James Whitmore did not introduce the idea of transforming Wannabe University. Nor did he introduce the "market ethos" (Karabel 2005) that faculty claimed to be characteristic of Wan U at the turn of the twenty-first century.[7] Often invoked, but rarely defined, that "market ethos" is said to involve the transformation of educational values into business values, including the imposition of hierarchical bureaucratic organization on the faculty. Before President Whitmore's arrival, Wan U was a respectable, regional research university. (In chapter 2, I will present a fuller description of Wan U.) Current administrators seem to agree that the state, the university, and its administrators had been late to join the national push to "rise" in such national standings as the annual rankings published by *U.S. News & World Report*. Similarly, they had been slow to respond to the relative diminution of legislative contributions to the university's general fund. To be sure, in the mid-1990s, state contributions were 35 percent of the operating budget, while some flagship universities in the West and Midwest limped along with state contributions of less than 20 percent. But Wan U did experience a financial pinch: its share of the state's general-fund budget had been cut almost in half—from 2.5 percent in the mid-1980s to 1.47 percent in the mid-1990s. That financial pinch was discussed in the business jargon associated with the market ethos, as administrators and trustees searched for new "revenue streams" and plumbed "key revenue drivers."

Being a late starter is often seen as a disadvantage. Wan U's trustees and administrators sought to turn it into an advantage. As administrators explained, they hoped to benefit from the experiences of other research universities that had gotten a head start. Through trial and error, others might discover best practices, and Wan U could learn from their successes and their mistakes. Indeed, Wan U's administrators brought back from conferences and seminars news about the "best practices" that other schools reported or that the committees of professional associations recommended.[8]

President Whitmore's predecessor, Ned Oakes, was often credited with beginning "to position" Wan U to claim a higher spot in the "substantial status hierarchy" (Clark 1983) of research universities. Perhaps because he loved athletic competitions, Oakes had identified athletics as what those who study higher education call "a lever of change."[9] (Oakes took a daily run around campus with the men's basketball coach, trying to match the taller man's strides. He also invited the coach and a key player to a reception for trustees.) With his ally, the director of athletics, Oakes encouraged his coaches to build teams that attracted national attention, such as in the supposedly revenue-bearing sports of basketball and football. Their success made the university seem to be more prominent. (At least it received more free publicity in the sports section of newspapers and on TV.) Also, both the director of athletics and President Oakes felt that success would "grow" ticket sales. Increased demand would mean that the price of basketball and football tickets could be raised.

Athletic success seemed to facilitate other changes. The legislature expanded the university's capital budget. Under the aegis of Oakes and a politically connected chairman of the board of trustees, Wan U had begun an ambitious construction program.[10] Even the membership of its board of trustees seemed to change. Successive members and chairmen seemed more cosmopolitan and less like the local boosters about whom the mammoth book of regulations of the National Collegiate Athletic Association insistently warns. The board's enthusiastic appointment of James Whitmore to his third college presidency seemed a logical next step in Wan U's campaign to fight its way to national prominence. After all, Whitmore was what the former provost of Tufts University calls "a professional president" (Gittelman 2004), one of those administrators who spent some years at one university before leaving for another supposedly better university, much as accomplished executives might jump from corporation to corporation

(Khurana 2002).[11] Dr. Whitmore had served in government, had political skills, was appreciative of corporate needs, and even was a member of the same political party as the governor. When James Whitmore was hired, Wan U was potentially positioned to join the ranks of the wannabes.

Although he reported to the trustees, who were themselves responsible to the governor and the legislature, President Whitmore was never foolish enough to announce that he intended to challenge the power of the faculty. From the first, he expressed appreciation of the faculty, his determination to support research, his wish to attract good students, and his desire to serve the state. Mainly, though, he talked about how Wannabe University was going to become one of the best research universities in the United States—a national, not a regional institution.

That theme, entering the "Top Twenty-five," was so ubiquitous that it almost seemed as though President Whitmore had found a way to discuss transformation that did not even hint at topics that might prompt the slightest conflict with the faculty. Professors also treasured being in the top twenty-five—preferably even higher. At Wan U, as at other universities, professors liked to boast of the status of their department in the disciplinary hierarchy. "Our psychology department is one of the sixteen best psychology departments in the United States," a professor might say. Or, when describing the university to a colleague teaching elsewhere, a professor might announce, "We have a particularly good psychology department and our biology departments are very good, too." Indeed, at first blush, the administrative and political decision for this state university to join the ranks of wannabes seemed simply an expression of its American identity. If one cannot be recognized as the best of all, then certainly one can aspire to be ranked at number twenty-five.

This celebration of top rankings is so ubiquitous that being "best" has become an American mantra—whether the topic under discussion is the Nielsen ratings, the weekend movie box-office take, the weekly Associated Press poll of college basketball or football rankings, or the yearly parade of singers on *American Idol*. At sports event after sports event, the fans sitting in the $100 seats and the $10 seats raise aloft an enlarged Styrofoam hand molded in team colors, its upright index finger gesturing "We're No. 1." As television cameras turn toward the fans, some scream, "Number one, number one." At other games involving lesser teams with problematic win-loss records, ambitious fans can only root for their team to enter the top twenty-five. Furthermore, being best or even near-best is fraught with meaning: in a particularly famous television commercial, the rental-car company Avis reported, "We try harder," because its volume of business was lower than that of industry leader Hertz.[12]

Rankings seem pertinent to higher education, because so many colleges and universities are chasing a higher rung in such national rankings as the *U.S. News & World Report*.[13] So many higher-education institutions present themselves as wannabes. Thus, when I told higher-education scholar Gary Rhoades that I was planning to write an ethnography of a wannabe university, he reminded me just how prevalent wannabes are: "A few years ago, I heard a fellow from a small public regional college in [the West] describe, with bitter disdain in his voice, how a new president at his institution had said that the college was going to become the 'Harvard of the [local] Valley.' :-)" (e-mail, May 12, 2006).[14]

The *Chronicle of Higher Education* concurs. It reported (Arnone 2003), "Whether driven by idealism, need, or greed, many universities have jumped on the bandwagon heading toward national recognition. . . . Aiming to become a national name-brand university," to be number one, the wannabes underestimate the difficulty of advancing up the educational ranks. "Ambition and arithmetic . . . are bound to collide because the number of aspiring institutions far exceeds the slots at the top of any ranking. No matter how hard how they try, 100 universities can't squeeze into the top 20."

Not every runner can come in first. Not every team can be the best. But every runner and every team can try to be number one. Sometimes, though, trying one's best may not be enough. Like other sectors in American society, higher education is highly stratified. A high ranking on the *U.S. News & World Report*'s "America's Best Colleges" seems to be associated with such American values as elite status and selectivity (MacTaggart 2007). "Elite" is a reference to social class, as is selectivity. Students from wealthy backgrounds are likely to attend expensive private residential colleges that have low acceptance rates, high "yield rates" (the percentage of accepted applicants who choose to attend a school that accepted them), and a high percentage of students graduating in four years (Attewell and Lavin 2007; cf. Stevens 2007). Indeed, such elite private universities as Princeton, Harvard, Yale, Stanford, and Duke sit solidly on or near the top of the *U.S. News & World Report*'s rankings of national universities. The highest-rated public university, University of California, Berkeley, does not poke through until number twenty-one. Nonetheless, both public and private colleges and universities compete to achieve higher rankings, as though they were competing for an athletic championship.

The competition of wannabes for a high ranking on the currently fashionable measuring stick may seem gamelike, but this competition is not a game. It does not involve "play," but is rather a dead-serious business enterprise. (Some scholars also argue that national sports championships are dead-serious business enterprises [Shulman and Bowen 2002; Bowen et al.

2003; Zimbalist 1999].) Rather, the search for recognition is an expression of business values that have become increasingly common in institutions of higher education. Some critics claim that rather than defining higher education as the development of critical thinking, the nurturing of civic responsibility, or the pursuit of knowledge—perhaps even knowledge for its own sake—contemporary colleges and universities see the purpose of education in more practical terms, such as preparing students for jobs (also known as "workforce development"). Furthermore, these critics continue, contemporary universities define both knowledge and job preparation as commodities, whose transmission is purchased by student customers (and their parents), when they pay tuition, room, board, and other fees. Increasingly, they also see themselves as a business. Thus, *Newsweek* quoted the provost of a wannabe university as saying, "We are a business. . . . Our shareholders are the faculty, the students and the state" (quoted in Kirp et al. 2003: 4). According to this view, education has become a market transaction.

Put somewhat differently, it is almost as though twenty-first-century higher education echoes Max Weber's characterization of the spirit of "modern capitalism." Weber wrote of the spirit of early twentieth-century capitalism: "Man is dominated by the making of money, by acquisition as the ultimate purpose of his life. Economic acquisition is no longer subordinated to man as the means for the satisfaction of his material needs" (Weber 1958: 53). Rather than making a profit being subordinated to man, man is subordinated to making a profit.

Universities appear to have undergone a similar inversion. As Roger Geiger (2004: 25) has observed, "A new standard of economic rationality . . . [pervades] . . . university decision-making." Rather than universities being subordinated to the production and transmittal of knowledge, knowledge is now subordinated to the needs of universities for profit and recognition. Seeking profit, the central administration engages in a "new managerialism" that undercuts faculty authority by implementing change from the top down. Chasing a sterling reputation, central administrators seemed to ask what they needed to say to garner approval. To some faculty, they seemed more concerned with the "image" used to market their product (a university education) to customers (students and their parents) and clients (the firms that would hire the university's graduates) than with the product itself.[15]

Our society has wedded the gamelike obsession with "achieving a high ranking" to higher education's market ethos. That marriage thrusts Wannabe University, like many other contemporary institutions, into an "audit society"—what Michael Power (1997) discusses as an "organizational order" linking governance and internal control systems through the new managerialism. As I argue in chapter 2, the "audit society" enables "coercive accountability" carried out in the guise of transparency, trust, and public service. As an organizational order, the audit society is dedicated to encouraging organizations (including governments) and their members to measure their aspirations, fears, and accomplishments against the hopes, worries, and activities of peers and competitors and to accept that those measurements have consequences. It entails both forced and voluntary surveillance, as individuals and organizations audit themselves and subject themselves to audit by others. Of course, to do so, they must make both their organizations and themselves auditable. That is, they must transform both their organizations and themselves into entities that can be defined, delineated, and measured. That transformation and the coercive accountability associated with both an audit society and its culture helps to constitute an *accountability regime*—a politics of surveillance, control, and market management disguising itself as the value-neutral and scientific administration of individuals and organizations.[16]

From Socrates to Freud, Western society has praised self-examination. The audit society might seem to be the apotheosis of self-examination, because it celebrates order and control through self-analysis. But this self-examination is antithetical to Socrates' famous pronouncement "The unexamined life is not worth living." Socrates' notion of self-examination stressed asking oneself about the ethical principles guiding one's actions. Audit does not assess how actions match ethical or philosophic principles. It is rather *a ritual of verification measuring if and how institutions and individuals have conformed to agreed-upon procedures of self-policing.* Besotted with these rituals, an audit society transforms itself into an accountability regime, where honor does not reside in a principled life but in being number one—or at the very least being in the top twenty-five.

WANNABES, RESEARCH, EDUCATION, AND THE STATE

Although the administration of Wannabe University, like that of other aspiring educational institutions, seems to speak more about status, rankings, and other points of pride than about knowledge, it is unfair merely to dismiss its attempt at transformation as ill-conceived ambition. Rather, Wannabe University has additional goals. These also resonate with American cultural themes. Most important is the vaunted association between education and economic advancement.

Officially, Wannabe University was to transform itself to solve a dilemma confronting its state. As the governor and key legislators declared in the state's newspapers: Too many students were leaving the state to get a college education elsewhere, and then they were failing to return. Indeed, more high school graduates left than returned. Like the countries that sent waves of students to the graduate science departments of Wan U, the state was experiencing a brain drain. The answer a powerful legislator had proposed was to improve the university. The availability of an excellent education (with a relatively low in-state cost) might diminish the brain drain, especially the departure of the best students. Also, through excellence in public higher education, the state might increase its prosperity. Indeed, perhaps the new mottos for the state might be "Through education, prosperity" and "Through higher rankings in the national education arena, even more prosperity." Here, too, the university was conjuring up American themes: Education may enable individual mobility. It may also facilitate industrial growth. An educated workforce serves industry. Industry requires educated and diverse employees, qualified to compete in the global economy.[17]

As discussed in public at least, all other goals were ancillary, seemingly designed to serve that primary goal of attracting the state's college students and fostering economic development. Such subsidiary activities might include raising more research monies by winning more grants and contracts, licensing the patents derived from faculty research, increasing the take from such auxiliary activities as athletic games and theatrical performances, improving the academic qualifications of high school students who apply for admission, and even marketing the ever-popular Wan U ice cream. I do not know whether university administrators and legislative leaders had concrete plans to achieve any of these goals. Although the department heads annually informed their faculty that funds were tight because of budget cuts, the administration and trustees certainly did not confide their fiscal plans to professors. Even the budget summary available to the trustees cut a sufficiently broad swath to conceal some specifics. For instance, an informant told me that the university spent more on improving the conditions for research animals than it did on counseling services for students, but I could neither confirm nor reject that claim from the summary data presented to trustees.

Search committees and trustees must have asked about fiscal matters, including revenue streams, when they interviewed candidates for university president. Certainly, they knew that the more monies raised through research, the more prestigious the university seemed to be and the less it might depend on state funds, which were becoming an ever-smaller percentage of its expanding budget. The better the university's key athletic teams, then the more ancillary income and national publicity generated; also the more applications for admission (including out-of-state applicants who would pay a higher tuition), the more selective the university could become. Even a university president who wasn't particularly fond of sporting events and often gave his basketball tickets to friends was enthusiastic about the institutional possibilities inherent in sports acclaim. All of these goals might help the university to climb up the national rankings, to transform itself from a regional to a national university.

Wan U did not officially declare itself to be on the path to national acclaim in order to halt the brain drain and improve the state's economy—although the state newspapers reported that the legislature felt that a flagship university with higher national status might serve those purposes. When President Whitmore first arrived, he had not proclaimed the motto "Through education, prosperity"—although rumors circulated through the liberal arts faculty that this new president was "oriented toward business" rather than toward "core academic values." Across departments, professors informed one another that President Whitmore had talked about alliances with business when he was introduced to the University Senate. At his inauguration, Whitmore emphasized both academic values and service to the state by educating people of all backgrounds and incomes and developing partnerships with such state institutions as businesses. Whitmore simultaneously affirmed: "Nothing is more important to the quality of life in this state than educational excellence. Nothing is more important to [this state's] economic development."[18]

The president's goals were to develop a university recognized across the nation for the excellence of its programs, the commitment of its faculty, and dedication to its students. He wanted

- a university that serves as [the state's] prime resource of excellence in a wide range of areas—from fine arts to the liberal arts, from social sciences to basic sciences;
- a university open to individuals of talent and aspiration who will, with the education they receive here, help build a better [state];
- a university that stands as the willing partner to the major institutions and enterprises of this state as we help [this state] move into the next chapter of a long and proud history.

As President Whitmore spoke, he positioned the university as an institution on the cusp of greatness:

I came to [this state] . . . firmly convinced that no public university in the United States is better positioned to improve, and improve dramatically, the level of excellence, access, and service it offers. I retain that conviction. [Wannabe

University] has been an important university for many decades. Now it has the potential to become a *great* university—one of the handful of public institutions that define what a state can do when it makes a commitment of resources and a commitment of will.

President Whitmore was also positioning the university as a wannabe. In his speeches and presumably in his discussions with legislators, donors, trustees, other administrators, and even some faculty, he aligned his ambitions for the university with the characteristics of a wannabe university.

As the *Chronicle of Higher Education* (Arnone 2003) has explained, a wannabe university yearning for recognition and approvals

1 wants to "translate a strong regional presence into national recognition and respect";

2 "push[es] . . . to spend hundreds of millions of dollars on new construction, while hiring well-known faculty members and recruiting top students";

3 develops "a slick advertising campaign . . . [that] portray[s] the institution . . . as being on the cusp of greatness";

4 speaks of aspirations "into the top [rankings] of the National Research Council [and] *U.S. News and World Report*"; and

5 explains that "becoming a national research university [is] vital to . . . [its] mission," since its region needs more research universities that act as engines for state economies."

At the height of ambition, it even

6 "dream[s] of nurturing the start-up companies for the next Silicon Valley or Research Triangle Park."

The central administration of Wan U, the trustees, the legislature, the governor, and some of the faculty lusted after fame, funding, and power.

A NOTE ON METHODS

Decades before this book was even a glimmer in my imagination, I had made the acquaintance of Wannabe University sociologists at professional meetings. We had delivered papers on the same panels. We had served together on committees and editorial boards. In the mid-1990s, like others, I was told that Wannabe University was transforming itself. By 2003, I was hearing tales of tension, conflict, and dissent: professors in four departments in the social sciences were feuding so badly that their departments might go into receivership. (The term "receivership" means that a department has lost its right to self-governance and the dean has appointed a senior professor from another discipline as its head.) People in two departments in the humanities appeared to have "arranged themselves into two camps"; some were barely talking to one another. Program reviews, some people told me, had exacerbated departmental conflicts, and in one or two cases had introduced conflicts where none had apparently existed. Other departments, I learned, had been promised specific resources as a result of favorable program reviews but had never received them, even when those promises were in writing.

I have always been interested in university politics, including how academic departments function. One must have a minimal interest in this topic to work in a university. So in 2003, after receiving approval to study Wannabe University from my university's institutional review board, I began interviewing key professors in the four social science departments that were supposedly being rent by dissent. I interviewed some of them over the phone and some in person. I took notes on these and other conversations I had with people who worked at Wannabe University, but as my university's institutional review board had specified, I never taped or took pictures of anyone or anything on the campus. I also started reading both the sociological literature and the management literature on higher education, as well as studies in the sociology of organizations. I assumed that the management literature presented a picture of how administrators think. I found that portrait of administrative thinking particularly valuable, since I had decided not to interview many high-level administrators. (I was, though, a faithful member of the audiences that central administrators addressed, charmed, and cajoled, and I did have regular interactions with several of them.)

The more I read and talked to people, the more I became convinced that an observational study of Wannabe University was a viable project. However, that decision created some problems. I knew that the reception of ethnographies had included attempts to identify their locale and even the identity of the people discussed in the book. The reception of Arthur Vidich and Joseph Bensman's *Small Town in Mass Society* is a famous case in point. Townspeople inscribed their pseudonyms in the Vidich and Bensman book on signs, hung the signs on themselves, and then held a parade.

Accordingly, to behave ethically, since 2003 whenever anyone has asked me the topic of my current research, I have explained that I am studying the transformation of Wannabe University. With each passing year, this project has become more real to me, and I have become more forthright about my research. As a result, social scientists familiar with participant observation have become quite careful about what they have said in front of me. People in the humanities, sciences, and professions have not been as careful as the qualitative social scientists. Some administrators even forgot a cardinal political rule: Say only as much as you need to say.

I have also tried to impede efforts at identifying my informants. So that my informants will not be placed in a difficult position, I am careful about both whom I quote and how I describe people. I have promoted some people by identifying associate deans as deans and I have demoted other people. To confuse matters more, now and again I used someone's correct title. I have not quoted my close friends. Nor have I quoted the sociologists who work at Wannabe University. Instructing me never to quote her, one sociologist suggested that Wannabe administrators would not be happy about my book and joked: "You may intend to retire when this book is published, but I do not." The comment of a white man who read part of a chapter for me indicated I was having some success at hiding identities. "That description was right on," he said. "Glad you thought so," I replied. "I was quoting you."

To protect informants, I have also avoided analyzing some topics, though information about them pops up here and there. Specifically, I have not discussed athletics. I have not analyzed the problems that women in the administration and on the faculty have faced at Wannabe University. Nor have I addressed the problems of people of color. Both women and members of racialized ethnicities face real problems. Quite a few men in the administration told me that Wan U is a difficult place for a woman to work. None of them was quite sure why, although a middle manager pointed to the "male" atmosphere—the pat on the back or the squeeze of the shoulder with which men greeted each other as they walked into a meeting. Sometimes women faculty spoke about how they coped with what they viewed as unequal treatment, from lower "merit raises" to the assignment of courses that their male colleagues viewed as not so important—or at least not as important as the courses that the men taught.

People of color frequently felt isolated. "When I came here over thirty years ago," an African American said at her retirement party, "there were very few of us and we were very isolated, each in a silo, one to a building at most." Many of those buildings are still in use. However, since some of today's new buildings are larger than those of the 1970s, that generalization does not hold as much. Nonetheless, it would be very difficult for me to quote any person of color on the Wan U campus without making her or him identifiable. To take a glaring example, were I to write about the perceptions and problems of an African-born professor or a librarian from India, people at Wannabe University would have a pretty good idea whom I was discussing. So even though I have heard professors use the word "racist" to describe a colleague, an administrator, or a situation, I have elected to avoid the topic of racialized ethnicity. However, here and there, an example involving this topic appears, just as I occasionally mention the Division of Athletics and its teams.[19]

In 2003 I also began participant observation of the meetings of important groups, especially those of the trustees. By 2004 I expanded my work by gaining access to college and university committees, whose meetings I observed. By fall 2006 I was observing six important committees, as well as the University Senate. I also observed a couple of executive committees. My notes are different from the official minutes of the committees that I observed. For instance, at meetings of the board of trustees, I kept track of how the president and the chairman of the board addressed people, who interrupted whom, and who held sufficient power or felt sufficiently powerful to interject jokes in their own comments.[20]

In general, I have tried to follow the journalistic practices I learned while doing research for my book *Making News*. Because I was attending so many meetings, more professors and administrators shared information with me. A few people made a special point of giving me information about professors and administrators whom they did not like. I analyzed their information the same way I analyzed other information. Two people whom I believed were in a position to know about a specific topic had to confirm salient details of meetings and actions when I had not observed those meetings or actions myself. When I did not have two sources for critical statements, I kept a record of negative comments so that I could get a better sense of the fault lines at the university. (I also discovered that a few professors in the so-called "dysfunctional departments" were keeping records about one another in case they ever wanted to lodge a formal complaint.) In addition, I wrote down the comments made by people whom I encountered when, say, I attended a dinner party or went to the supermarket in Ashton. I have *not* interviewed current administrators, though I did feel free to ask them informal questions when I encountered them on campus or at committee meetings. On the whole, even though I have done my best not to quote friends or sociologists and to mask people's identities, I have followed a key rule: "Everything's data unless it will harm someone."

I have used another data source often omitted from ethnographies, news reports. As I explained in *Making News* (1978; cf. Gans 1979; Fishman 1980; Gitlin 1980), institutionalized ideologies are embedded in the very processes of gathering and disseminating news. How the news media disperse their resources, including their staff, reveals what they believe matters. What media identify as "fact" defines not just what can be facts, but also the criteria determining facticity.

Like all contemporary organizations, Wannabe University did its best to control how the news media portrayed it. It sent news releases to the media and posted them on its website. It also posted on its website the favorable coverage it received from the news media. (Somehow the critical coverage rarely if ever was posted.) I paid special attention to how Wannabe wanted to be seen. I filed all stories about the management of Wannabe University that were published in both local newspapers and the important state newspapers, especially the *State Capital Record*.

I also paid special attention to three more sources of information disseminated by Wannabe administrators. One is the *Wannabe Weekly*, a widely distributed newspaper published by Wannabe's Office of University Relations—what in a less euphemistic era might have been called its public relations department. The minutes of powerful committees suggested the importance of this publication. For instance, the records of decisions and actions taken at one of the most powerful committees on campus occasionally indicated, "Place a story about [this matter] in the *Wannabe Weekly*."[21] Additionally, many stories in *Wannabe Weekly* are identical to the news releases on the website labeled "Wannabe press releases." (Multimedia feeds are also available through University Relations.) I also used Wannabe's general website, which University Relations maintains. The last is e-mails sent by administrators to students, staff, and professors. I view all three sources as announcements of how administrators want others to view both the university and its administrators.

I am all too familiar with the inaccuracies endemic in news coverage. For my purposes, those flaws do not matter. Rather, news coverage is an expression of what Dorothy E. Smith (2005: 13) calls "relations of ruling," "forms of consciousness and organization that are objictified in the sense that they are constituted externally to particularly people and places." As she explains, "We are ruled by people who are at work in corporations, government, professional settings and organizations. . . . Though they are, of course, individuals, their capacities to act derive from the organizations that they both produce and are produced by. The relations and organizations in which they are active are also those that organize our lives and in which we in various ways participate" (18). These relations are both omnipresent and mundane.

> Watching television, reading the newspaper, going to the grocery store . . . taking on a mortgage for a home, walking down a city street . . . these daily acts articulate us into social relations of the order . . . called *ruling* as well as those of the economy. . . . These transactions aren't with people we know as particular

individuals. . . . The functions of "knowledge, judgment and will" have become built into a specialized complex of objectified forms of organization and consciousness that organize and coordinate people's everyday lives. (18)

Modes of organization and coordination are not random. Policies are not accidents. Neither are rules and regulations. Institutions govern people through policies carefully wrought by the individuals, committees, and other groups at work in institutional bureaucracies. As a member of the pertinent committee reminded me, a group in the College of Liberal Arts and Sciences spent almost two years writing that college's mission statement and strategic plan. Essentially these are policy and planning documents about the business of the college. Not only do the university, its colleges, and its schools each have a mission statement, but the central administration had asked every department, even the mailroom, to write one, for all were involved in the bureaucratic business of the university.

Organizations, including universities, often announce their rules, regulations, and policies in newspapers, which the institutions publish both to present themselves in a positive light and to promote compliance. Indeed, the rules and regulations—and the formal accounts of them disseminated in newspapers and on the web—are so important that Smith specifically identifies them with ideology and social regulation. In essence, in our bureaucratized and centralized institutions, these written policies and the procedures associated with them become objectified as the essence of social regulation—as relations of ruling (Smith 2005: 15ff., 69). The *Wannabe Weekly* and the Wannabe website exemplify the sorts of official information that Smith discusses.

I have relied on Wannabe's official publications for accounts of some events. Sometimes I have also used these official statements rather than my own data, for the printed statements will not encourage people at Wan U to say, "I wonder who told her that." Also, the official accounts reveal more than either what Wannabe's administrators want people to believe or what they want to hide.[22] They also highlight the administration's dedication to spin (cf. Frankfurt 2005). In conversations with me, administrators have praised their colleagues by saying that he or she had found "a really good way to spin it." Spin seems so important that I suspect that sometimes the decision to publish a specific version of an occurrence may have been reached at President Whitmore's weekly Wednesday 9:00 a.m. meeting with his vice presidents and directors. (The provost and the dean of the medical school were the only "academics" routinely included in this meeting.) I have assumed that the administrators' news spin is telling; that is, it informs me of what the administrators may want others to believe.[23]

One final note: I have written in modified temporal order. I began collecting data and writing in 2003, when James Whitmore was president and Tyler Johnson was provost. I allude to events before Whitmore's presidency. Whitmore resigned when I was completing a second draft of this book. A new president, Richard (Rick) Daniels, arrived as I was working on a much revised chapter 7. I began writing President Daniels into this book in 2008, when Provost Wesley presented the faculty with a new strategic plan. I do not cover the transition from Whitmore to Daniels. Nor do I generally discuss how presidents and provosts decided to leave or were advised to leave Wannabe University. Like students and faculty, administrators are entitled to privacy.

PLAN OF THE BOOK

As all institutions of higher education are, Wannabe University is operating in a new environment. In the mid-twentieth century, higher education was a public good; now the distinction between public and private is not so clear (Gumport and Snydman 2006). In 1970 Wan U did not charge tuition; its undergraduates paid only "fees." Now compared to the other public universities in the region and compared to its "peers," Wan U is a bargain. But it is an expensive bargain. Its tuition has been creeping up; its out-of-state tuition resembles that of some private universities. Its administrators are on a perpetual search for new and increased revenue streams. As a chairman of the board of trustees repeatedly said, although research universities are not businesses, they can be business-like.

This book is about how being "business-like" has affected today's public research universities and how the changes in universities are, in turn, revealing emerging aspects of American life. It argues that the new emphasis on business has introduced new sorts of administrators who have different kinds of relationships with the professoriate. Increasingly, they try to govern them rather than to govern *with* them. As a result, the process of auditing has become ever more important, as administrators create situations in which faculty members must account for themselves. Indeed, these administrative actions appear to be encouraging an *accountability regime*.

In many ways, Wannabe University is typical of an ambitious American public research university, as chapter 2 explains. It situates Wannabe University geographically and historically and also in the context of contemporary American higher education. Some changes have emerged in research universities, as they have immersed themselves in the audit culture and accountability regime that are coming to dominate many American institutions. These changes include declining support from legislatures coupled with increasing legislative interest in higher education as preparation for the workforce; an increased emphasis on research that could be transformed into a revenue stream; an emphasis on pleasing customers (undergraduates and their parents); reviews of departments to improve "quality" (or at least ranking in a discipline); an increase in the number of full-time professional staff per full-time faculty; and an increase in part-time instructors. Wannabe University also suffered a bad case of "middle-status conformity" as it sought to institute "best practices" that would increase the "three e's" associated with an audit culture: economy, efficiency, and effectiveness.

Chapter 3 highlights Wannabe University as a "middle-status conformist" that simultaneously seeks to conform to what other public research universities do, while it develops its own distinctive "brand." I pay special attention to how Wan U participates in the corporatization of higher education, transforming the faculty's research into a revenue stream (as other research universities do). I include here some of the techniques used to persuade professors to earn money for the university and to dissuade professors from shirking. These activities involve new relationships among administrators and professors, who were once thought to share the governance of universities.

As academic administrators have increasingly followed the corporate pattern of achieving vertical mobility by moving from one employer to the next, professors have reconsidered both the meaning of being an administrator and the relationship between the professoriate and the administration. Chapter 4 argues that many professors feel that the "outside" administrators are "corporate administrators" more concerned with power and their own careers than with the fate of Wan U. Put somewhat differently, according to many professors, by helping Wannabe University climb a rung up the ladder of American public research universities, the "corporate administrators" help themselves clamber up the stairs of a managerial career in academe.

Adherents of the "new managerialism," Wan U's administrators seek to improve organizational rationality to maximize economy, efficiency, and effectiveness. To accomplish this rationalization, they are modifying the administrative structure of Wannabe University by engaging in centralization. Some changes have been accomplished through a gradual concentration of power; others by seemingly sudden fiat. Chapter 5 discusses the politics of centralization. It focuses on the "academic restructuring" (the elimination of three schools), the departure (retirement, firing, and career movement) of most of the deans, and some of the methods that professors use to deal with administrative fiats. These include both direct and indirect bureaucratic methods and ritual compliance.

Chapter 6 reports how professors reacted when, over a ten-year period, the central administration began to emphasize the need to improve the instruction of undergraduates. That emphasis on teaching undergraduates and auditing how instructors perform this task highlights an essential contradiction in contemporary American research universities. As professors see it and as has been the case at American research universities since the post–World War II period, research universities stress research. Professors' careers are based on their contribution to the scholarship of their fields. However, to sell the quality of their education to potential students and their parents, research universities boast of how they rank in the annual *U.S. News & World Report* publication "America's Best Colleges." To produce its ratings, that magazine uses indicators that stress aspects of undergraduate education, not research. Chapter 6 includes some discussion of the innovations (or "tricks") involving instruction that Wan U introduced to improve its ranking.

Chapters 7 and 8 discuss how the central administrators tried to implement some of the changes that would improve its ranking. In chapter 7, I discuss how the central administration encouraged instructors to make themselves auditable by introducing techniques for assessing both what undergraduates learn and how well professors teach. To some extent, external forces coerced it to do so. Its Regional Accreditation Agency not only mandated that it have such business documents as a mission statement and a strategic plan, but also that it institute student outcomes assessment. The chapter asks whether Wannabe University is conflating education and lifestyle, and whether its concern for students is simply part of "doing business." Chapter 8 discusses the impact of these changes of faculty, stressing how the shift of emphasis from one provost to the next leads to inconsistency and confusion. It asks about the mission of a public research university, noting how the characterization of higher education as both a public and a private good produces organizational ambivalence. That ambivalence was particularly clear as Wan U's specific policies about "managing" diversity shifted when one provost replaced another.

But there is much continuity. Chapter 9 considers some ways of making the faculty accountable, including the use of external reviews and "data-mining" about graduate programs to eliminate graduate departments. I discuss how much the faculty at Wannabe University is already being audited, although the professors do not identify the forms that they submit either to be granted promotion and tenure or to receive merit raises as structures associated with an accountability regime. I also contrast the American accountability regime with the highly centralized system introduced to British higher education in the 1990s. Although the centralization and rationalization being imposed on American research universities is less marked than the practices now found in the British system, the American accountability regime developing in higher education resembles the regimes imposed in other fields with ideological content as well as in health care. Why, I ask in chapter 10, has the faculty has been so compliant?

2

Situating Wannabe U

When President James Whitmore declared that Wan U was an "institution in transformation," he did not bother to explain why the university needed to change. Nor had he done so in his inauguration speech. Then he had referred to "our mission as a land-grant university" to promote "excellence," "access to all [state] residents," and "service to the state and beyond."[1] He had also invoked the possibility of greatness. Apparently, President Whitmore assumed that everyone at the academic convocation—politicians, trustees, faculty, students, and reporters—knew why change was necessary.

Gathered in the university's largest auditorium, the audience paid close attention to Whitmore's formal address. The faculty seemed informed about Whitmore. After all, it was in their best interest to have some sense of his character and preferences. Before the speech, a few professors whispered among themselves about the new president's decision to buy a home close to a pocket of wealthy donors rather than to occupy the on-campus presidential house. Everyone knew that the house needed repairs, but a scientist knew enough about the Whitmore family to tell those sitting near him that repairs were not the only issue. Teachers at the local school were making too big a fuss over the president's children to please his wife. (She wanted them to be treated like everyone else.) Some professors seemed less enthusiastic about Whitmore's emphasis on business. They preferred to define "service" in terms of the intellectual and moral growth of their students.[2] However, politicians and trustees applauded heartily as Whitmore announced that the university's "capacity to translate that concept [of service] into ongoing, working, profitable partnerships with [the state's] major public and private institutions is already beyond question." And that "the University cooperates with more than 200 companies and provides a point of service for hundreds of thousands of the state's citizens."

Three groups of the faculty might have known the justification for transformation and the emphasis on business: professors who specialized in the field of higher education; those who regularly read the *Chronicle of Higher Education*, as did some department heads and directors of research institutes; and those who served on university committees that discussed university finances. In other words, most of the faculty did not know why the university had to change. As Whitmore, quoting Clark Kerr, had implied, faculty "entrepreneurs" seemed more attuned to their own research and to their own disciplines than to the institution that employed them.

What's more, not only were some professors ignorant about why the university should change, but as several administrators and ambitious young faculty were to comment in the coming years, many of the faculty did not want change. At least, they did not want to change their own routines and priorities. "The only thing wrong here," one first-rate humanist said, "is that the older faculty don't want the university to get better." Echoing complaints heard in university communities for decades, one Ashton psychologist, who was not employed at the university, described assistant professors in his neighborhood: "At cocktail parties the assistant professors complain that the tenured members of their departments demand that we publish a lot . . . [to receive] tenure, but they're not willing to work any harder than they've ever done and that hasn't been very hard."

The administrators cared about the recalcitrant professors and criticized them when they chatted among themselves. They assumed that faculty attitudes toward change were important because professors could impede "progress." Some administrators, who had once served as faculty members, retained vestiges of faculty attitudes toward "shared governance." ("Shared governance" is the idea that faculty should participate in key decisions about teaching, research, and the quality of academic life at the university.) They worried that organized opposition from the professors who dominated the University Senate might impede the adoption of specific measures.[3] Other administrators had learned from consultants hired by the university that the cooperation of faculty would ease administrative tasks. Yet others had attended national workshops where "experts" maintained that a research university can only introduce lasting cultural change *if* the faculty buys into the process.[4] Although their degrees were in neither the social sciences nor management and they probably could not define cultural change if challenged to do so, these administrators were happy to announce to various forums: "It takes a long time to change a culture,"[5] and even said, "You have to break eggs to make an omelet."

James Whitmore was not the first administrator to try to prepare a first-rate omelet. In the early 1990s, President Ned Oakes had wondered whether sports provided the path to national renown (and possibly increased income). When he arrived in 1994, Provost Mike Tremaine started to reorganize the administration, to increase the emphasis on the faculty's research productivity, and also to reorganize undergraduate teaching.

WANNABE UNIVERSITY IN 1996

James Whitmore arrived at Wan U when the university was in its fourth reincarnation. It had started as a two-year agricultural "school" in the late nineteenth century, well after Congress had passed the Morrill Act, which had established land-grant colleges. (The land-grant institution in its state was a private university some sixty miles down the road.) It was to become Ashton Agricultural College, then State Agricultural College. Finally during the Great Depression, it became Wannabe State College and ultimately Wannabe University. It was also to wrest the status of the state's land-grant institution from its private university neighbor. Historians of the university credit Wannabe's president in the 1960s with transforming the university into a research institution, replete with a research foundation, mechanisms for internal research grants, and medical and dental schools.[6]

By the time James Whitmore arrived on campus in 1996, Wannabe University was the state's flagship institution of higher learning, included thirteen schools and colleges at its main campus in Ashton, separate schools of law and social work within twenty-five miles, five regional campuses throughout the state, and schools of medicine and dentistry about forty miles away. The university taught roughly 12,000 undergraduates, 10,300 of them on the main Ashton campus. It employed roughly 900 full-time professors in Ashton. For a public research university, it was small. It served a small, but prosperous state—at least the state seemed geographically small compared to, say, Oregon or Minnesota. Compared to the roughly 20,000 undergraduates who attended Texas Tech in 1994 or Ohio State's undergraduate enrollment of over 35,000 on its main campus, Wan U's enrollment was minuscule. Indeed, within two years of President Whitmore's arrival, consultants advised that the undergraduate enrollment should expand. It was to increase by roughly a third.

Expansion of the undergraduate student body was part of the attempt to "transform" Wannabe University. The consultant's study commissioned by the administration maintained that Wan U was simply too small to make it into the ranks of the big-time universities. Expanding the student body, including the number of students from out of state, would supposedly increase the university's resources. Not only did out-of-state students pay higher tuition and have higher Scholastic Aptitude Test (SAT) scores than in-state students, but their presence would open other possibilities.[7] To maintain an adequate student-to-teacher ratio, Wan U would need a larger faculty. More professors in some departments would translate into a richer intellectual environment and so potentially increase the revenue stream resulting from faculty research. Indeed, the size of the undergraduate body was to increase by 17 percent in academic 1998–99, President Whitmore's second year and Provost Tremaine's last year at Wan U. In all, it was to increase by a third on the Ashton campus. (I discuss more about this expansion in chapter 6.)

When President Whitmore arrived, as true of Ashton and the surrounding rural communities, the university was almost essentially white. Although the university's records report that in 1994 about 14 percent of the student body belonged to an "underrepresented minority," the main campus was "whiter" than the regional campuses and Asian Americans were the largest "minority" on all of the campuses, although almost of the "minorities" in the state were either African American or Latino. Together these two groups were roughly 20 percent of the state's population. In 1994 roughly 8 percent of the undergraduates on the main campus were either Latino or African American. The other 6 percent were Asian American, although Asian Americans were only about 2 percent of the state's residents. As characteristic of many schools that play sports in the National Collegiate Athletic Association's Division IA, a goodly percentage of the black men on the Ashton campus were athletes. In 1994 not quite 6 percent of the faculty were people of color. Most of them were Asian Americans. Asian Americans, mainly the children of graduate students from abroad, were also the dominant "minority" in Ashton's public schools. The Ashton campus and the nearby exurban communities were so white that basketball coaches competing with Wannabe University for first-rate players would warn black recruits about the boredom, isolation, and whiteness of the area. I do not think they mentioned the extraordinary seasonal beauties so characteristic of the region.[8]

I first saw Wannabe University in the early 1980s. I remember returning to New York (I then lived on Manhattan's Upper West Side) and mumbling, "I can't believe that people live like that!" At the time I was more entranced with how the late afternoon light fell on some of New York's tall buildings than the verdure of rolling hills formed by receding glaciers. And Ashton does indeed seem isolated. When national magazines run stories about Ashton, they usually point out that one has to travel almost ten miles to get to a movie theater. The nearest McDonald's is just as far. So is the nearest Burger King. But the region has miles of walking trails replete with waterfalls that were harnessed to factories in the nineteenth century. Then a few local industries had grown quite prosperous and had even been world leaders in the manufacture of some items. These industries were also early participants in the movement of factories from the North to South in the 1950s, leaving the area with pockets of unemployment, underemployment, and decided poverty.

Although one can find spurts of institutional ambition throughout its official history, Wannabe University was a "Johnny-come-lately" to the "reputational arms race," the battle for national and international recognition. Until the early 1990s, as one ex-administrator put it, its trustees tended to be graduates who loved the university as opposed to loving what they could get from the university. Supposedly, being a trustee was also a political and a social plum. Then in the 1990s, the governor, the legislature, the trustees, and the administration decided to step onto a national stage. By the time it announced its desire to transform itself, other regional research universities had begun to strive for national status, and the national research universities had entered into sometimes bitter combat for research funds and international recognition. With endowments and investment portfolios smaller than most of those of the private research universities, the "publics" had a harder row to hoe.

When James Whitmore arrived at Wannabe University, the school had already won its first national sports title. A politician had used that accomplishment to organize the legislature, which had received the team on its floor with whoops of joy. Inspired by athletic success, the legislature had already announced a massive and expensive building program. The board of trustees had effectively marginalized the past university president by placing budgetary matters in the hands of an ambitious provost, who was eventually to move on to the presidency of other universities, one of them a top-notch research institution. Presumably the possibility of making his mark on an institution poised to grow had attracted James Whitmore to Wannabe University.

As true when there are shifts in the top management of any major corporation, when President Whitmore took charge, politics ensued. As president, James Whitmore regained control of the budget. He staved off seemingly self-centered attempts of high-level administrators to gain personal perquisites, such as the right to live in a university-owned house that Ned Oakes, the past president, had occupied. Supposedly at the behest of the board of trustees, President Whitmore had moved to a location more convenient to the legislature and to contacting and entertaining donors. The large house was left vacant.

Early in James Whitmore's presidency, Provost Mike Tremaine continued to work to transform Wannabe University and so to make a name for himself. Until he left in 1998, Provost Tremaine declared many initiatives.

He set out to increase the number, the size, and the scope of the grants and contracts that the faculty received. He also inaugurated a wave of program reviews[9] and set out to integrate the new technology into campus life. Provost Tremaine was not the first person to inaugurate program reviews. An earlier provost, now viewed as an "insider," had done so in the 1980s and had even visited every department to discuss his findings with its faculty. Provost Tremaine did not visit departments.

With Mary Matthews, Provost Tremaine also campaigned to improve the quality of undergraduate teaching by increasing the status of teaching. When Mary Matthews was appointed vice provost for education and instruction, other universities already had more sophisticated technological infrastructures and had begun to experiment with ways to maximize both the research dollars obtained by the faculty and the quality of undergraduate teaching. For instance, in the late 1990s Mary Matthews proposed hiring "teaching professors," people who did not publish, taught more than research professors, and could be construed as "master teachers." At Duke University, by 1987 such "Professors of the Practice" had been language instructors who freed research professors for other tasks (Fogg 2004).

Some efforts failed; some succeeded. Vice Provost Matthews's attempt to introduce master teachers failed; the faculty blocked it. Other programs were a grand success. As *Wannabe Weekly* reported in 2001 when Mary Matthews left to be provost of a small liberal arts college, Wan U's first vice provost for undergraduate education and instruction had "spearheaded the creation of a new set of General Education Requirements . . . , reorganized the academic advising system . . . , opened a dialogue with community colleges [to facilitate their students' ability to transfer to Wan U], . . . and worked with [the director] of the Institute for Teaching and Learning, to develop effective mechanisms to help improve teaching, especially through the use of information technology in the classroom." She had also addressed plans (later completed) for a building dedicated to undergraduate teaching. Among the programs eventually housed there were the Institute for Student Success, the Institute for Teaching and Learning, the Honors Program, the Individualized Major, and First-Year Programs. When successful, the programs expanded. In ten years, the Institute for Teaching and Learning (ITL) grew to ten subunits employing forty people, some plucked from other units. For instance, the Writing Center relocated from the English department to ITL. By 2007 there had been so many initiatives and so much expansion of existing programs that it was difficult to find a vacant office in the Building for Undergraduate Education (the BUE).

Provost Tremaine's wave of program assessments supposedly succeeded. (Evaluation of these reviews depends on whom one asks. In 2007 a vice provost complained that almost every assessment contained a variation of "With more faculty, this department could expand, or improve, or specialize more, or . . .") What matters here is that these first attempts to transform Wannabe University from a regional to a national institution introduced conflicts.

It may be a truism that to make an omelet, you have to break a few eggs, but many older professors did not like to view themselves as eggs in need of breaking. Some of them resisted change. In contrast, some newly arrived professors, both acclaimed scholars and newbies fresh from graduate school, had a tendency to say, "If those old-timers would just stop interfering, this could become a great university." Indeed, one accomplished scholar expressed this opinion to me twice.

Program reviews had revealed deep conflicts in some areas of academic inquiry. Many of these fields were the kind where one would expect to find conflict. Either figures in the field had historically battled about theories and methods, as is true in many of the social sciences; new developments in the field had engendered conflicts about appropriate topics and methods of inquiry, as has occurred in English and in history departments around the country; or the attempt to "improve" by introducing new paradigms and rewarding research much more than teaching had fanned the flames of discontent. (Later the attempt to balance the relationship between research and teaching would again provoke unhappiness.)

Soon after a program review, four social science departments in the College of Liberal Arts and Sciences were either placed in "receivership" or narrowly escaped receivership. In three of those departments, the dean and department head had pressed to alter the department's academic emphasis so that it would be more mainstream (and potentially lucrative).[10] Supposedly, the dean wanted departments to conform to the direction that the mainstream of their disciplines were taking. Some professors claimed that especially in departments with serious conflicts, the department head or the dean of the College of Liberal Arts and Sciences had also encouraged reports that would limit the directions of specialization in more eclectic (or heterodox) departments. The dean had done so by choosing the external reviewers from a list carefully prepared by department heads (and often the head's departmental allies). These external reviewers would examine the department's materials; interview professors, students, and administrators; and write the report. Although geographically sprawling, academic fields have relatively few people compared to other occupations. Its members regularly run into one another at professional meetings so that "everyone" knows the sympathies of prominent practitioners. It is probable, but not inevitable, that a scholar can predict the academic sympathies of someone in her field. Thus, through the choice of reviewers, deans could influence the direction of academic fields (Trow 2003). When members of one department complained that the dean "is trying to make us a clone of every other department in [our field]," they were asserting that *academic structure can have a profound effect on academic inquiry* (Lohmann 2004).

At Wannabe, after the reviewers had submitted their report, the department made an official reply. With the dean and provost, the department prepared a "memorandum of agreement" that specified how the department would develop; for instance, what kind of specialists it would hire. Although everyone in a department could enter into the process of responding to the reviews and commenting on the memorandum of understanding, some departments handled this process in a fairly oligarchic manner. Dissenters were ignored. Although the department head signed a memorandum of agreement with the dean and provost, oligarchy encouraged severe nastiness among the professors. As one person put it, "People wrote in e-mails things they would never say face-to-face." The head of one unhappy department took a job on the other side of the country. (The dissenters claimed that the dean helped him to find a job.) Several people in a second department split off to form their own department. A third department not only went into receivership, but the dean also brought in a mediator to engage in conflict resolution. In a fourth department, everyone worked at home, so that individuals never had to speak with one another. (Years later, when that department finally went into receivership, the acting head imported from the humanities observed, "Working there is like working in a mausoleum.")

There were also other casualties. A humanities department had campus-famous squabbles. A science department was dissolved. In the School of Engineering, younger and older professors (some say non-tenured and senior) supposedly had seriously disagreements. Eventually, they contributed to (but did not cause) the forced resignation of a dean. In one department that had spent over a year in receivership, some conflicts became a joke. "What's going on?" someone asked at a department meeting. "I thought the dean was angry at us, and now you're saying he likes us." The answer captured the spirit in many departments: "Yeah, he thought we were awful. Then [another department] went into receivership and had the same acting head as us. The dean thought we were awful until [the acting head] told him about them." Others simply said, "They make us look good." Or, "What's happening in engineering makes liberal arts look good."

In *Taking the Reins* (2003), Eckel and Kezar stress how important it is to involve all groups and all factions if a higher-education institution wants to transform itself. George Keller (2004) tells a similar tale in his "story of a little-known college's strategic climb to national distinction." At Wannabe University, "transformation" was imposed, not chosen. Few people came to forums called to discuss proposed changes. "You can call a meeting to discuss changes," a then-member of the provost's staff said, "but almost no one comes." Relatively few elected senators entered debates at the University Senate. Deans and vice provosts rarely expressed their disagreements in group meetings with the provost. One chairman of the board of trustees did not hesitate to criticize anyone publicly or privately; but almost everybody was afraid to criticize him.

I do not want to give the impression that the university was "fractionated" any worse than other contemporary universities. (As is frequently true of the politics of large formal organizations, university politics are sometimes brutal.) In the 1990s, some departments were downright congenial, and they continue to provide friendly, even convivial places to work. People forge friendships in their departments and across departments. They greet one another at their children's soccer games, the middle school dances, high school plays, concerts in the university's grand auditorium, and also at university athletic events. They meet at Christmas parties and block parties. Overall, professors mostly say, "Wannabe is a good university, and the Ashton area is a fine place to live."

When James Whitmore arrived, the area was not at its most prosperous. The region's search for new industry was faltering. The university was widely recognized as the largest employer in the region, the mainstay of its economy and its source of theater, music, and dance. When recruiting new faculty, the academic departments tended to downplay this cultural fare that the School of Fine Arts provided for the region. Rather, they stressed proximity to major cities with some of the finest museums, music, and theater in the country. Even the area's minor cities had superb cultural fare.

The undergraduates didn't care about the art, classical music, and avant-garde theater that many professors so valued. That was all so irrelevant to student life—"BORING!" as then-undergraduates might have said. In 1996 the students who came to Wannabe University were concerned with the price tag, growing national recognition of the school's sports teams, the well over one hundred subjects (including professional training) in which one could major, and, probably, the weekend parties. Both in-state and out-of-state tuition were a real bargain. The university reeked of school spirit. Some of the professional schools had good reputations. And, just as SUNY Stony Brook, also set in the middle of nowhere, was a party school in the 1970s, so too had Wan U established a reputation as a school where students partied hard. Eventually, the faculty and the administration were to take steps to counter that reputation by finding ways to cut down on students' alcohol consumption, such as sponsoring alternative activities and even joining the town of Ashton to sponsor the construction of a "downtown area" of shops, housing, and entertainment.

The "downtown" area also had another more serious university-related purpose: to increase the percentage of students admitted to Wan U who chose to go there. As the vice provost for enrollment management informed the University Senate in September 2006, for some years the university had collected proprietary data about admitted high school students who had decided *not* to attend Wannabe University.[11] When surveyed, many of these students indicated that the isolation of Ashton had contributed to their decision to go elsewhere. As discussed in chapter 6, the percentage of admitted students who choose *not* to attend a university or college lowers its ranking in *U.S. News & World Report*'s annual survey of colleges. So the university hoped to mimic some of the East's university towns by providing at least the simulation of a city center. (The administrators understood that they could not hope to imitate a Cambridge, an Amherst, or even a Northampton.)

Wannabe University had some top students; several professors were members of either the National Academy of Sciences or the National Academy of Engineering, but Wannabe was not a top university. It could not even pretend to be one. In 1995, when the National Research Council published its rankings of the quality of doctoral programs in the United States,[12] only one academic department ranked in the top twenty in its field—and there were only forty-one departments in the country granting a degree in that field (Goldberger, Maher, and Flattau 1995). Mostly the standardized scores of departments in the arts and humanities, in engineering, and in the physical sciences and mathematics were below the national mean.[13] In the biological sciences and the social and behavioral sciences, a few departments scored near the mean or one or two points above it. Other public universities in Wannabe's region did not fare much better, for the area had long emphasized its stellar (and even not-so-stellar) private institutions. It would be fair to describe Wannabe University in 1996 as a good public institution within its region, but a mediocre research university when considered in the national context. To quote an acclaimed sociologist of education who prefers to remain unnamed, "As a state university in a small state that has not had a long focus on public education, Wannabe U starts from a different place than does an Ohio State, a Texas Tech, or a University of South Carolina." Certainly some people associated with Wannabe University would like to think differently, but as the sociologist succinctly put it, nationally Wannabe University is of "middle status."

As briefly mentioned in chapter 1, officially the state's politicians were ambitious to bolster Wannabe University, because the state was experiencing a "brain drain." Although the state was home to many colleges and universities, most of them were small; that is, each enrolled well under five thousand undergraduates. They could not accommodate the 60 percent of the state's high school graduates who went directly to college even had they wanted to do so. Many did not wish to do so. Like many eastern private colleges, they tended to have a national orientation. They favored competitive national admissions, and if they could not attract stellar students nationally, they were happy to poach students from nearby states by offering more attractive scholarship possibilities than those other states did.

More high school graduates left the state to attend college than came to it for that purpose. And the best and the brightest were most likely to leave. Some legislators described the situation as a crisis, for if the state was going to be able to compete in the new international financial markets and technological and pharmaceutical sectors of the global economy, it needed more of its most promising high school graduates to stay in the area. Once an excellent student left home to attend college, she might never return.

Wannabe University administrators agreed. At least, almost all of them were happy to accede to the desire of important state legislators to put Wannabe University on the national map and so to decrease the state's brain drain.[14] They expressed tactical concerns. How could they bolster the research excellence of the faculty? What did they have to do to increase their national recognition so that more of the state's "best" high school graduates would compete to attend Wan U instead of defining it as a "safety school"— a "college of last resort" where one was sure to be admitted? How could the administrators raise the visibility and national perception of Wan U's quality so that it could attract the best students? Also, what did they have to do to attract more out-of-state students, who paid considerably higher tuition?

WANNABE AS A MIDDLE-STATUS CONFORMIST

Wannabe University is not the only institution of higher education to ask such questions. Indeed, reading the management literature about higher education, one learns that such questions were quite common. Coupled with its middle status, that very "commonness" makes Wannabe University quite sociologically interesting. It implies that administrators at Wannabe University might be expected to engage in the same practices that other universities were introducing to improve their status.

In the 1950s, social psychologists wrote about the *motivation* to conform. Their experiments on small groups of individuals indicated that middle status is associated with conformity; people of either high status or low status experience less pressure to conform than do people of middle status. Low-status actors are not invested in what others think of them. High-status actors may successfully signal to others that despite their limited nonconformity, they remain important members of a particular social scene.

In 2001 Phillips and Zuckerman successfully tested the applicability of those generalizations to firms in stable (though not fixed) markets—that is, they tested them for members of "status hierarchies that give security to the highest-ranking actors and render the lower-ranking actors observable outsiders" (390) and where actors' placement in these hierarchies has not changed appreciably over time. They chose two economic markets, law firms in the Silicon Valley and securities analysts, and found that firms with middle status were indeed more likely to conform to industry norms.

Logically, these findings about motivation, status, and conformity should also apply to research universities. Universities participate in a relatively stable, but not fixed status hierarchy. After all, status means standing, reputation, or the honor that one is accorded. Universities accumulate this honor as they compete for students, for research grants and contracts, and for top faculty. This market-like competition enables analysts to construe research universities as members of a higher-education market or industry (but see C. Smith 2004).[15] And although there are some universities that gained high status relatively quickly, the approximate placement of universities in a status hierarchy has been relatively constant for some time.[16] That is, no research universities have fallen from the top quintile to the middle quintile. Asked to rank universities, most professors at research universities would probably agree which universities are roughly as good as one another—including which ones are superior and which decidedly inferior. More technically, their rankings would probably have a fairly low standard deviation.

Accordingly, when James Whitmore arrived to transform Wannabe University, he, his "academic" senior staff (provosts and deans), and his "administrative" senior staff (directors and vice presidents) might be expected to introduce the same "innovations" that other middle-status research universities were introducing. Wannabe University did not have the clout to launch innovations that were "too innovative"—that varied too much from the norm. Indeed, now and again, conforming administrators even tried to eradicate institutionalized local practices that departed too much from what "everyone else" was doing.[17]

Wannabe University's middle status and its conformist tendencies make it an ideal place to study the transformation of American research universities. The practices it introduced illuminate the norm. As we will see in chapter 3, if other research universities prospered by setting up a university park for emerging industries, Wan U tried to set up a university park. If other universities established an institute to "incubate" faculty inventions, Wan U created an "incubation unit." If other research universities created a revenue stream by building multistory parking garages, Wan U erected parking garages.[18] Wan U conformed.

Wannabe University's adherence to conventional practices also demonstrates the usefulness of theories about how organizations adapt to their environment. Rather than exploring the motivations to conform, these theories concern the *process* of conformity. Indeed, where administrators see themselves as introducing innovations to their university, sociologists see these same administrators as conforming to what others do or have done. For instance, discussing Provost Mike Tremaine, one relatively high-level administrator said, "He shook things up." However, a list of Provost Tremaine's accomplishments during his tenure at Wan U is also a roster of what other universities had done or were doing.

THEORIES OF HOW ORGANIZATIONS CHANGE

Two sets of sociological ideas are particularly important to understanding conformity and the process of change at Wan U. One group of sociologists stresses that change involves *adaptation* to a "technical environment" (Thompson 1967). It says that higher-education institutions come to resemble one another, because they adapt to similar external or environmental stimuli.[19] Similar structural problems may result in similar structural solutions, especially if the decision-makers believe that they have limited choices (Scott 1981). Take the problem of staffing a full complement of courses when under budgetary constraints. If one does not teach enough courses, students may not attend the college and so the college will become bankrupt. But one cannot offer courses without paying instructors, and if one pays instructors too much, the college will become bankrupt. The problem may be exacerbated by contractual constraints governing the employment of full-time instructors. Customary contracts require that (a) full-time employees must receive expensive fringe benefits and (b) after a set number of years as a provisional full-time employee, a faculty member must be evaluated for tenure. Granting tenure to a professor is a commitment to a long-term expense, for many contracts between institutions of higher education and such faculty groups as the American Association of University Professors specify that a tenured professor may only be fired for individual malfeasance or if the institution faces a particular kind of financial crisis.

Universities with budgetary constraints have two obvious solutions: (a) hire more part-time faculty and (b) hire some full-time faculty with the understanding that their contracts are for a specified number of years and they will not be eligible for tenure.[20] In the past two decades, throughout academia there has been an increase in part-time instructors and in visiting instructors. They have no hope of tenure. Their status may be viewed as a change in university employment patterns, an increase in its "contingent labor force." From the viewpoint of adaptation theory, such structural change is a rational response to structural problems in a technical environment.

Instead of analyzing the technical environment (such as budgetary constraints) to which organizations respond, another group of scholars asks about how *institutions learn from each other*. Proponents of the new institutionalism (DiMaggio and Powell 1991) emphasize stability rather than change. They try to explain why so many organizations end up having the same structure (isomorphism), even though they evolved in very different ways. To answer this and related questions, the new institutionalism emphasizes components of institutional environments, including such "social forces as norms, standards, and expectations of stakeholders in the relevant organizational field" (Kraatz and Zajac 1996: 812). Although many sociologists discuss norms, values, and expectations as aspects of culture rather than as aspects of structure,[21] the theory has clear structural elements. The new institutionalism emphasizes that institutions are embedded in organizational fields and also that the organizations in that field influence each other's activities by setting common norms and values. These norms and values define legitimate ways for the organizations to operate. They even define how people within the organizations conceive of the alternatives they face. As the people in these organizations and the organizations themselves conform to these conceptions, they become increasingly homogeneous. They are adapting to the environment they create for one another as much as, perhaps even more than, the economic challenges or the technical environment that any one organization may face.

For instance, under certain conditions, one might explain the behavior of enrollment managers by referring to the new institutionalism. Suppose that while at a national convention of administrators, the vice provost for enrollment attends a series of workshops discussing how to decrease the dropout rate of first-generation Euro-Americans who are first-year students at large state universities. The vice provost initiates the recommended programs on his campus. He has acted as the new institutionalism had predicted; indeed, even the definition of "the dropout rate of first-generation Euro-Americans" as a problem is an affirmation that shared conceptions are a characteristic of organizational fields.

Examples of such imitation are more than hypothetical. For instance, in 2007 and 2008, the provost of Wannabe University presented a draft of a new academic plan that sought, among other things, "to create an academic infrastructure that coordinates, integrates, and sustains proposed activities" concerning research, education, and outreach about the environment. To enact that strategy, the plan proposes to "explore options from what exists at other institutions" and to "identify and implement the structure most appropriate to the goals at Wan U." Over a decade earlier, a different assistant vice provost had used the same strategy to improve the university's academic counseling services for intercollegiate athletes. He had surveyed the gamut of arrangements at other universities that had first-rank teams or aspired to have them, and then he had chosen a structure used at a top basketball school. As do theories that stress adaptation to the environment, neo-institutionalism does a better job explaining the process of conformity than do theories of either radical or long-range social change.

CHANGING UNIVERSITIES IN A CHANGING SOCIETY

Trustees, presidents, provosts, vice presidents, and deans understood that change was necessary. The administrators of one university actively sought—even plotted to gain—a competitive advantage over other universities, because in the last quarter of the twentieth century colleges and universities were facing series of crises that were often fiscal. Quite simply, costs were rising, but income was not. Even the average price of maintaining a parking space (estimated to be $600 per space at Cornell University in the mid-1990s) was higher than what a university could then charge its students and staff to park their cars (Ehrenberg 2000; cf. Smith 2000). Administrators framed both these crises and their potential solutions in terms of management: What did universities have to do to market the product called "higher education"? (See, e.g., Zusman 1999.)

Another set of social scientists analyzed the crises in rather different terms: They did not ask about the processes of day-to-day or even decade-to-decade change. Rather they inquired about trends over thirty or forty years or even over centuries; these scholars try to figure out where Western societies are headed, and universities have long been a central part of Western societies. For these scholars, what matters is the following: Are the problems facing higher education indicative of the problems confronting other institutions as the socioeconomic structure of Western societies has been changing? This rather large question is irrelevant to the day-to-day concerns of most educational administrators. An answer to this intellectually interesting question is, to use the popular idiom, "merely academic."[22]

It will not solve such key practical problems as balancing the budget, wooing legislative allies who will argue for budgetary increases, or finding ways to quell the arguments of opponents.[23] Nonetheless, theories of long-term social change matter. If nothing else, by telling us where we have been and suggesting where we might be going, these theories feed the human spirit, augment a collective sense of social responsibility, and illuminate pitfalls we might try to avoid.

SOCIAL SCIENTIFIC EXPLANATION OF LONG-TERM ACADEMIC CHANGE

To spot trends of long-range societal development, academic researchers have explored both early modernity and late capitalism. Just as there are schools of sociological thought that offer competing, but related, theories about institutional processes, so too are there schools of long-range change. Some reached back to early modernity to place contemporary patterns and practices in historical context. For instance, following the work of Foucault, some British anthropologists and historians have argued that surveillance, a key aspect of social control in contemporary societies, had its roots in early modernity and could even be found in key British universities (see Strathern 2000). Before 1790, students attended universities, read, took oral exams, and left. Strathern (1997; cf. Evans 2004) argued that administrators began their surveillance when, in 1792, a member proposed that at Cambridge University "all answers in the tripos examination should be written as well as verbal" (Evans 2004: 21). Quoting Strathern (1997), Evans notes: "With measurement came a new morality of attainment. If human performance could be measured, then targets could be set and aimed for. What is became explicitly joined with what ought to be" (21). This system of surveillance can be called the beginning of the rationalization of British higher education and the assignment of worth to a now-quantifiable degree.

Others do not take such a long view. They cite the reorganization of universities in the late nineteenth century. That reorganization combined aspects of collegiate education, research, and practical education (as discussed more fully in chapter 6). In an award-winning history, Barrow (1990) has argued that trustees and administrators at American universities introduced changes without educational justification. They simply wanted to increase efficiency; they wanted universities to run more like the emerging corporatized industries. Before reorganization, Barrow claimed, at some universities professors could organize any course they wanted to teach merely by announcing its existence and where and when it would meet. Not only did this system lack any semblance of uniformity, but because the meeting times of courses were not coordinated, students faced what we would today call enrollment conflicts. To "correct" such loose practices, trustees and administrators rationalized scheduling. They introduced uniformity—so many credits for so many hours of class, with meeting times and places to be regulated by a central agency. Barrow claims that these men "industrialized" higher education.[24]

I do not want to adjudicate now among these thematic treatments of the history of higher education. Indeed, some have argued that surveillance, rationalization, industrialization (or corporatization), and modernity are interrelated processes, potentially affecting one another.[25] One might also maintain that some of these processes are homologous—arising from the same causes, but not causing one another.

DE-CHURCHING UNIVERSITIES

Here's what matters: These and other treatments of grand trends insist that *higher education is one of the last revered Western institutions to be "de-churched"*; that is, it is one of the last to have its ideological justification recast in terms of corporatization and commodification and to become subject to serious state surveillance. Universities are no longer to lead the minds of students to grasp truth; to grapple with intellectual possibilities; to appreciate the best in art, music, and other forms of culture; and to work toward both enlightened politics and public service. Rather they are now to prepare students for jobs. They are not to educate, but to train.[26] To be sure, some of the great American private colleges and universities—such as Harvard, Yale, and the much younger Duke—still discuss past values when they define their current missions.[27] But even when Nannerl Keohane, the liberal political theorist and past president of Duke University and Wellesley College, expresses her admirable vision for the education of students at research universities, she seems to be differentiating between the sort of *education* that may be offered at the elite private colleges and universities and the kind of *training* available to everyone else.[28]

Although they use different grand narratives, many sociological commentators agree that since the last half of the twentieth century, many once-sacrosanct institutions have been "de-churched." Law and medicine are probably the two most studied examples, for both professions have undergone extensive reorganization. Whether he is a doctor or a lawyer, the lone practitioner in business for himself is no longer prototypical. Most lawyers are salaried; the lawyers with the most prestige practice in large firms with a corporate clientele (Sandefur 2001). Law firms may have over twenty partners, all of whom are subject to the organization's rules and regulations. Indeed, the law firm defines how its partners and associates should get work done.

The immense change in medical practice is well-known.[29] The lone practitioner whom Norman Rockwell so often portrayed on the cover of the *Saturday Evening Post* is now all but extinct. So is the kindly older doctor teaching a younger man, the fatherly Robert Young of the 1970s television show *Marcus Welby, M.D.* Today doctors are commonly organized into multi-doctor practices that pay to belong to the "health maintenance organizations" (HMOs) that insure their patients. These HMOs set policies concerning the procedures they will approve and the conditions under which they will do so. They also oversee how individual doctors practice. One Ashton physician jokes about how HMOs supervise his work, for they check to see whether he is giving appropriate care to patients. For instance, calling the practice "assessment," those companies evaluate the doctors by calculating the percentage of their diabetic patients who receive appropriate tests every six months and who go for an eye examination at least once a year. The companies then reward or punish the doctors for their patients' behavior.[30]

DEPROFESSIONALIZATION

Another sociological way of analyzing these changes in law, medicine, and academia is to say that lawyers, doctors, and professors are being "deprofessionalized." They are losing their hold on self-determination—their ability to recruit, certify, and expel practitioners. Social forces are also weakening both their license and mandate (Hughes 1958); that is, their ability to define their own rights and responsibilities (Freidson 2001). Instead, they are increasingly being supervised and made accountable to others. Calling professors "managed professionals," sociologist Gary Rhoades has cited some pretty basic responsibilities that professors do not have:

> [They do not] manage college and university budgets. They do not set the salaries of administrators or themselves. They do not have final authority over who gets laid off. They do not decide whether to approve or eliminate academic programs. By and large, they do not control how many full- and part-time faculty members are hired (nor how many students are admitted). Faculty do not purchase and set up new instructional technologies. Faculty neither set nor enforce outside employment policies. They must negotiate with the organization regarding intellectual property rights. (Rhoades 1998: 5)

Placing this trend in the context of the development of contemporary capitalism, Dorothy E. Smith (2004: 36) identifies deprofessionalization with "new forms of regulation that undermine the autonomy of the professions and increasingly subordinate the practice of the professions . . . to the demands of capital accumulation for lower taxation, reduced government deficits, and extended privatization."[31]

By citing such factors as "the demands of capital accumulation for lower taxation," Smith is placing the new forms of regulation in the context of contemporary forms of capitalism and is implying a grand narrative. In essence, like Slaughter and Leslie (1999; cf. Slaughter and Rhoades 2004), she is arguing that contemporary versions of capitalism, as personified by the agents of such neo-liberal practices as supply-side economics (Harvey 2005), are increasing their surveillance of work done by the traditional "liberal professions" and are calling them to account.

Other theories of deprofessionalization also stress a quite different aspect of the term "account" without linking accounts to such contemporary phenomena as neo-liberalism, supply-side economics, and privatization. Rather they talk about accounts, accounting, and accountability within the context of changing social systems. Abbott (1988) provides the key discussion. He situates the deprofessionalization of any specific job in the division of expert labor within a system of professions. Each profession is bound to other professions through its ties to the system. Therefore, when the jurisdiction over tasks changes from one profession to another, the entire system must adjust. What one profession loses, another may gain. A profession that claims new rights and responsibilities might abscond with those of another profession. A profession that sticks to its own niche (such as the job of "railroad engineer") may cease to be a profession when the importance of its niche in the system evaporates—or when significant social change occurs.

The system of professions is itself affected by larger forces, whether these are called the rise of the state, increased rationalization, or commodification. Thus, for instance, Abbott (1998: 227) argues that in the late nineteenth century, the rise of "large corporations and the national capital market helped create the American accounting profession [and] the rise of interventionist governments built the work of statistics." The insurance company's quantitative "assessment" of the doctor (whose patients do or do not follow his advice), the law firm's review of an associate's "billable hours," the provost's and vice provost's review of how students rated a professor's qualities as an instructor—all represent the expansion of accounting and statistics within the system of professions. Indeed, just as accountants audit tax returns, so too the philosophy of accounting has invaded other professions, whose practitioners must provide some kind of "account of themselves." (In my mind's eye, I hear a parent asking a child, "How do you account for your behavior, young lady?" or a police officer asking a suspect, "Can you account for the missing hour? Where were you? Who were you with?")[32]

Administrators at Wannabe University care about accounting. As have other administrators at other universities, they have established specific offices that audit the university's finances and activities (provide internal audits), and they annually hire corporate bodies (firms of external auditors) to check the validity of the processes associated with these internal audits. These external auditors file reports that wend their way to the desk of Wannabe's president and then become the subject of discussion at meetings of the Wannabe Board of Trustees. When they do not do so, there may be harsh consequences. When President Whitmore claimed that he had never received a key audit, the vice president responsible for presenting that report to him was "severed" from his employment at Wannabe University.

External audits are not firsthand evidence. In preparing them, the external auditors do not check the original (internal) calculations. Rather, they do a secondary audit; they check the processes by which the internal auditors checked others' actions. Each new level of auditing represents the expansion of accounting accomplished through its incursions on the activities of other workers, including professionals. Put somewhat differently, each time an auditor checks on the activities of other professionals, the auditor is proclaiming, "I am authorized to supervise the processes through which you do your work."

Supposedly each new level of accounting makes more transparent (or observable) the processes associated with the operation of a corporation or university.[33] Thus, when in 2003 the head of a social science department told the chair of a search committee in charge of hiring an assistant professor, "I want this search to be transparent," the department head was saying: "I want every step that you take to be so aboveboard that someone who decides to examine your every action will find that you have followed every rule and regulation that this university has established to manage hiring procedures." It is almost as though the department head were saying, "I want you to proceed as though no one trusts you and as though every step you take affirms your obeisance to rules and regulations, and so affirms your worthiness to be head of this committee." Transparent procedures supposedly provide a reason for trust, but they are a form of surveillance, based on the idea that you cannot trust anyone. If one could trust anyone and everyone, there would be no reason for audits. Thus, audits present themselves dialectically. At one and the same time, they are displays of both trust and distrust.

A society typified by this dialectic is *an audit culture* (Douglas 1992; Strathern 1997, 2000; Power 1994). As Michael Power (1994: 13) explains: An audit culture emerges when trust has broken down. "And yet the spread of audit actually creates the very mistrust it is meant to address. . . ." Audit creates "a 'regress of mistrust' in which the performances of auditors and inspectors are themselves subjected to audit." Audit becomes what Shore and Wright (in Strathern 2000: 79) call "coercive accountability." "It encourages a form of 'reflexivity,' but the reflexive subject is caught within tightly fixed parameters that appear to render opposition futile." This "coercive accountability" is a *regime of accountability* or an *accountability regime*. Indeed Dorothy Smith (2004) uses that term in her discussion of how deprofessionalization is historically situated in neo-liberalism. Strathern (1997, 2000) and Power (1994, 1997; cf. Douglas 1992) take a broader view. They suggest that an accountability regime may be found in a variety of societies, not just those that are neo-liberal. They also believe that accountability regimes will be one of the defining characteristics of the society that we are becoming. More simply, undergoing epochal change, we are "buying into" an accountability regime.

This conception of an accountability regime appears to resemble Foucault's panopticon—a surveillance machine akin to a prison constructed so that a jailer can see all of the prisoners, but none of them can see him. Since a panopticon is hierarchical, both aspects of that description are important. Some people see, but cannot be seen. Others are seen, but cannot see. Administrators seek to audit the behavior of the professoriate; however, the professors cannot see the activities of the administrators, which may be hidden behind the curtain of transparency (Gawley 2008). Strathern and others argue that an accountability regime is a structure characteristic of a historical era and associated with a particular kind of (audit) culture.[34] I will be using the term "accountability regime" in its broadest sense and in association with the concept audit culture. I follow Strathern and others by suggesting that an accountability regime is working toward the "de-churching of universities." It is drawing on the audit culture to do so.[35]

Wannabe University administrators do not discuss accountability and audit in such theoretical ways. But they do seem to see the "accountability regime" characteristic of an audit culture as a form of protection. Sometimes by imposing an audit on themselves, they may protect themselves from government supervision and so claim limited independence. They are self-monitoring before a governmental agency monitors them. Sometimes auditing protects them from scandal. When asked about possible malfeasance or scandals, administrators cite their auditing procedures as well as the rules and regulations (published on the university website), which, if followed, would ward off negative audit reports.

Administrators also seem to see news reports as a form of audit that may hold them accountable. They recognize that, because they are not quantitative, news stories differ from the work of formal auditors. But as true

of auditors, one purpose of the fourth estate is to keep institutions honest. Administrators seem to feel that news reports can be just as dangerous
as formal statistical reviews that criticize their activities. Using the Office
of University Relations (public relations), they try to plant positive stories
about the university and to prevent negative stories from appearing. They
do not want to read negative items about Wan U in the news media. More
important, they do not want either local, state, or federal officials to learn
about occurrences that cast students, professors, staff, or administrators in
an unfavorable light. If unsavory accounts of university activities are spread
by the news media, the administrators want to be able to prove that they
had done everything possible to prevent those occurrences, including such
accepted forms of surveillance as promulgating "transparent" rules and
regulation and auditing how they are used.

Negative publicity costs money. Learning that students or professors have
behaved improperly or that administrators have engaged in some form of
unethical conduct or in malfeasance, donors complain. They may even
withdraw gifts. Politicians complain, too. They do withdraw funds. Thus,
when a national news show reported that a provocative and nationally
known conservative had provoked liberal students into bad behavior when
she spoke on campus, the Office of University Relations was besieged by
phone calls from donors. The donors were not interested in the provoca-
tion; they called to condemn the behavior of the liberal students and to
question university policies toward outside speakers.

Negative publicity costs power. Learning about problems at the university
from the news media, legislators launch public investigations. Powerful legislators and governors may even give top administrators deadlines by which
they should resign.[36] Administrators may sometimes comfort one another
that a scandal will eventually die down. However, they do not accept the
dictum that any publicity is good publicity, because in due course people
will forget the scandal, but remember your name. That dictum, they seem
to feel, suits Hollywood and the entertainment industry, not the higher-
education industry.

Wannabe University has had its share of scandals reported in state media,
especially the *State Capital Record*. A few of them have also been reported
in the *Chronicle of Education*, though most have not. One or two of these
scandals have involved audits: Had the administration paid sufficient attention to auditors' reports? Had the university spent money wisely? Were
students getting their money's worth? Were students safe? Do dormitories
conform to fire codes? Administrators warn subordinates *not* to provide
the news media with negative information. "I don't want to read about the
problems in your department in the *State Capital Record*," one dean told

members of a social science department, when he refused to replace their department head. "I have an idea who put that in the paper," another dean said drily after the *State Capital Record* carried a story saying that most of Wannabe's deans had either been fired or resigned and specifically included a negative comment about him. "There are reporters in the room," special presidential assistant Peter Lynch warned, as the chairman of the board of trustees convened a twenty-minute meeting of trustees being conducted via conference call.

Auditing and reporting-as-auditing have become conventional forms of surveillance. A bad audit—a negative report—announces that an institution does not conform to accepted practices. A middle-status university, such as Wannabe University, cannot afford to be deviant. Being deviant might affect the budget. It might affect a university's standing in the market. Eschewing deviance, the Wan U administrators want the university to conform by adopting the latest "best practices" lauded by its peers. As we will see, the central administrators behave as though they want Wan U to "fit in" with other public research universities, yet simultaneously to stand out for its special qualities. They want Wannabe University to be the same yet different, as are Coke and Pepsi, Toyota and Honda, Harvard and Yale, Apple and Microsoft. The central administrators behave as though Wannabe University is a brand. Indeed, they constitute it as a brand.

3

Conforming, Branding, and Research

What are universities about? "It's all about money," a central administrator told me, as we discussed Wan U's priorities.

It's about branding. "We're doing what we can to preserve our brand," the director of athletics informed a university group, as he spoke of the problem posed by rip-off T-shirts being sold illegally at football games. At the time, he was replying to an inquiry about why the philosophy department had not been permitted to produce Wan U T-shirts when it played host to a special symposium several years earlier.

It's about being distinctive. "As we work on a new academic plan, we are developing signature programs," the provost told the Wannabe University Board of Trustees.[1] He seemed not to hear the unspoken reference to a restaurant's signature entrée, a jean-maker's signature fit, or the logo design on the signature fabric of a handbag.

As the administrators and managers associated with Wannabe University sought to imitate the "best practices" of other institutions in the higher-education industry, they simultaneously tried to distinguish Wan U from other research universities—to "enhance revenues" by establishing their brand. The administrators of Wannabe University are not the only administrators in higher education who are trying to define a brand. Indeed, "branding a university" conforms to current "best practices." To attract students and donors and to please legislators, today's university presidents may ask: "How does this campus gain distinction without twisting itself into an unnatural shape merely to be distinct?" Posed more positively, "How do we magnify the collective characteristics that define a [university] experience and make it unlike that of its peers?"[2] Branding has a peculiar aspect: it encourages minute variations that supposedly distinguish one product from another. Sometimes these microscopic variations between brands produce distinction without difference, as occurs when subjecting colas to a taste test or comparing some textbooks to others. More important, branding—the search for individuation—is part of conformity.

Analyzing conformity as the result of the dialectic between imitation and individuation, Georg Simmel (1972: 295) noted the appeal of imitation: "It . . . gives to the individual [or firm] the satisfaction of not standing alone in his [or its] actions. Whenever we imitate, we transfer not only the demand for creative activity, but also the responsibility for the action from ourselves to another. Thus the individual [or firm] . . . appears as a creature of the group, as a vessel of the social contents . . ." (cf. DiMaggio and Powell 1991). "Conversely," he suggested, "wherever prominence is given to change, wherever individual differentiation . . . and relief from generality are sought, there imitation is the negative and obstructive principle" (295). The war between the principle of conformity and that of individuation is so historically pervasive, Simmel argued, that "the antagonism between both principles has been reduced to a form of cooperation" (296).

Examples abound of students' conformity—simultaneous imitation and individuation. A Wan U graduate student, who in 1995 pierced her eyebrow, explained self-righteously that the piercing expressed her "individuality." She had not, after all, pierced her nose or placed a fifth piercing on an earlobe as had many of her contemporaries. There are similar distinctions among tattoos, as a male graduate student implied in 2007 when he explained to me the difference between his tattoo sleeves and those of another student. One of them had used a Japanese style, the other, "old-style Americana of the 1920s and '30s." By engaging in the fashionable practice of getting extensive individualized tattoos in known styles, each man had conformed.

Ultimately, branding and conformity reveal some of the ways that higher education is a business—an "industry," to use the term that administrators prefer (Kirp et al. 2003). After discussing three aspects of academic conformity—management fads, advertising, and web pages—I will concentrate on Wannabe University's early attention to what academics identify as the two basic aspects of their job, research and teaching, and also on a matter clearly within the realm of administration, finances. All three factors are intertwined. Both the managerial and sociological literatures insist that financial concerns are implicated in how universities have changed their policies about research and teaching. As Patricia Gumport (2002, 2006) explains: Over the past twenty-five years, public high education has introduced a new institutional logic—it has come to view itself as an industry rather than as a social institution.[3] As this change has occurred, public research universities, including Wan U, have adapted corporate management fads, have marketed their brand, and have sought both new efficiencies and new ways to increase "revenue streams." As Washburn (2005) and Kirp et al. (2003) point out, research is very much a revenue stream. It has been corporatized. It concerns profit, as much as advancing "knowledge in the abstract."

ACADEMIC BRANDING

MANAGEMENT FASHIONS

It may seem peculiar to create an analogy between piercings, tattoos, and research universities, but all three involve imitation, individuation, and conformity. As true of tattoos and piercings, academic administration and management are a matter of fads and fashions (Birnbaum 2001). Since the 1960s, one managerial fad has replaced another, often arriving in academia just after fading out of corporate life. Thus, since the 1970s, a host of books have recommended specific strategies. Birnbaum (2001: 24) cites "*The Managerial Revolution in Higher Education* (Rourke and Brooks, 1966), *Quantitative Approaches to Higher Education Management* (Lawrence and Service, 1977), *Implementing Management Information Systems in Colleges and Universities* (McManis and Parker, 1978), *Management Science: Applications to Academic Administration* (Wilson, 1981) and *Applying Corporate Management Strategies* (Fecher, 1985)."

In higher education as in the corporate world, managerial methods may supplant one another: "Management by objectives" yielded to "zero base budgeting"; "strategic planning" gave way to "benchmarking," which led to "total quality management" or "continuous quality improvement," as that technique came to be known in higher education (Birnbaum 2001; cf. Kirp et al. 2003). Sometimes these techniques coexist. Thus, like many other research universities, Wannabe University has a "mission statement" that is helping it to set programmatic goals (strategic planning). It assesses its accomplishments against those of "peer institutions" as it engages in "benchmarking" to determine "best practices."[4] It also has adopted methods of assessing classes, departments, institutes, and programs so that it can engage in "continuous quality improvement." (Or, as a new chief operating officer and vice president put it in fall 2003, when he visited a variety of campus groups to introduce himself: "I believe in CQM" [continuous quality management]).

The Wan U administration also conformed to management practice when in 2003, at the request of its board of trustees, it introduced benchmarking. The provost's staff, including vice provosts and some vice presidents, had meeting after meeting to define the appropriate "metrics" with which to compare Wan U to "peer institutions." It worked hour after hour considering which eight public research universities were its peers and "aspirant" peers. (Only one of those schools is relatively close by; the others are in the South or the Midwest, where land-grant universities supposedly carry more esteem.) And then, because it had selected too many ways to measure its transformation, these officials spent considerable time discarding and refining the eleven items eventually used to analyze the undergraduate educational experience, graduate and professional education, diversity, resources, and national reputation.[5] Ultimately, a comparison of Wan U and its peers fit on a one-page table, a terse executive summary that might highlight both Wan U's progress toward transformation and the specialties associated with its brand.

THE WEB PAGE AS BRANDING

One sees how skillfully University Communications sold the university when one examines the Wan U website. According to *Wannabe Weekly*, University Communications was to "establish . . . a marketing and strategic communications approach for the University." The program was to "position the University to function in what has become a highly competitive environment, and will emphasize that the University should be the first choice for [in-state] students. It . . . also work[ed] to increase recognition of the University as a resource for the state, and to improve the University's national reputation."

To better "serve" its customers, the Wan U website was altered in the early years of the new century. First, the university had one generalized website. Later, like other universities, it developed separate sites for such separate customers as students, parents, and potential students; such constituents as alumni who might donate to Wan U;[6] as well as faculty.

In *Wannabe Weekly*, the newspaper that the university used to present its official version of occurrences, the head of the University Communications department publicly explained: "The University's web philosophy has evolved over time. At one time, we didn't know exactly who was using our website. All we could do was imagine the various audiences and try to offer something for everyone." After using surveys and focus groups to learn how consumers (students, parents, prospective students), constituents (alumni who might donate to Wan U), and workers (faculty and staff) used the website, University Communications designed a series of parallel sites that shared design elements but facilitated each group's use of the ten or fifteen links its members were most likely to use. The revised websites were more than efficient; they were designed to appeal to customers.

In 2006 the "parents' website" offered a fairly subtle appeal to consumers. Wan U presents itself as ideal for all sorts of families and as a university with school spirit where parents and children can have safe fun. The parents' page has three pictures: a white mother and son on the top front step of a cozy-looking dormitory (perhaps this is a single-parent family; perhaps the father took the photo, as fathers usually do); an Asian American family posing by sitting in front of a flower garden containing a sculptural icon of the university; and a white family clad in Wan U sweatshirts sitting near the Wan U band in the stands of the soccer stadium. The thirteen "useful links" for parents also demonstrate that "the University knows" what parents care about. They include the university's parents' association, the pages for students and potential students, the visitor's center, the campus hotel, the admissions center, the bursar's office, driving directions, and a page on campus safety.[7]

Simultaneously, the Wan U website casts students, prospective students, and parents as potentially fickle consumers whose applications and allegiance (measured in tuition, fees, residence and meal contracts) the university must woo. Wan U's appeal to these groups is a form of simultaneous imitation and individuation, for Wan U does not stand alone. Its management practices conformed. Its website conformed. It introduced special sites for special people the same year that other colleges and universities were doing so. It also advertised.[8]

SELLING THE BRAND

To promote its brand, Wan U advertised itself during its televised basketball and football games. (During these games, each of the competing universities airs a commercial promoting its school.) The ads were supposed to make Wan U seem special by stressing qualities that might induce high school students to apply and attend.[9] The administrators who approved the commercial also wanted the parents of those potential students to consider Wan U favorably. Accordingly, at the turn of the century, University Communications depicted Wan U as a school of high academic quality, whose faculty do first-rate research and also value teaching; as a school with a great diversity of programs and also diversity of people; and as a school where both faculty and staff care about students. One series of television commercials shown during breaks in athletic games presented a modern red-brick campus with state-of-the-art technologically sophisticated classrooms and laboratories, where professors and students from a variety of racialized ethnicities interacted with one another in an atmosphere of respect and caring. A few years later, the commercial focused on an athlete who was both first-team all-American in his sport and also in academic accomplishment. For the next few years, the commercial featured a student playing a guitar. As he strummed, he enumerated Wan U's many "Points of Pride." Then, staring at his musical instrument and the pick held between his fingers, he announced: "Great pick." (His tone of voice might have announced: "This is a best buy!") Less expensive to produce than films of campus activities, as did the television commercial that featured the academically accomplished athlete, this ad might appeal to students with outstanding academic records by convincing both them and their parents that Wan U was not simply a party school. Through its television advertising, Wannabe University simultaneously imitated and individuated. It tried to be memorable.

Indeed, even Wan U's architecture conforms to current fashion and aims to please students. Take the "new" (renovated) student union. On July 11, 2003, the *Chronicle of Higher Education* featured a story on how the student unions recently built on American campuses resemble suburban malls (Lewis 2003). When in 2004 Wan U reopened its revamped student union, it featured a food court. Its fast-food stations seemed sure to attract students, for they included among others a Wendy's, a Blimpie, and a Panda Express that students might frequent when meals provided by the university's Dining Services did not appeal. (The fast-food franchises rented their space from the university.) Similarly, the athletic department proposed building a new fitness center so that Wan U could compete for students with other universities. As a professor suggested when the director of athletics raised the issue at a 2005 meeting of the Athletic Advisory Committee, "My daughter is applying to colleges and is receiving lots of brochures from schools. They feature their new fitness centers and my daughter cares about sports. If we are really trying to implement best practices, we need a better fitness center."[10] (The board of trustees approved planning for the building in 2007.) Imitating and individuating—conforming—Wan U presents itself as part of a changing industry.

A CHANGING INDUSTRY

As true of any business, colleges and universities must at least break even to stay afloat. But the business of higher education changed radically in the last half of the twentieth century. First it expanded. Then it faced the possibility of drastic contraction.

THE TRENDS

After World War II, state and national policies favored higher education. Through the 1970s, higher education was a "growth industry" (Levine 2001: 39). Enrollment rose every year. "The primary and most persistent demand that government made on higher education was to increase capacity. . . . Rising government support was the norm. Public institutions of higher education multiplied. Government aid was targeted at private schools to promote expansion. Few questions were asked" (39).

During this period, the federal government also promoted university research (LaPidus 2001: 250), partly by funding graduate education, partly through competitive grants and contracts. Congress established and funded numerous agencies, such as the National Science Foundation (1945). It expanded others, such as the National Institutes of Health. Various departments—from defense to agriculture, transportation to the National Aeronautics and Space Administration, education to the treasury—funded university research, especially in the sciences and engineering. Industries and private foundations provided research monies as well.

By the 1980s the growth industry had "leveled off" and became a "mature industry,"[11] as the United States went from a system of mass higher education to one of almost universal higher education. By then, more than 60 percent of American high school graduates were attending some form of higher education (Levine 2001: 42). By 2007, 80 percent of high school graduates were enrolling in some form of higher education within eight years (Attewell et al. 2007). But they were not members of the demographic group, white men, that had dominated American campuses since their establishment.

University-management expert George Keller captured the importance of the demographic transformation in his classic *Academic Strategy* (1983). First he warned of an impending crisis, and then he introduced demographic and financial explanations. As Keller put it in a famous passage: "A specter is haunting higher education: the specter of decline and bankruptcy" (3). For,

> America's 3,100 colleges and universities are living through a revolution. It is as profound a change as that which crushed the early nineteenth-century world of tiny religious colleges and created the new era of universities, state land-grant colleges, graduate schools, coeducation, research, deans of postgraduate education for the professional classes at the turn of the [twentieth] century. (viii)

As Keller explained, higher education was beginning to lose its traditional customers; for the first time since the Civil War, American colleges had to "deal with a prolonged decline in potential students" (12). Because of a drop in the birth rate between 1961 and 1975, fewer young people were graduating from high schools and applying directly to colleges and universities. This drop was particularly dramatic—a plummet—for higher education's traditional students: white men. Indeed, increasingly high school graduates would include people of color, and college students would include a plurality of women and "non-traditional students," who had graduated from high school years before.

The fall in the birthrate had been less dramatic for African Americans. Immigrants were increasingly people of color, born in Asia, Latin American, and the Caribbean. Indeed, the demographic transformation that Keller anticipated was so complete that "less than a quarter of the undergraduate population" in 2006 "entered college immediately after high school, attended college full time, lived in dormitories, and rarely worked for pay because they were financially dependent on their parents" (Attewell and Lavin 2007: B16). As Paul Attewell and David Lavin observe, "College is no longer a phase of youth to be enjoyed before real life begins."

If a college or university were to attract a traditional customer base, it had to compete with other higher-education institutions. To enroll the upper-middle class and elite students who were determined to earn a degree and were more likely to do so than students from less fortunate backgrounds, a research university, such as Wannabe University, had to find ways to compete with the more than 150 other research universities. It had to compete with some private and public colleges as well. "Enrollment managers" knew that wealthier students were more likely to have good educational backgrounds and to graduate in four years.[12] Similarly, they knew that only 20 percent of the institutions of higher education in the United States have competitive admissions. (The other 80 percent accept any qualified candidate who applies.) Competing with one another, with private universities, and with liberal arts colleges, public research universities were claiming a spot in the elite sector of the higher-education industry. To maintain that claim, Wannabe University, like other universities, had to market its product.[13]

The position of the public research universities, such as Wannabe, was not secure, because the track was not level. At least twenty private research universities were supposedly more elite than almost all public flagship universities: The "privates" had larger endowments, more students with wealthy parents as well as very good high school grades and SAT scores, and more alumni who boasted considerable wealth and achievement. They had a better reputation. In the first years of the twenty-first century, private research universities elbowed public research universities out of the top twenty spots in *U.S. News & World Report*'s "America's Best Colleges."[14]

To make matters more difficult, public colleges and universities had to market education in the context of reduced state support. A variety of observers claim that the decline in state support was symptomatic of neoliberalism (see Harvey 2005). Others say it was a result of global competition. Yet others say that the state had too many other priorities. To an administrator, the ultimate cause may not matter. To be sure, sometimes knowing the cause of a problem may help to solve it, especially if that "cause" is within the control of an individual or institution. What counts is the problem one must solve and how one can go about solving it. Even though he had been the CEO of a Fortune 500 company and a college president, the head of a board of trustees could not solve the "problems" of neo-liberalism, global competition, or state priorities. At best, a skilled administrator can struggle with the practical problems arising from such significant socioeconomic changes.

PRACTICAL SOLUTIONS

Administrators are "practical people."[15] Whatever the ultimate "cause," the immediate and practical problem facing research universities was clear: by 2000 in some states, particularly in the West and Midwest, the percentage of the budgets of public universities provided by the state sank so low that a few universities spoke of themselves as "state-affiliated universities" rather than "state universities." State contributions might be less than 10 percent of a university's general fund, though it must be noted that sometimes this dip in the percentage of state support resulted from increased university spending coupled with decreased state funding. Additionally, a decreasing share of states' general budgets was spent on higher education. Instead of spending money on higher education, states invested in such items as K–12 education, transportation, and prisons. As one Wan U professor who studies education quipped, "The university may be having problems, but the prisons are doing fine." Indeed, in Wan U's state, punishing criminals was such a growth industry that the state shipped some convicts down South.

In dollars, both state support and tuition increased during President Whitmore's tenure. However, overall expenses swelled so much that state support constituted a smaller portion of revenues. Students' tuition took up much of the slack. Why did expenses increase so much? What could Wannabe University do to raise more money? The answers to these questions are intertwined.

As anyone who owns a business knows, "you have to spend money to make money." I will start by talking about attempts to make money. Some of these were costly and, what's worse, did not work. The university could, for instance, hire people to intensify its efforts at fund-raising; Wan U established the Wannabe University Foundation, which did indeed significantly increase the university's endowment. A university can also increase its revenue by raising tuition (and/or increasing the number of students); pushing faculty to increase the number and monetary value of the grants and contracts for which they apply and (with a bit of skill and luck) receive, increasing how the university may profit from those awards; or increasing auxiliary income—such as revenue from sports or from products that the university may license or co-produce. (I am using the term "license" to indicate both revenue derived from selling permission to put the university logo on such products as T-shirts, and monies derived by patenting faculty research and selling permission to use those patents in some way.)[16] Reorienting itself to increase its revenue streams may also involve shifting the allocation of resources within the university, such as the proportion of employees who are faculty or staff.

THE RESEARCH PUSH

I start with the administrative push for more grants and contracts, which would produce income and underwrite some of the costs a university incurs by sponsoring research, but not all grants and contracts result in a profit.[17] Here's how universities had made money from some faculty research from World War II until the 1980s.

Then, as now, when a professor applied for a grant from the federal government, she made out a budget that requests that the grantor pay her for the time she will devote to doing the research. The sum may include her time during two months of the summer. It may also include monies to release her from some of the time she is supposed to devote to teaching during the academic year. (By not teaching, she can devote more of her effort to research.) These summer and release-time monies are subject to a multiplier effect. The grantor not only pays the researcher a stipend based on her university salary, but also pays fringe benefits at a predetermined rate that has been negotiated between the agency and the higher-education institution. Once calculated together, the benefits and salary are added to requests for equipment, travel, and specific services (such as postage) and are called "direct costs." (Not all agencies will fund the same items as direct costs.) These are subject to another multiplication. By prior negotiated agreement, universities may charge the granting agencies a percentage of the "direct costs" as "overhead" or indirect costs. (This process is sometimes called "recapturing the indirect costs," to indicate that the university is out of pocket for mail service or maintaining duplicating machines or even heating the room or laboratory housing the research. Universities have negotiated agreements with agencies about the percentage of direct costs that may be identified as indirect costs.)

The rules of how a university can profit are clear. Universities are not supposed to profit from indirect costs, and all indirect costs are supposed to be associated with research. When universities have used indirect costs in other ways, scandals have resulted.[18] Nonetheless, universities can profit.

When a granting agency subsidizes a professor's salary for two summer months, the professor earns two months' additional income. (Professors at most colleges and universities earn nine-month salaries.) The university receives the overhead on that additional salary. When a granting agency "buys" some of a professor's teaching time from the university, the university has to find someone else to teach that professor's course(s). Most often, it hires a graduate student or an adjunct professor, each of whom earns much less than a professor. The monetary difference between the costs associated with the professor's salary and fringe benefits and the stipend paid the substitute teacher is profit. So, too, the university may use some overhead to subsidize internal grants to professors, especially when those relatively small internal grants may result in applications to external funding agencies. And it may "kick back" some of the overhead to the researcher who received the grant, her department, and the dean of her school. (The university generally has an agreement specifying what share of the overhead customarily goes to which party associated with the grant.) The researcher, department, and dean are supposed to use their share to generate more research.

The possibilities became more complex in 1983, when Congress passed the Bayh-Dole Act, also known as the University and Small Business Patent Procedures Act of 1980 (see Mowery et al. 2004). Before the act, some, but not all, federal agencies had permitted universities to patent inventions made by its researchers while pursuing research funded by those agencies. The Bayh-Dole Act introduced a uniform federal patent policy. It extended that right to discoveries resulting from grants from any federal agency. It specified that

- a university *must* file a patent on any discovery that it chooses to own;
- a university could collaborate with commercial concerns to promote the use of inventions;
- the federal government had a non-exclusive license to produce the invention around the world and that it also had "march in" rights; and
- small businesses have priority to licensing relevant inventions.

It also established uniform guidelines for licenses.

The act virtually announced that university research can be a commodity. Indeed, some say it represented the commodification of university-based research. But sociologists, economists, and management experts disagree about what prompted the Bayh-Dole Act. Some argue that socioeconomic policies associated with neo-liberalism gave birth to the commodification of scholarly research (see Harvey 2005; Slaughter and Leslie

1999; Slaughter and Rhoades 2004). As these scholars see it, neo-liberalism decreased the monies available for higher education, "and what new money was available was concentrated in technoscience and market-related fields in what amounted to a higher education version of supply-side economics" (Slaughter and Leslie 1999: 37). They maintain that in a world characterized by new forms of international economic competition, "post-secondary education was directed toward national 'wealth creation' and away from its traditional concern with the liberal education of undergraduates." Research universities became part of the "academic capitalist knowledge/learning regime"; to wit, internationally, universities embedded themselves in corporate and global purposes and practices (Slaughter and Rhoades 2004). Etzkowitz, Webster, and Healey (1998) use different concepts and build a model that emphasizes how state activities are intertwined with those of industry and academia in a "triple helix." (They use the term "triple helix" to discuss how government, corporations, and universities are intertwined and affect one another.) However, all of these researchers concur that the processes associated with globalization have prompted universities to promote the *transformation of knowledge into capital*.[19]

Another school of researchers believe that the commodification of knowledge emerged because of how the fields of biology, biochemistry, and pharmacology had developed in the last half of the twentieth century (Mowery et al. 2004; Powell and Grodal 2005). Pharmaceutical and chemical industries had long profited from academic research, but they had largely done so in one of two ways—under a system of open patents or under a system of patents managed by an agency that simultaneously served many universities. As biotechnology flourished during the last decades of the twentieth century, the possibilities for profiting from that research increased—not only for industries but for universities as well. In the 1970s, the University of Wisconsin was patenting biological discoveries associated with federal grants. Also in the 1970s, Stanford University's new Office for Intellectual Property realized that the university would profit if it managed its own patents and, even better, if it insisted that its researchers patent their findings rather than publish their findings to be used by anyone who cared to do so. Open publication raised the possibility that some firm might patent a university researcher's openly published finding, so that the firm profited, but the university did not.

Biomedical research flourished; computer technologies took off. According to Powell and Grodal (2005), the nature of these expanding and ever-changing fields fostered the possibility for profit. Admiring how Stanford University, Duke University, and the University of North Carolina at Chapel Hill had aided themselves as well as enhanced the economic development of their regions, more public and private research universities emulated them. They sought to create new revenue streams by establishing research parks and offices that "incubated" faculty discoveries. Once appropriately nurtured, the discoveries would supposedly hatch into profitable firms owned by the researchers and the university or the researchers, the university, and a non-university-based corporation. The dream of such awesome profit is inherent in the *Chronicle of Higher Education*'s list of the attributes of a wannabe university. Recall, as discussed in chapter 1, at the height of ambition, a wannabe even "dream[s] of nurturing the start-up companies for the next Silicon Valley or Research Triangle Park." Wan U dreamed, too.

Before James Whitmore set foot on campus, President Ned Oakes tried to start a research park on some unused land relatively near the science complex. He hired the father-in-law of a local legislator to head it. His task was quite complex. Not only would the university have to construct buildings to house potential firms, but it also had to build roads so that the research park would not add to the increasing traffic congestion around the university. (Recall Wannabe University is located in rural Ashton, which defines "traffic congestion" differently than would an urban area.)

The attempt failed, although why it did so was never public knowledge. And, to some extent, this attempt to start a research park—early for Wan U, but late for other universities—was misguided. What was to stop an incubated firm from picking up and moving to an urban area with a more suitable workforce than that found in the Ashton vicinity? Indeed, why should the young people thought to be the potential discoverers and manufacturers of products want to stay in Ashton? During the area's industrialization in the nineteenth century, Ashton had a record of its best and brightest young people moving elsewhere.

Heading his third university, President James Whitmore took a different tack. With Mike Tremaine, the provost in place when President Whitmore arrived, he pushed the virtues of faculty research. A series of "corporate" vice provosts for research beefed up all aspects of research administration. President Whitmore and Provost Tremaine "encouraged" the deans to increase the grant activity of their school or college.[20] The deans "encouraged" department heads and professors. The deans tried to mold eclectic departments into more conventional paths in the hope that they would thus garner more research monies. (Recall that one social scientist had complained that the dean was trying to make his department a clone of a respected department.) The deans established centers and institutes that might facilitate an atmosphere conducive to funded research. External grants and contract funding increased dramatically.

Some of these centers, especially in the sciences, did generate an increase in external funding. Even a humanities center took steps toward financially justifying its existence. To apply for a research fellowship at the center, a professor had to submit an application that mimicked the application for a fellowship from the National Endowment for the Humanities. Science departments that generated more discord than grant activity faced the possibility of being replaced by interdisciplinary institutes that might generate more research monies, as happened at least once.[21]

President Whitmore, his provosts, and his deans kept up with the national identification of potential revenue streams, especially those associated with biology—the field whose development had supposedly prompted the 1980 Bayh-Dole Act. Throughout the country, research universities anticipated the possibility that research on stem cells, fuel cells, and nanotechnology might produce the next equivalent of the Silicon Valley. Provost Tyler Johnson had begun to invest in stem-cell research as early as 2000, when he invested $20 million (including five faculty position) in the Center for Regenerative Biology. The School of Engineering's Center for Fuel Cell Research, founded in 2002, attracted $20 million in its first five years. The Wan U administration and board of trustees were eventually to identify stem-cell research and nanotechnology as "priorities for investment," as Provost Gerald Wesley explained to a meeting of the faculty of the College of Liberal Arts and Sciences in December 2006.[22] Investment included hiring faculty whose work was pertinent to those fields and equipping them with (very expensive) state-of-the-art laboratories.

PROFESSORS IN THE AUDIT CULTURE

The drive for more funded research involved more than improving institutional resources. To thrive, an audit society must foster a culture that encourages individuals to audit themselves—or at least to make themselves "auditable." Top administrators pressured the faculty, especially scientists, to transform themselves—or at least to measure themselves by their academic accomplishments, much as administrators measured them. Those assessments were to include getting grants. Thus, at a reception, the vice provost for research introduced me to a professor by saying, "Tom is one of our biggest grant-getters" as opposed to "Tom does terrific work" or "Tom has a daughter a little younger than your son."

Managers initiated a series of probes, some more gentle than others. Many of those measures involved individual rewards for individual accomplishments. Some of these were unfunded. In 2003 the vice provost for research introduced to the board of trustees a half-dozen professors who had received $1 million or more in external funding, and during one convocation, snapshots of "outstanding faculty" who had received many grants were sequentially projected onto a large screen. No one asked why it was an honor for a professor to meet the members of the board of trustees or why anyone would want to have their picture flashed on a giant screen during the convocation ceremony. Rather, the central administration seemed to assume that professors value meeting trustees, much as members of the upper classes value being appointed as trustees (Daniels 1988). In a status-conscious consumer culture, who wouldn't want to meet important people? Who wouldn't want to be recognized as outstanding?

Administrators introduced monetary rewards as well. The university created research professorship (no teaching for a year) to honor outstanding scholars. It added a new title, Board of Trustees Distinguished Professor, to be awarded to top scholars who were good teachers and had served on university committees. (Distinguished professorships offered some bonus pay.) Often using a PowerPoint presentation, each year the new Board of Trustees Distinguished Professors gave a synopsis of their work at a board meeting and were feted after the meeting at a reception with top-notch hors d'oeuvres. (Department heads nominated their "best researchers," since having a Board of Trustees Distinguished Professor was also a form of recognition for the department.)

Many professors at many institutions of higher education value such recognition. I recall attending a memorial service where I encountered a professional acquaintance whom I had not seen for years. "How are you?" I asked warmly. "I'm the University Professor of Sociology at Private College," my acquaintance replied. At national meetings, some professors happily boast to others of the publications and recognitions they had received that academic year.

At Wan U some professors found the new distinguished professorships an exciting possibility and others found them irrelevant. Some professors found them a way to engage in one-upmanship with competitors, as indicated by a social scientist's comment that "applying doesn't seem worth the effort, but it would be great to see the look on Jim's face if I got one." Others found them a cause for envy and dissatisfaction. Thus, one humanist replied to a letter asking him to apply for an endowed chair after he was not asked whether he wanted a larger office recently vacated by a retiree and a departmental competitor was nominated for a Board of Trustees Distinguished Professorship, but he was not. (When professors feel appreciated, they are not as likely to respond positively to inquiries about their interest in positions at other schools.)

Provost Johnson also introduced a "research incentive award," whose terms were to be modified under Provost Wesley's tenure but were instead discontinued. Here's how it worked. Recall that professors at Wannabe

University receive a nine-month salary, paid biweekly over twelve months. Applications for research grants and contracts may include two months of summer salary as well as two months of fringe benefits. Both the salary costs and fringe benefits affect the size of indirect costs associated with a grant or contract, since "indirect costs" are based on percentages periodically negotiated by the university and granting agencies associated with, say, the federal government. The rule is simple: the higher the salaries, the higher the fringe benefits, the higher the indirect costs. Under specified conditions and with federal agreement, a professor might have applied for a "research incentive award" totaling an extra month of summer salary. In the College of Liberal Arts and Sciences, the condition was that their application requested at least $500,000. In the School of Engineering, a researcher who funded six graduate students qualified for a research incentive award. (The researcher then employed the graduate students as assistants in her laboratory.)

On the books for several years, the research incentive award was reviewed after the federal government found that its wording did not comply with federal regulations (and fined Wan U over $1 million).[23] In the name of efficiency, the central administrators wanted a uniform rule to apply to all researchers in all schools and colleges, to be approved by the Deans Council, and to be acceptable to the federal government. Once it was reintroduced to the appropriate committee of the University Senate, some faculty argued it was unnecessary, even harmful, while others argued that it was a just reward. A subcommittee, including an associate vice provost and several department heads, met six times until the representative from one school conceded that it was unnecessary to set a policy for the five professors in his school who were the only ones applying for such large grants, especially since they would continue to do so even if they did not receive a research incentive award. One possible implication of the committee's rejection of having research incentive awards on the books is that money does not motivate many professors as much as both the deans and the central administrators had thought it did. Another is that the professors had yet to transform themselves into fully auditable individuals. They were not all judging themselves and others by either the money they earned or the fanciness of their titles.

Provost Johnson also introduced "disincentives" or punishments. Professors who did not do enough research, as indicated by publications and grants received, might not be living up to the "Policy on Faculty Professional Responsibilities" published on the provost's web page. Its provisions specified that departmental colleagues might "audit" research activity and punish some colleagues as "shirkers." They might be suspended from the doctoral faculty. Even worse, they might be asked to teach more courses each semester than professors whose grant activity and publication rate were deemed satisfactory. (Those whose research activity was exemplary might qualify for a "merit raise" distributed within departments and also by deans and the provost.) In this model, as several professors noted after a badly attended faculty forum about assessing the quality of instruction, research is rewarded and teaching is treated as a punishment (see chapters 6 and 7).

From fiscal 1997 through fiscal 2007, the research revenue stream doubled—although it remained lower than at larger research universities. Funding associated with the College of Liberal Arts and Sciences increased more than sevenfold. Monies raised were not the only yardstick for judging faculty. As had traditionally been the case at some research universities, they were also the measure of schools and deans. Each year when deans went before the Central Budget Committee to request funds, they reported their school's performance—the number of students taught, papers published, grants received. Professors thought that these indicators also influenced the deans' reappointments. Deans are reviewed for reappointment every five years. When one dean was up for his fifth-year review, some scientists and social scientists predicted that his reappointment was a shoo-in. "How could he not be reappointed?" social scientists asked. Grant activity in his school was way up. "His" professors were bringing in significantly more money. Friction within departments and an increasing student-faculty ratio were simply not as important as increased grant activity, these scientists and social scientists explained.[24] "The university is pushing for more funded research. It is not demanding harmony among colleagues," one explained to me.

Professors are not the only people hired to support funded research. Nor are they the only people who transform inventions into incubating corporations. Satisfying ever-more complicated government regulations required an ever-larger staff of managers. Incubating inventions also required staffing. As we will see, since salaries and fringe benefits are the most significant items in any university's budget, hiring more staff may mean that a smaller percentage of the faculty is composed of full-time employees. If finite funds cover more full-time staff, monies are not available for more full-time faculty.

President Whitmore did indeed hire staff to promote research. In 2002 *Wannabe Weekly* announced: "A for-profit entity [the Wan U Research and Development Corporation] has been revitalized to help the university create start-up businesses using technologies developed by faculty." It was to "work closely with the [university's] Center for Science and Technology

Commercialization" (whose head gave a PowerPoint presentation to the board of trustees to explain the center's incubation of businesses). Periodically, the *Wannabe Weekly* announced that professors were profiting from their research. In 2006 it reported: "A new technology in insect pest control may lead the way to a new generation of safer insecticides." A specific corporation was investing over $1 million "for the development of insecticides that will exploit molecular targets first identified in the laboratory" of a Wan U professor. It announced a discovery by some researchers at the dental school. And the *Wannabe Weekly* made it clear that research scientists were not the only professors who could profit. Some well-known professors in the School of Education had produced computer programs to enrich the classroom experience of grammar school students. They were working with the university's Research and Development Corporation to market these programs to schools and school districts and so to turn a profit for both themselves and Wan U.

Such news articles have a taken-for-granted aspect. By "taken for granted," I mean they report the commercial development of faculty research—commodification—as though it is "perfectly natural" for professors' work to be patented and sold rather than reported in academic journals (cf. Kirp et al. 2003). Challenging the "right" of both the faculty and the university "to incubate businesses" and so "to turn a buck" simply seems un-American. Indeed, in conversations at faculty gatherings, professors seem to take for granted scientists' ability to profit from their research. They will question how people spend their money, but not the right to earn it, as seen in the following conversational snippet:

> **Q:** He moved to that block? Those are McMansions. They must be at least 3,500 square feet. I thought those were built for people commuting to [the nearby city].
>
> **A:** He's in engineering. He made a discovery that the university is developing. My brother made that mistake. You know, some people think that those large houses will bring happiness.

Nor will they question the need for staff to manage grants and to promote inventions.

THE COST OF PROMOTING RESEARCH PROFITS

At Wannabe University, as elsewhere, the administration's appointment of more personnel to "manage" its business interests has resulted in the expansion of the university's staff. Rhoades and Sporn (2002a) report that nationally the hiring of staff has outpaced the hiring of faculty, as seen in table 3.1, calculated from data collected by the Department of Education's National Center for Education Statistics.

The data available for Wannabe University suggest a similar pattern. These data start three years after the Rhoades and Sporn data end and seem to continue the trend that they outline: a shift in the nature of professional employment on college campuses. From fall semester 1998 to fall semester 2005, the percentage of professional staff who were full- and part-time faculty decreased, as seen in table 3.2.

However, the processes that produce this pattern are more complex than the simple hiring of more non-faculty professionals (professional managers) than of faculty. These categories are government-defined. The definition does not take into account shifts in the character of the labor force. Today the job titles and duties listed by an "office of human resources"[25] are meant to attract college-educated personnel. Thirty years ago, a woman with only a high school education and specified skills might have been called a "secretary" and defined as "classified personnel." Today a woman with a college education, some of those same skills, and additional skills might be called some variant on "program assistant," "educational assistant," or even "executive assistant" and classified as a "non-faculty professional." That change in job titles, qualifications, and duties increases the number of non-faculty professionals at universities.

Nonetheless, Rhoades and Sporn (2002a, 2002b) are correct in pointing to a shift in distribution of employees across categories. At Wannabe University, as at their example, University of Arizona, there has been a decided increase in professional managers who engage in "quality assurance," who are engaged in "development activities" (fund-raising), and who "incubate" faculty discoveries. From 1996 to 2006, the number of people serving as the staff of the Institute for Teaching and Learning also increased—from two to forty. (I consider changes in teaching in a later chapter.)

Hiring staff may impede hiring faculty. Not only is hiring "non-faculty professionals" often an expensive proposition, but hiring senior administrators is even more costly. Moreover, the replacement of senior administrators tends to be more expensive than the replacement of senior professors. Here's how a scientist explained it to me:

> The cost of administration increases. When a senior person leaves a department or retires, the usual pattern is that the department is authorized to replace that person *at the entry level*. Senior hires are usually the result of explicit decisions to strengthen a department, not of routine personnel transitions. On the other hand, within the administration, a senior official is *never* replaced by an entry-level person. . . . I would bet that people are invariably replaced by people who cost more.

TABLE 3.1
Total numbers (full- and part-time) of professional staff, 1976–1995, at U.S. colleges and universities

	1976 # (%)	1987 # (%)	1989 # (%)	1991 # (%)	1993 # (%)	1995 # (%)
Executive/administrative managerial	101,263 (11.1)	113,719 (10.5)	144,670 (10.6)	144,755 (10.4)	143,675 (9.7)	147,445 (9.6)
Faculty (instructional & research)	633,210 (69.3)	793,070 (62.1)	824,220 (60.2)	826,252 (59.1)	915,474 (61.7)	931,706 (61.0)
Nonfaculty professionals	178,560 (19.6)	349,772 (27.4)	398,883 (29.2)	426,702 (30.5)	425,319 (28.6)	449,807 (29.4)
Total	913,003 (100)	1,276,511 (100)	1,367,773 (100)	1,397,709 (100)	1,484,468 (100)	1,528,958 (100)

Source: From Rhoades and Sporn (2002a: 17). Their cited source: National Center for Education Statistics.

TABLE 3.2
Total numbers (full- and part-time) of professional staff at Wannabe University*

	Fall 1998 # (%)	Fall 2007 # (%)
Faculty	944 (42.2)	1,113 (37.3)
Executive/Administrative/Managerial	75 (3.4)	88 (2.9)
Nonfaculty professional	1,219 (54.5)	1,783 (59.8)
Total	2,238 (100.1)	2,984 (100)

*Excludes classified personnel.
Source: Calculated from data reported by the Office of Institutional Research, Wannabe University.

The scientist suspects there is probably an exception to this practice, promotion from within. A department head who becomes a dean is probably paid less than a dean recruited from outside. Thus, he continues, the savings accrued through internal promotions "would seem to be a powerful inducement to a prudent administration to promote from within." But administrative decisions are not necessarily rational decisions. He asks:

> Who wants to serve in an administration with people who share responsibility but are earning below the norm? By definition—there is no other definition in the administration—they are inferior in status. Job security is non-existent for administration officials; there is no equivalent to the recognition that comes with publication or even the praise of students; and the only thing remaining is

symbolic—the Bigelow [carpet] on the floor, the snacks at the retirement party, and, most importantly, the cogent evidence of the esteem of one's peers and superiors as expressed in one's salary.

By spending money to pay staff, including senior administrators, a university has fewer funds to hire full-time professors. To compensate, like many other research universities, Wan U has increasingly hired part-time instructors rather than full-time faculty. Some are graduate students who pay for their education by serving as teaching assistants. Some are adjunct professors, academics trapped in the geographic area without a full-time academic job. When Wan U does hire full-time faculty, the deans authorize a search for assistant professors. They also give precedence to professors who will best advance the university's mission as defined in its strategic plan.

Adapting corporate management techniques, branding the university, promoting research revenue, incubating firms, balancing the budget, administrators increasingly present themselves as corporate managers. Like high-level corporate managers, they want to do their jobs so well that they can leave for even better jobs. "I want to thank you all," Provost Tyler Johnson graciously told the crowd at the party marking his departure for the presidency of another research university. "When I interviewed at [My Newest State] University, I told people about the wonderful programs you introduced here. The trustees [who hired me] were very impressed with these programs and with your work. They want me to introduce these programs there. I am proud to have worked on these programs with you."

4

Outsiders and the New Managerialism

"I hear this is a good university to move from. People have left here for really good places," the central administrator explained, when asked the reason for accepting a job at Wannabe University. Among professional administrators, Wannabe University has established a reputation as a good stepping-stone for a hardworking person with talent, skill, and ambition. Because promising and accomplished administrators are both coming and going, the management of Wannabe University reveals some ways that higher education is growing to resemble corporations.

WANNABE AS STEPPING-STONE

Since the 1980s, with one exception, Wan U presidents have been professional presidents (Gittelman 2004) whom the board of trustees hired after a national search. Since the early 1990s, Wan U presidents have appointed internal search committees headed by a high-level administrator to hire provosts, deans, and some vice provosts from a national pool. Depending on the position being filled, they were sometimes given funds to call on the help of consulting firms (headhunters). People come to Wan U because its reputation as a good stepping-stone seems warranted.

People who have held key jobs at Wan U have gotten even better jobs elsewhere. Consider recent provosts. One man had been in place when President Whitmore arrived; he left for the presidency of a good public university and is now one of the highest-paid state university presidents in the nation. Another had recently left for the presidency of an acceptable state university. (While chatting with a union official at the meeting in which the trustees gave President Whitmore a raise, an administrator joked that President Whitmore's salary was being increased so that it would be higher than that of his ex-provost.) Even the fellow who had twice served as acting provost had left for a presidency, albeit at a minor and distant state college.

Others have done well, too. One of the three past presidents abandoned administration. However, the other two left for the presidencies of what rank-conscious administrators and faculty identified as "even better" research universities than Wan U. One vice provost for education and instruction left to be the provost of a quite good women's liberal arts college. A vice provost for student affairs accepted a position with the same title at a university with three times as many students.[1] She explained to the student newspaper, "In my field, this is considered a promotion."

However, the possibility of satisfying ambition is not a sufficient reason to take a job at Wannabe University. In an era when almost every research university presents itself as a wannabe, the ambitious professional university administrator has lots of jobs from which to choose. In January 2003 the *Chronicle of Higher Education* named an ambitious wannabe university in virtually every area of the United States: Texas Technical University, University of Utah, Oklahoma State University, University of Cincinnati, the University of Connecticut, the University of South Carolina. Each of these schools might present itself as a stepping-stone to bigger and better jobs.

Wannabe University also attracts professional administrators because it sits in an attractive area of the country, has good schools, has access to major cities, and offers very competitive administrative salaries. The average pay for a professor at Wan U is well above the national average for a public research university and a little over two-thirds the average pay of a professor at one of the state's private research institutions. Ashton—as faculty, administrators, and staff tell prospective colleagues—is a fine place to live.

Situated amid farmland, hills left by retreating glaciers, and hiking trails that wend through woods, past waterfalls, and besides rivers, Ashton is also located near important interstate highways. It is close to four large airports that a traveler can choose among when deciding a departure point. Looking for urbane entertainment, a resident of Ashton can also select among opera companies and symphonies, outstanding art museums, and excellent theater.

Ashton's location—smack in the middle of the concentration of colleges and universities in the northern United States—makes it unusual among public research universities. Northern public universities have all found one or two boasting points, but on the whole, they are the poor cousins of the great private universities that claim international status. In the Midwest, such schools as the University of Michigan and the University of Wisconsin battle with one another for eminence. Although the campuses of the University of California must contend with the competition from Stanford University and the University of Southern California, they do not have as much local competition as the northern institutions of higher education.

In the North, public research universities must contend with Harvard, Yale, and Princeton, as well as with renowned liberal arts colleges, whose graduates hold key positions in the national government and in the international corporate complex. As is true of graduates of many state universities, alumni of Wan U people the state legislature, but alumni of private colleges represent both Ashton and its state in the governor's mansion and in Washington, D.C. Wan U is close enough to the great universities and private colleges for its top administrators to command excellent salaries, so that they and the trustees who set their salaries can hold their heads up when they encounter the top administrators from relatively nearby private institutions of higher education.

Sometimes the administrators of Wannabe University—even the university itself—seem to have an inferiority complex. Unlike the television commercials for Avis car rentals, the central administration does not brag about the possibilities inherent in being second best. Rather, it seems simultaneously to boast and to apologize for itself. Indeed, the university reminds me of one of the university's well-published professors: he informed a central administrator that when he was a newly minted assistant professor teaching at Yale, he would have gotten tenure had his wife not gotten pregnant and family life had not interfered with his work. (He, of course, claimed no responsibility for the pregnancy.) Many central administrators seem cocksure of their own abilities, especially when they compare themselves with people whom they knew in their youth or with the administrators who never left Montana or Mississippi or Maine. But they seem simultaneously defensive when they place themselves in the context of the outstanding private colleges and universities that populate the northern landscape. While they take credit for their successes, they do not seem to accept blame for their failures—unless the news media trumpet their failures so widely that there's no one else to accuse of wrongdoing and nowhere else to hide. Nonetheless, when dealing with Wan U's faculty and with the few administrators who have been promoted from within, the professional administrators present themselves as people who have been around. "He's not worried about the responsibility of being a university president," a central administrator, who had come to Wan U as an assistant professor, once said of James Whitmore. "This is the third time he's been the president of a university."

LOCALS, COSMOPOLITANS, AND OUTSIDER ADMINISTRATORS

Many administrators, who had been drawn from other colleges and universities in the 1990s and later, seemed to identify themselves as "cosmopolitans" and to think of the people who have made careers at Wannabe

University as "locals"—although they did not use these customary socio-logical terms. (The terms "cosmopolitans" and "locals" are generally used to distinguish professionals who have opposing orientations toward organi-zational loyalty, commitment to specialized skills, and orientation to out-side reference groups [Gouldner 1957].) Conventionally in this distinction, locals show organizational loyalty, are oriented toward reference groups within their organization, and often have a commitment to generalized skills, while cosmopolitans demonstrate the opposite characteristics.[2]

By identifying themselves as cosmopolitans, administrators who have been hired from the national labor pool rather than "promoted" from the faculty imply their superiority to the faculty. Cosmopolitans have an unfor-tunate tendency to believe themselves superior to locals. In essence, these administrators implied that they understood the issues universities across the nation were facing and that most Wan U professors did not. Suppos-edly since much of the Wan U professoriate had only taught at Wan U or had taught there for over a decade, these faculty members did not have firsthand knowledge of how national and local issues were intertwined and could not understand the problems facing Wan U and other research uni-versities. To these so-called cosmopolitan administrators, too many people at Wan U were simply "locals."

However, by sociological criteria, many of the professors at Wannabe University are just as much cosmopolitans as the outside administrators. (Some would angrily mutter, "More so.") In their work and behavior, they, too, are oriented toward their professional peers and dedicated to the spe-cialized skills and knowledge of their discipline, though they may feel loy-alty to Wan U. Within academic departments, about the worst statement that a newcomer holding senior rank can make is: "You people don't un-derstand how things are done nationally—at leading research universities." By tone of voice and body language, that senior newcomer conveys, "You people are just locals," or even, "You people do inferior work." To be sure, nationally the movement of senior professors from one educational institu-tion to another had abated by 2005, as universities sought to hire less ex-pensive assistant professors rather than more highly paid associate and full professors. However, members of the faculty, who have complained about the new administrators, do belong to their national organizations, present papers at their meetings, and publish in good journals. According to their local and national colleagues, some are very good at what they do, maybe, but not quite, eminent.

I will use the term "outside administrators" and "outsiders" to identify administrators recruited from other universities, generally through a na-tional search. Thus I use the terms to indicate a career path, a location on an occupational structure. Structural positions have social-psychological consequences. They shape how people think about themselves and others—and also how others think about them.

Of course, sometimes after a while, status as an outsider may become irrelevant. For instance, although the dean of one large college was recruited after a national search, he has been at Wan U for ten years. (At one point a faculty rumor claimed that he had stayed at Wan U because he wanted to be provost.) Any faculty member in this dean's college who had been hired within the past ten years does not think of him as an outsider. That dean is simply "*the* dean." That professor would care whether the dean had enough power to deliver on the promises he had made, whether the dean kept his word, and whether the dean said he listened to faculty members ("I have an open-door policy"), while he paid attention only to a select few. However, many faculty who have been at Wan U for over ten years view the outside administrators with some distrust.

THE POWER OF OUTSIDERS

Many faculty members know that the professional managers may view Wan U as a rest stop in a productive career. They may informally bet on how long a specific administrator will last. (Some give the current provost two more years; after all, there have been four provosts and/or acting provosts in ten years.) They know that the pattern at Wan U is typical. Its pattern of turnover resembles the acknowledgments in James Duderstadt's *A University for the Twenty-first Century* (reproduced in fig. 4.1): so many provosts and associate provosts, so many deans of students, so many vice presidents.

Because they are strangers who may leave tomorrow,[3] outsiders often find it easier than people promoted through the ranks to disband colleges and to dismiss subordinates. The new managerialism follows corporate practice. Because outsiders are not part of existing organizational culture (and to bolster stock prices), many corporations seeking new CEOs and other top executives have turned to outsiders. Here's how a retired CEO contrasted the promotion of organizational insiders with hiring outsiders:

> There are so many constraints on the internally-promoted individual. There is so much baggage! Organizational boxes, the people in the boxes . . . commitments to people on what their future will be. [As an insider,] you are part of the process. Now that you are on top, you cannot be a Magnum Prick. . . . You don't see many examples of internal candidates getting to the top of the system and then laying waste to the existing culture. (Quoted in Khurana 2002: 65)

Outsiders, this management theory maintains, are more likely to introduce radical change. Some faculty scuttlebutt suggests that the outsider administrators were hired because they were not bound by loyalty or friendship

FIGURE 4.1
Senior Administrators at the University of Michigan Whom President James Duderstadt Thanks
for Help during His Decade-Long Presidency

PROVOST: Chuck Vest, Gil Whitaker, Bernie Machen
VP-CHIEF FINANCIAL OFFICER: Farris Womack
VP-RESEARCH: Linda Wilson, Bill Kelly, Homer Neal
VP-STUDENT AFFAIRS: Henry Johnson, Mary Ann Swain, Maureen Hartford
VP-UNIVERSITY AFFAIRS: Walt Harrison, Lisa Baker
VP-DEVELOPMENT: Jon Cosovich, Tom Kinnear, Joe Roberson
DEAN OF THE GRADUATE SCHOOL: John D'Arms, Bob Weisbuch
SECRETARY OF THE UNIVERSITY: Dick Kennedy, Harold Johnson, Roberta Palmer
VICE PROVOSTS AND ASSOCIATE VPS: Bob Holbrook, Doug Van Houweling, George Zuidema,
    Chuck Moody, Lester Monts, Rhetaugh Dumas, Harold Jacobson, Tom Butts, Paul Spradlin,
    Bill Krumm, Norman Herbert, Chandler Mathews, Randy Harris, and Cynthia Wilbanks
CHANCELLORS: Blenda Wilson, Clint Jones, Jim Renick, Charlie Nelms
ATHLETIC DIRECTORS: Bo Schembechler, Jack Weiidenbach, Joe Roberson
ASSISTANTS: Robin Jacoby, Shirley Clarkson, Connie Cook, Ejner Jensen
SECRETARY TO THE PRESIDENT: Nona Mustard

Source: Duderstadt 2000: xiii.

to the faculty and so might have greater freedom to introduce potentially radical changes. Other professors say that, for whatever reason, the current top administrators don't want anything to do with faculty who served Ned Oakes, the predecessor of the current president—although they recognize some exceptions to that rule. Embodying its ongoing disagreement with faculty, administrators produce yet another version: they claim that these administrative hires were considered on a "line-by-line" basis. One central administrator said that a particular dean was not recruited from the outside to impose radical change, but rather because there were no viable internal candidates for the position. Where faculty members (managed professionals) see patterns, the administrators (professional managers) whom I interviewed do not. But then subordinates may pay closer attention to patterns than superordinates do. An underling's occupational future may depend on understanding the boss's desires, but the boss may not need to pay a lot of attention to his underlings in order to succeed.

THE FACULTY VIEW THE OUTSIDERS

Among themselves, professors discuss the new professional managers as outsiders. Faculty members who are now over the age of fifty also view these outside administrators as members of a new breed. However, many professors in their thirties and forties have only worked under the new managerial regime and so do not complain.

OUTSIDERS LIKE POWER

Echoing Brint's findings (1994), older faculty members state that the new outside administrators are more concerned with *power* than with *service* to their colleagues. Service was supposedly the motivation of the inside administrators of yesteryear. Additionally, these professors claimed that the new outside administrators are very concerned—too concerned—about their career mobility, especially their ability to get a better job at another higher-education institution. Significantly, although professors speak this way about outsider administrators, they do not talk this way about other professors who might see Wan U as a stepping-stone to an even better job in an even better department at an even better university.[4]

OUTSIDERS ARE CORPORATE CREATURES

Professors do not envy the outsiders. In conversations with friends, many wonder why anyone would want to go into administration and still see administrators as failed academics. Many also feel that becoming an administrator entails a loss of freedom. Professors work long hours, but mostly they can decide when they want to do their research or to prepare their classes. Administrators work long hours, but other people set their timetable. Within certain limits, professors wear what they please. The limits placed on administrators are more stringent. At Wan U, both male and female administrators wear suits. The women also wear the sorts of dresses and "coordinates" sold in the "career corner" of department stores. Indeed, on becoming an associate dean, one humanities professor—who had previously dressed in good taste—"spent her raise" on suits and dresses. Within limits, professors can say what they please. They can publicly criticize or question a superior. An administrator simply cannot engage in such behavior. Or, as a central administrator said when a faculty member apologized for being too critical at a committee meeting, "You're a professor. You can say what you think. I can't do that." (This particular administrator treated her boss in a deferential manner. Seeing them together, a manager, who had just been hired and had yet to meet the relevant players, thought that they were married.)

In many ways, being a member of a university's administration resembles being a corporate manager. In both spheres, professional managers follow many of the same rules. These include such behaviors as loyalty to one's boss, discretion about one's work, being attuned to practical decision-making, and not talking out of turn at meetings (Jackall 1988). Indeed, when an assistant called out to correct a vice provost at a meeting of the board of trustees, there was a sudden pall in the room and the vice provost looked aghast at his underling's behavior.

In part because the press of meetings requires solving immediate problems rather than planning for the future, in part because managers' days are
an interminable round of meetings (cf. Hochschild 1997), constraints may
lead corporate managers to reach for short-term instead of long-run gains.
Jackall's (1988) description of this plight of corporate managers resembles
Wolverton and Gmelch's (2002) description of the typical day of a typical
dean: a round of meetings and interminable e-mails that leave little time to
think. One provost at Wannabe University received as many as a thousand
e-mails a day. (That job was eventually redefined.) An associate vice provost was known to answer e-mails as late as one in the morning. The director of athletics routinely worked late and on weekends; he attended home
games and chatted it up through halftime with trustees, key boosters, and
other people who mattered, such as a coach's agent. The professional managers worked hard, with long hours, and their activities were frequently
constrained.

Some faculty members do not see the administrators' plight so sympa-
thetically, especially not that of the outsider administrators who have been
hired within the past fifteen years. They seem to resent the outsiders imported to help "improve" Wannabe University. They say that their publications are weak and that they are overly concerned with their own individual
advancement, as opposed to the long-term goals of the university.

To faculty members, one central administrator serves as the prototype of
the new administrators: he took credit for innovations, while overspending
his budget, and then left for a higher-paying job. Jackall (1988; cf. Khurana
2002) might say that as corporate administrators do, this person "milked
the system" and left others to deal with the consequences of his mistakes.

OUTSIDERS AS OUT-OF-TOWNERS

One can think about outsiders either social-psychologically or structurally.
For instance, in the small Iowa town that Naples studied (1996), "outsider"
is a social-psychological status. Even people who have lived in the town
for decades may think of themselves as "outsiders." At Wannabe University,
"outsider" is a structural status, in part because of how the university and
the town connect with each other.

Wannabe University and Ashton intersect structurally and culturally. Individuals fill multiple roles. In 2006 a past president of the Wannabe chapter of the American Association of University Professors sat on the Ashton
Town Council. Before he retired to Florida, another past president of the
AAUP had also been elected to the town council. The mayor has a managerial job at Wan U. For over a decade, the administrative assistant of a past
dean of the graduate school was the head of the Ashton Democratic Party.

The president's main assistant, Peter Lynch, sits on Ashton's "municipal" development committee.

In Ashton/Wannabe, multiple allegiance and ways of knowing people are commonplace. Those overlapping allegiances and roles also seem to exclude the "outside administrators" from some aspects of the local culture shared by members of both the university and the town. Outsiders have not met "their" faculty at local parties; they did not attend local churches; their children have not been in school together. They have not been active in the local union. (At Wannabe University, the local union had previously served as a source of administrators, and with service on university committees and membership in the town's institutions, had facilitated knowledge of who influenced whom; who kept his or her word; who was an asset to a committee.) Rather, to a surprising extent, what the outsiders know about individual faculty members (and even departments) depends on what other administrators, including department heads, say about them. Conversely, many professors do not feel that they know these outsiders well enough to discuss potential problems in an informal setting, such as a chance meeting at a grocery store or a university art show.

PUBLICATIONS OF THE CORPORATE ADMINISTRATORS

Many outside administrators do not inspire respect for their academic accomplishments. Older professors were dismayed at the relatively poor publication records of the outsiders. Indeed, some faculty members contrast the academic qualifications of the corporate and the insider administrators. In the eyes of many, the corporate administrators do not have strong publications, although they claim that inside administrators have been well-published. The contrast is particularly telling, when older faculty reel off the academic qualifications of some administrators of previous decades. A former provost was a member of the National Academy of Sciences. Another provost was "a son of a bitch," but also "a first-rate social scientist" whose research was "awfully good." A former dean was one of the most distinguished members of a distinguished department.

Too many of the "outside" administrators have not been distinguished scholars, some professors say. A department head said that the publications of one top administrator are "weak at best." Of another, a different department head said, "When he wants to discuss research, he has to talk about his dissertation. He apparently hasn't done any research since then." Of a third: "I don't know how many times I have heard him mention that he is a biologist. It's as though he mentions his field when he talks to [a group of faculty leaders] so that we will know he is intelligent." Put somewhat differently, and professors have put it this way, these administrators have not distinguished themselves in the very areas that faculty use to evaluate one another and that these administrators use to evaluate faculty. To paraphrase yet another former department head, if these administrators had been recruited by the academic departments in which they have been given tenure, almost none of them would have been considered for a senior position.

WANDERLUST

Perhaps professors who talk this way are simply turning the tables on administrators. Generally, members of a group do not like to hear that they are not qualified for what might be viewed as a promotion, and that generalization should apply to faculty as to anyone else. By consistently running national searches for top administrators and eliminating local professors from the competition, the central administration is implicitly insulting its professoriate. To be sure, Wannabe professors may be the only candidates considered for jobs as *associate* vice provost or *associate* dean, but they are rarely included in the search for provosts or deans.[5] In the corporate world, outsiders are more likely to move from one organization to another, collecting stock options along the way (on executive mobility, see Khurana 2002; cf. Jackall 1988). The careers of many of these "outside" administrators follow the corporate model: they have moved around the country seeking advancement, which they supposedly deserved because of the splendid job done at a previous and current institution. To invent an example, someone might have received a doctorate in Montana, served as a faculty member and department head in, say, Oregon, a dean in Texas, and an associate provost in Illinois, spending three to five years in each administrative post.

To be sure, some "inside" administrators had also done five-year stints in a succession of jobs. A former and academically distinguished administrator explained at lunch with some senior faculty, as they recruited an outsider for the central administration, "You know, I was chair of my department for five years, then dean, and then provost for five years. I figured five years and then I'll see what happens." Those at the lunch interpreted his statement to mean: "I thought I would see how far I could go, whether I wanted to seek a presidency, and whether I could do so." Nonetheless, among academic administrators, the current degree of movement around the country (the corporate model) is relatively new—a feature of the last twenty years.

CORPORATE WANDERERS AS BAD COPS

Some analysts (Gordon 1996; Phillips 2003; Khurana 2002) argue that in the business world, this pattern of vertical movement between firms has hampered corporations. More than organizational culture is at issue here. Rather, some argue, this career model encourages people to look out for themselves in the long run and to look out for the corporation in the short term (Jackall 1988; Gordon 1996: 80, 81; cf. Khurana 2002). Put somewhat differently, those who concentrate on individual advancement may work to increase the worth of their stock options rather than introducing changes that fundamentally affect a corporation's long-range profits or improve the lot of workers or communities (Phillips 2003: 148). Corporate managers may "milk" their job and move on to the next promotion before their mistakes have become evident. At Wannabe University, faculty—especially older faculty—say that the new "corporate administrators" are not motivated to provide service to their colleagues as the former inside administrators supposedly had done, but rather they allegedly seek to exercise power and move on to a better job. For instance, some professors knew that a former dean had seen his job as that of a traffic cop: he was to make certain that departments took their turn at the stoplight as they waited for resources. The new deans, they announced, were not traffic cops. They were more like police chiefs, expecting their subordinates to obey.

Two stories capture the shift in deans' attitudes toward authority over the past twenty-five years. Professor Jack Jacobs recalled his first year as department head over two decades before. He had submitted recommendations for merit raises to the dean, and the dean suggested giving one person more and another less. Even after Professor Jacobs stated that he knew the discipline better than the dean did, the dean persisted in his recommendation. So, Professor Jacobs scrawled a letter of resignation and handed it to the dean. Asked what he was doing, he explained, "You hired me to run this department. If you want to run it, you don't need me." The dean relented on the merit raises, and Professor Jacobs recalled, "He didn't bother me again." Professor Jacobs added, "That wouldn't happen anymore."

Now when the dean tells department heads what to do, they obey. For instance, a dean wanted to transfer two faculty members to another department. The members of the department were happy to accept one of them, but not both. (They viewed one as a troublemaker who sparked intense dissension.) Nonetheless, after the dean attended a department meeting, they welcomed both men. Commenting on what had happened, a member of the department told a committee meeting, "The dean forced us to take them both." When I asked the head of another department whether the dean would have threatened to decrease the recalcitrant department's resources, he replied: "No. The dean probably didn't have to do that. You haven't heard him," or, to paraphrase, "You haven't seen how he treats people when he wants them to do something." Some professors feel that the dean is a bully. Others say he is a micromanager.[6]

Professors in several disciplines feared that in a time of diminishing resources, their dean would cut funding to their department if they did not go along with his instructions. That dean made such threats when he visited uncooperative departments. At department meetings in that school, department heads routinely tell their faculty, "The dean wants . . . If we do not go along with him, the dean may not give us [a variety of resources]." Professors believed the threats, because the dean was known to have even mocked his (female) associate deans at meetings of the department heads of the college.

Ultimately, it doesn't matter whether the dean, the provost, or the chairman of the board of trustees is a bully. The social perception is the social reality. All that matters is that these outsiders have engaged in conduct that professors find to be the personification of being a bully. Moreover, few professors and department heads believe they can successfully challenge the dean. Deans seem to find it difficult to challenge the provost repeatedly and to maintain their job, as will be discussed in chapter 5. The provost and the president seem to obey the orders of the chairman of the board.

Once upon a time, the administrative/business sector of the university was a bureaucracy, and deans supposedly occupied an uncomfortable position: members of a bureaucracy, they were nonetheless supposed to represent "their" faculty in "their" departments to the central administration (Wolverton and Gmelch 2002). Now, a department head joked, the chair of the board tells the president and provost, who tell the deans, who tell the department heads, and at department meetings, we all sit around trying to figure out how we can do what they tell us to do and maintain academic integrity.

Also, the consolidation of centralized power supports the faculty perception of the administrators as bullies. More professional managers can "produce" more supervision. A retired central administrator explained that in the past decade, during James Whitmore's presidency, administrative supervision had increased. "Things were more decentralized [when I was in the central administration]. There was less administrative oversight. The people in the provost's office had so much to do. . . . Don't get me wrong; there was oversight. But we didn't have enough time to look closely over the shoulders of program directors." On another occasion, he noted, "Today there are so many vice provosts and their staffs have grown so large that they have regular meetings to coordinate their activities so that their staffs will not step on one another's toes." Hiring more professional managers enabled the centralization of authority, and such centralization in turn facilitated the strength of bureaucratic rule. The legitimation of centralized authority even enabled some managers to be bullies.[7]

Again, the pattern does not appear to be idiosyncratic to Wannabe University. When I discussed the decreasing power of department heads with the head of a humanities department who had been at Wan U for thirty years, I was told, "It's not just here, you know. I speak to my friends at other universities. This [realignment and centralization of power] is going on everywhere." Other people made similar comments.

A DISGRUNTLED FACULTY?

Are these professors a particularly disgruntled lot? Sometimes the answer seems to be yes. Some of the faculty's claims do not apply to an administrator whom many scientists dislike. "A series of articles that I did" have been cited so often in scientific journals, that administrator told me, that "I am one of four people on campus who is among the top 1,500 citation leaders in the *Science Citation Index*."[8] Many social scientists say of a dean, "What has he ever written?" However, they do not know that before he became a dean at an unusually young age, he was on the fast track to becoming a leader in his field. His academic record before he was a dean was very promising. By downgrading the dean's previous accomplishments, these professors indicate a willingness to dismiss outsiders.

However, other evidence suggests that nasty criticisms of outsiders *qua* outsiders are not a characteristic of the culture of Wannabe University. Professors criticize some former deans who were insiders. "Sure," one scientist states of a retired insider dean, "George seemed to keep his word" when he was dean, but "he favored his own department and gave them better resources." One person, who had once served in the central administration, described a powerful insider as "a man without a compass, but with rabbit ears," meaning that he had no ideas of his own, but was very sensitive to the minutia of the larger political atmosphere.

Conversely, although professors criticize the academic records of many corporate administrators, professors who report to one corporate dean heap ecumenism on him: "He is the real thing," one said at dinner. "He has lots of publications, lot of awards, and he's wonderful to work for." The professors seem to be distinguishing administrators by their academic records and behaviors, not by the geographic location of their previous job.

I suspect that although many professors are complaining about specific people, they would criticize any group of administrators and trustees who initiated so many changes without asking their views. Frequently, these administrators (and even the faculty committees that they appoint) act without asking. Indeed, the task force charged to design a strategic plan was co-chaired by a professor and a member of the administration. But, the deans reported, they were neither asked about their college's strengths and weaknesses nor consulted about the task-force recommendations. Nor were departments. Nor were divisions. Nor were institutes. Ultimately, it seemed, the task force was responsible to the provost, the president, and the board. The strategic plan was indeed a business tool, a product of the new managerialism that had been sweeping through higher education. It was not an academic matter.

THE POLITICS OF MANAGEMENT

As generally happens at large institutions, when professional managers and managed professors "do business" with one another at Wan U, they assess each other's rank, status, and power. At Wan U, one aspect of the politics of power seems to be weighing the status that faculty grant administrators and, even more important, the status that administrators attribute to one another.

ADMINISTRATORS ON ADMINISTRATORS

Because status matters to administrators, a few managers spoke as though they believed that by denigrating others, they were commending themselves. However, on the whole, the administrators were very careful about speaking badly of one another. Those who knew about my research were especially careful around me. Too many had experienced disloyalty from faculty in whom they confided. When someone repeated a manager's confidence, he or she diminished that administrator's power. None of the administrators wanted to make enemies. Nonetheless, when speaking with me, some administrators promoted their own abilities. They introduced what might be called "national criteria" to elevate their own claims to recognition. (As the "new institutionalism" might predict, they were using the norms in their "organizational field" to set conceptions of what mattered.)

Perhaps because so many of them had once been professors, administrators shared with the faculty notions of which research universities are "really good." Like faculty, they could array key colleges and universities on the ranked rungs of a constructed "educational ladder." They could assign a rung to the colleges and universities at which various administrators had once been employed. The administrators who had served at "good schools" distinguished themselves from the administrators who had served at "weak schools." Recalling the splendid rankings of the leading institutions with which they had once been associated, these managers might recall that their former school had followed different procedures than those used at Wannabe University and that those procedures were superior—more professional or more business-like than the procedures at Wan U.[9] Generally, those who made such unfavorable comparisons felt that their colleagues did not appreciate their ability or knowledge.

For instance, a central administrator severely criticized how his colleagues set budget priorities, particularly the assignment of new academic lines to a department. (The term "line" refers to the line of the university's budget that a person occupies.) He believed that permission to hire ("new lines," or professors) should go to the academic departments that were the most capable of turning those lines into revenue streams. He explained that departments that had achieved a high national ranking and whose members had been awarded significant outside funding (preferably from such agencies as the various units of the National Institutes of Health) should "receive lines." Granting new lines to those who did not meet these criteria was "a waste of resources," especially if they did not teach many undergraduates. He continued that at Wan U "small politics—who likes whom and gets along with whom"—interferes in what should be rational decisions.

This administrator even criticized a Wan U push into a new scientific area as a potential waste of money: the federal government had already identified several universities as leaders in that field and was expected to pump research funds into those universities. Wan U was not one of those universities; furthermore, the administrator continued, the relevant academic department was not even close to being a leader in the field. Therefore, investing in that department was a waste of money and an example of how Wan U administrators and trustees did not base decisions on appropriate criteria. Almost passionately, he explained that the National Research Council ranked that department well below its peers and that the department had graduated only six seniors a year. Giving it resources was not a good investment.[10]

Of course, not all outsiders were actively boastful. I found it almost impossible to elicit criticisms of administrators from other administrators. Sometimes administrators simply referred to practices at their previous universities, because people often carry their past experiences as templates for making decisions in the present. For instance, asked about a program that straddled his school and the School of Business, one dean explained that at his previous (prestigious) university the program had been in the School of Business. Similarly, one central administrator spoke approvingly of a possible movement of certain funds from the graduate school to the central administration. (A significant portion of the faculty was opposed to that structural change in responsibility.) He did not justify that movement by citing the increased power over resources that the central administration would have. He simply said, "That's the way it's done at most good research universities."

ADMINISTRATORS IN PROFESSIONAL ORGANIZATIONS

Some administrators know "how it's done" because of their involvement in professional associations. Indeed, professional associations seem to play an important role in the "new managerialism." For almost twenty years, the "professional presidents" who have led Wannabe University had pushed other administrators—whether insiders or outsiders—to be professionals. In the late 1980s, a president who eventually left to head a leading research university virtually commanded deans and associate provosts to attend the meetings of a national organization designed for top university administrators. By the 1990s, many administrators were members of other professional organizations as well, for there are national organizations for deans of students, directors of residential life, and directors of career services—just to mention some of the managers who work in the Division of Student Affairs. Administrators who hold offices in their professional associations are proud of that accomplishment. They list their offices on their résumés, to use the corporate term, or curriculum vitae, to use the academic label. In conversation, they might explain the procedures recommended by a national committee on which they serve.

At professional meetings, administrators engage in some of the same activities as professors do at their conventions. They hear papers, they participate in panels, they gossip. When sufficiently angry, they might even repeat nasty gossip. Thus, a central administrator repeated gossip when he compared President Whitmore's behavior at Wan U with that at his last job. He criticized the president for currently playing favorites among the faculty and for meeting weekly with a small group of administrative favorites to make decisions. (He called them "the secret-handshake club.") He explained, "At his last job, the president did the same thing. If you weren't in either the academic or administrative club, he had no use for you. . . . It was no secret in that [region of the country]." The administrator explained that "people in education" get to know one another and that he had heard about this gossip at a national meeting, while speaking with a "well-respected" guy who held a job for which James Whitmore had applied but had been rejected.

It is quite possible that this angry gossip has no merit—that President Whitmore did not behave in the way described, that he had never been considered for that other job, that my informant had never spoken with the current job-holder. The quality of information is not the issue. What matters is the exchange of information—the existence of a national network on which the outsiders may draw or may claim to draw. For outsider administrators, as for many professors, involvement with a national network signifies worthiness.

Other sorts of professional meetings seem central to the "new managerialism." There are meetings about trends in assessing (auditing) teaching. There are meetings about improving diversity among students and faculty. These are special conferences for which a university must submit an application delineating what staff needs to learn and where, on the last day, the staff must summarize what they have gained from the conference. Sometimes, attending their professional meetings, the administrators of Wannabe University will even encounter representatives of professors' professional organizations.

As more and more disciplinary organizations tackle such professional issues as teaching in addition to promoting the exchange of information about research, the concerns of professionals in disciplines merge with the concerns of professionals in administration. For example, after attending a national meeting, one administrator gave me documents that someone from the American Sociological Association had distributed at a session about teaching that he had attended. The documents were packaged in an attractive ASA folder. On another occasion, administrators attending a series of workshops about a specific pedagogical concern found that the "faculty member" leading a parallel workshop about diversity issues was a member of the Wannabe administration. As an adherent of the theory of new institutionalism might put it, the professors and the administrators are becoming stakeholders exposed to similar norms promulgated by groups in their organizational field.

TRUSTEES AS UNIVERSITY PROFESSIONALS

The new managerialism has also included changes in boards of trustees. Trustees now have their own national organizations, such as the Association of Governing Boards of Universities and Colleges, where they attend sessions on the problems universities face. Also, I have the impression that at Wannabe University, trustees seem to be drawn from different occupations than was true fifteen or twenty years ago. Then, as now, many trustees are either politicians or are politically connected. But others hold key positions in financial institutions and have experience with universities. Changes in boards involve more than personnel. One informant recalled the boards of previous decades as "ladies and gentlemen," because they stayed in their place. That informant had also implied that members of the current board did not stay in their place—out of the hair of the administrators. (The *Chronicle of Higher Education* is more subtle: it discusses the problems that occur when boards engage in micromanagement.) One person mused: "I don't know whether the board has changed the university or the changes in the university have affected the board. It's probably a little bit of both."

I observed such changes at meetings of the Wannabe University Board of Trustees, although I do not know whether those changes are characteristic of this university, symptomatic of the personalities of specific people, or indicative of a general trend. At board meetings in 2002, the chairman of the board was relatively inactive. He delivered his report and called on people to speak, but I had a sense that President Whitmore exercised a real influence on the course of trustees' meetings, for he acted as though he were the most important person in the room. Ever so politely, President Whitmore interrupted speakers. (The man who was provost in 2002 was interrupted so often that I decided he was losing power.) He might add a comment about a problem after a subordinate had delivered a report. He was the person who thanked a vice president or vice provost for a concise report. He proffered witticisms.[11] Indeed, one ex-administrator claimed that this chairman of the board did not do a good job reading reports and that before trustees' meetings, a group of central administrators would meet with the president to plan how to control the chairman. They worried that he might table as meaningless a matter that the administrators thought was crucial.[12]

At meetings of the trustees held in 2005, the next chairman of the board, Bill Hardway, clearly controlled the administration. He made the jokes and thanked those who gave reports. President Whitmore spoke when Chairman Hardway called on him to do so. Chairman Hardway also did his best to control media reports. At one public meeting, where the governor, Chairman Hardway, and President Whitmore faced reporters, Chairman Hardway stood up to answer a question that a reporter had addressed to the president. It had clearly been the president's task to answer that query.

Some of Chairman Hardway's attempts to control media reports about Wannabe University seemed to express his experiences as a high-placed corporate officer. Education and political reporters regularly attended meetings of the board of trustees as part of their beat, just as business reporters attend the shareholders' meeting of a corporation vital to a state's economy. Early in his tenure, Bill Hardway wanted to gather all of the vice provosts and vice presidents before the formal meetings of the board of trustees so that they could rehearse the flow of the meeting. He wanted to make sure that the news media learned what he preferred them to learn. When it proved difficult to gather so many people on a regular basis, Chairman Hardway devised another procedure. For years, before the public portion of some meetings, the board and key administrators had gone into "closed session" to discuss pending legal issues and personnel matters. Under Chairman Hardway, the board sometimes did discuss legal cases when it met in private session. According to some central administrators who were excluded from the closed meetings, at other times board members prepared their public discussion of what reporters might view as a controversial matter, such as a deficit in a key revenue stream. After one rather long closed session, the chairman paced near the back of the room as trustees asked an administrator about a budgetary problem that had been reported in the news media that week.

When one trustee criticized Chairman Hardway's corporation, the chairman placed a cell phone call and alerted someone to that criticism. Sitting close enough to the pacing Chairman Hardway to hear his phone conversation, I could not help but be impressed by his desire to control. After the meeting, I had a sense that he was succeeding.

People mingle before they leave the meeting room. Often who chats with whom about what is telling. For instance, a dean, known to be in the midst of an ambitious campaign for donations, seemingly rushed to tell the chief financial officer that the committee they had discussed "is set." A high-level central administrator sat down to chat with a trustee's personal assistant. The beat reporter for the *State Capital Record* went into a hallway to call her editor. Chairman Hardway exchanged pleasantries with trustees, as did President Whitmore; but more people gathered near the chairman than near the president.

Everyone attending the meeting of the board of trustees knew how carefully both the agenda and speakers' comments had been scripted. Although the university bylaws required the trustees to discuss and to vote, the trustees' meetings are ceremonial affairs. "There are no surprises and . . . no real decisions have to be made in public" (Morrill 1995: 102).[13] The meetings of the trustees are choreographed. As true of other rituals, these meetings were imbued with unspoken politics.

5

The Politics of Centralization

Like trustees' meetings and retirement parties, "introductory receptions" are both ceremonial and political affairs. They announce how power is distributed at the university. Refreshments at the reception to introduce Gerald Wesley to the faculty were simple—fruit, vegetables, dip, the pink punch. The parties for key administrators were said to have been more elaborate. Truly important people had been invited to meet the new provost at a dinner party.[1]

The arrival of a new provost is the occasion for a new round of internal politics, much as the arrival of a new chief executive officer or division head signals a new onslaught of political activity at a corporation. Because academia is geographically far-flung but socially compact, many Wannabe professors routinely check with colleagues at the last university where the latest powerful administrator had previously worked. Making his first report to the University Senate during his fifth week on campus, a powerful central administrator said, "I expect that by now, you have all heard from your colleagues at [my former university]." Conversely, professors fully expected to hear from colleagues at other universities when someone leaves Wan U for another job. Some scientists had heard from colleagues at My Newest University within weeks of Tyler Johnson's departure to assume its presidency.

At the faculty reception for Gerald Wesley, both President Whitmore's introduction and the newest provost's response reminded those attending how much of the collective life of universities is composed of layers of politics. There are external politics: A public university depends on public officials. It also tries to influence reporters to protect itself from media, legislative, and gubernatorial criticism. There are internal politics: Central administrators try to please and to influence the trustees.[2] They jostle one another for information about happenings at the university that may help them either to gain an advantage over their competitors or to consolidate power.[3] Also, the central administration makes demands on the deans. The deans try to curry favor with the central administration or to find another way to acquire more resources for their school or college. Simultaneously, departments politely elbow one another to gain resources from the dean and in some, but not all academic departments, professors vie for good resources.

Internal and external politics may interact. As DiMaggio and Powell put it (1991: 67), sometimes coercive forces, such as external political actors, influence how an organization acts, including whether and how it copies the activities of comparable institutions. External politics may derail the enactment of internal policies. Thus, some legislators objected when Wan U wanted to contract with an Arab nation to build a campus in its capital. They were concerned about whether that campus would be accessible to both Jewish Americans and Israelis. To counter their opposition, as the provost explained to a Senate committee, the central administration worked through Jewish interest and political groups whose leaders favored the association.

Sometimes internal matters can influence public perceptions of the university and so external politics. Administrators want to avoid negative publicity—in part to protect their own jobs. Thus, when several women accused their department head of racism and sexism, the dean informed them that he did not want to read about the accusation in the *State Capital Record*. He did not want internal politics to become public knowledge. Also, another administrator suggested, the dean did not want his superiors to think that he could not maintain a collegial atmosphere in the departments under his jurisdiction. As this central administrator explained, that "dean has a problem: too many of his departments are having serious problems and it's becoming public knowledge." For an administrator, the pertinent issue may not be whether a particular subordinate, such as a department head, makes racist or sexist decisions, but rather whether others question his administrative ability. Similarly, the issue is not whether an Arab state prevents Israelis from traveling within its borders, but whether the politics of the Middle East will have an impact on the provost's desire to forge international relationships so that more undergraduates will choose to study abroad.

Put somewhat differently, as professors see it, administrators address practical problems, not philosophic issues.[4] So far as the professors can see, intra-university politics concentrate on what is happening at the moment, not what might happen years in the future. Administrators strategize; they do not philosophize. They act; they do not develop a philosophy of education. Certainly, the administrators at Wannabe University were not trying to define and enact an educational philosophy. Rather, observing them at meetings and receptions, I felt that for almost all of them the only political concern that mitigated their emphasis on immediacy and short-term consequences was jockeying to gain an advantage in the next moment. For almost all of them, "a long time from now" is the foreseeable future, which seems to be defined as an extension of the concerns of the present, much as a planner may hope that the graph line of a multiple regression equation represents incremental, but decided progress. Like corporate planners, the Wannabe administrators try to assess "where we are now," so that they can set reasonable goals for where they would like to be "five years from now" and can develop a strategy to get from here to there.

Here are three examples. Each involves a practical matter that the Wannabe central administration faced. One revolved around strategizing to maximize resources. In late 2007, administrators knew that federal funding to finish a half-completed road would be available in 2009. (Administrators and faculty called it "the road to nowhere.") Top administrators and members of the powerful Building and Grounds Committee knew that once the road reached its intended destination, it would provide easy access to thirty acres of land supposedly belonging to the School of Agriculture, but that "Athletics ha[d] its eye" on that site for its own future expansion. For them, any discussion of "the road to nowhere" entailed the politics of maintaining or reassigning the right to use the thirty-acre parcel. It involved practical politics.

Even advance planning entails practical questions. When the central administration expanded the undergraduate enrollment, it faced a housing shortage for undergraduates.[5] In 2003, after the *State Capital Record* reported that thousands of undergraduates could not get a room on campus, a local corporation interested in developing on-campus undergraduate housing at universities throughout the country visited President Whitmore to explore building apartments on campus. President Whitmore advised the company's principals that the university's plans did not include expanding on-campus housing, but he apparently suggested that private firms were building student-housing complexes near many universities. As the company's principals were to report to a neighborhood group in 2007, the university's plans had not included "bonding for housing."[6] Instead the company's partners bought undeveloped land almost adjoining the university and in 2007 submitted its plans for housing 632 students to the Ashton Planning and Zoning Committee. When neighborhood residents virulently opposed the complex, presidential assistant Peter Lynch worked to convince both the residents and the town government that the development would help keep students from renting houses near the university (and so degrading that local housing stock). But, apparently, no one at the university examined the impact of university development on other areas of Ashton, just as no one had apparently discussed how completion of the "road to nowhere" would affect the streets it joined or traffic on the other side of town. (Cars do not remain segregated in a one- or two-mile-square radius.)

Ultimately, even advance planning for issues that strike at the heart of the university raises practical questions, albeit practical questions with some intellectual substance. Addressing the University Senate in late 2007, Provost Gerald Wesley explained that the central administration was trying to develop a series of metrics with which to compare the research enterprise at Wan U with research at its "peers" (other public universities with which it compared itself). "That way," he explained, "we can set our goals and make plans to achieve them." At least as Provost Wesley explained it, planning for the future did not require a reexamination of how research is implicated in education or of the meaning of education.[7] Planning required solving the practical problem of identifying suitable metrics.

Concentrating on the moment may isolate administrators from some of the implications of their actions. Absorbed in surviving today to compete again tomorrow, the administrators may engage in a politics that obscures the larger picture, much as concentrating on the proverbial trees hides one's view of the forest. Of course, different members of "the Wannabe community" may offer competing identifications of the larger picture. For instance, professors may see the larger picture as a snapshot of their academic department's standing against a collage of leading departments in their discipline. Central administrators seem to frame the larger picture as a portrait of Wannabe posing against a forest of other public universities. Both groups may fail to notice that their emphasis on specifics is obscuring a still larger landscape affected by global warming or continental drift. Intent on the many immediate levels of university politics, professors and administrators may *not* notice that they are accepting the principles of the audit society and are participating in an accountability regime. As C. Wright Mills put it, "Caught in the limited milieux of their everyday lives, ordinary men often cannot reason about the great social structures—rational and irrational—of which their milieux are subordinate parts. Accordingly, they often carry out series of apparently rational actions without any idea of the ends they serve" (quoted in Morrill 1995: 217).

When Gerald Wesley became provost, he did as other provosts had done: he increased the amount of power concentrated in the central administration. Many professors assumed that he did so to make his job easier. By circumventing some of the mechanisms of shared governance, he made managing the university less cumbersome. Ultimately, I will suggest, the centralization of power facilitates an accountability regime. At least, the centralization of power facilitates the task of convincing colleges, departments, and individuals to make themselves auditable. To track the centralization of power, I turn back to Gerald Wesley's arrival in 2005. I examine some policies he initiated and some actions he abetted, including the dramatic departure of deans. Then I discuss how, if at all, the Wannabe professoriate responded to increasing administrative centralization.

INTRODUCING THE LATEST PROVOST

President Whitmore's introduction of Provost Wesley to the faculty raised the possibility that the latest provost might try to increase the power of the central administration. When introducing Provost Wesley, President Whitmore was as charming and gracious as ever. Speaking off the cuff, President Whitmore thanked a local legislator who had helped the university on several matters. Referring directly to recent critical newspaper reports, he smiled, and then in a serious tone noted, "If you never do anything, no one ever attacks you." He spoke indirectly about published news that a state college wanted to offer a doctorate that seemed to compete with a degree offered by Wannabe University. Indeed, President Whitmore waxed philosophic about competition among different public universities in some other states and the degree of intense competition that had developed in those states. He then praised the search committee that had identified Gerald Wesley as a leading candidate. (He also managed to praise the head of the search committee, "my friend" who held a chair in science, for President Whitmore was a good guy who liked to say kind words in public.) And then he turned to Provost Wesley.

President Whitmore explained how delighted he was to have Provost Wesley aboard. He described Provost Wesley—his education, his wife, his children, his on-the-job experience—a dean in one university, a provost in another, both located in what easterners view as the Heartland, both academically inferior to Wannabe University. "Gerald" had experience leading a public research university in dire financial straits, much worse "than ours." He had a "strong hand." President Whitmore smiled and commented that because Provost Wesley had joined Wan U, the president would be able to be the "good cop." President Whitmore did not say who would be the "bad cop." But next President Whitmore reminded the guests that previously the academic plan was being "carried out in an ambivalent manner," and then he glanced meaningfully at Provost Wesley. Everyone laughed. (The president did not mention who had displayed a weak hand, though he clearly implied that both the departed Tyler Johnson and the more recently departed acting provost had done so. One high-level central administrator told me later, "If the president keeps saying things like that, the provost is going to think that it's his job to fire people.")

The new provost's short remarks were also revealing. Gerald Wesley spoke about the recruitment process—how at one point he had been asked to write a short statement about his view of universities. "I wrote about people," Wesley told the group; "a university is its people." And then Wesley praised people whom he had met. He mentioned President Whitmore, the trustees, the vice presidents, and members of the faculty. He had kind words for the members of the search committee. He said it was a pleasure to get to know such capable people.

Wannabe University's "new cop" seemed to have kind words for everyone except the deans. Some professors attending the reception wondered whether that omission had been accidental. Tyler Johnson had struggled for power against at least one of the deans. He and the dean of the largest college were said not to like each other. Some administrators had even spoken of their mutual antipathy as a "problem for President Whitmore." "The new provost didn't mention the deans," I said later to an administrator. "I noticed," he very quietly replied. (Later in this chapter, I will consider a massive turnover in deans that resulted from resignations, retirements, a "negotiated reassignment," firings, and the elimination of three schools.)

When he had visited campus as a job candidate, Provost Wesley had glossed over some aspects of his past jobs, but some faculty and administrators learned about them relatively quickly. Provost Wesley had not been politically secure at his last job as provost and chief academic officer of Respectable Research University. Supposedly when he had arrived at Respectable, he had formed an alliance with its president, but the state legislature's cutbacks of Respectable's funding had been so severe that the president had resigned, departing a scant year and a half after Wesley's arrival. According to some accounts, Respectable's next president, Ralph Long, did not like Wesley. Other accounts of politics at Respectable University did not claim to know President Long's personal preferences or predilections. They merely specified that for whatever reason, Long did not give Provost Wesley the title of "executive vice president," which is traditionally awarded to a university's highest-ranking academic officer. Instead, President Long had given that title to a vice president on the business side. In response, those accounts continued, Wesley had started looking for another job.

Some administrators move from job to job in the spirit that other people move from marriage to marriage. On national television, a comedian once joked that he understood what had gone wrong with his first marriage and tried not to make the same mistakes in his second. Unfortunately, he had said with a shrug, his second wife presented a different series of preferences and issues. With his third wife, he tried not to behave in the manner that had so doomed his first and second marriages. But his third wife cared about yet another set of issues and so left him for a different set of reasons than had his first and second wives. Intent on the idea of pleasing, he had not noticed a principle associated with the act of pleasing: Pay attention to who your current partner is and what she wants.

Provost Wesley brought to Wannabe University the experience of having been hired by one president and passed over by another. Administrators and professors who had heard this information tried to use it to predict how Gerald Wesley would act at Wan U. All assumed that Wesley would take rational steps to protect his position within the university. Some people felt that Provost Wesley would do James Whitmore's "dirty work" to maintain the president's approval: they feared he would play "bad cop" to the president's "good cop." Others assumed that Wesley might look for a political sponsor who was more powerful than a "mere" president. For instance, he might express fealty to Bill Hardway, the chairman of the board, who now clearly steered the trustee meetings that President Whitmore had once dominated.[8] Administrators claimed that Hardway liked to be thought of as "tough" and valued administrators whom he felt to be "tough." But whether his primary organizational loyalty was to President Whitmore, to Chairman Hardway, or to both men, like the managerial outsiders who move from corporation to corporation (Khurana 2002), Provost Wesley was not bound by loyalty or by friendship to the other vice presidents, the deans, his other subordinates, or the faculty. Provost Wesley "is going to shake things up," one middle manager with an office in Top Hall predicted.

THE GRADUAL CONCENTRATION OF POWER

As true of other research universities, the "managerial side" of Wannabe University is a "mechanistic bureaucracy," a strict hierarchy that can be nicely summarized in an organization chart. With its thirteen schools (excluding medicine and dentistry) and six campuses, the "academic side" more nearly resembles a cross between a series of hives and a matrix system. I have called it a system of hives, because although all of the deans report to the provost, supposedly one dean never interferes in another dean's or school's activities. Unless a member of a trans-university committee, each dean supposedly limits his or her activities to his own hive (or "tub").[9] The "academic side" is a matrix system inasmuch as faculty on "regional campuses" pledge allegiance to both their academic (subject) departments (which are organized under deans) and to the associate vice provost who manages their campus and reports to the vice provost for education and instruction. As at other institutions of higher education, at Wannabe University these systems coexist with unions, interest groups, and standing committees (within departments and within colleges, and across colleges and schools) as well as ad hoc committees and task forces organized by either deans or central administrators. The result is a complex pattern of organizational interactions that, as Burton Clark (1983) notes, can be quite unwieldy and difficult to manage.

Despite the obvious complexity, it is possible to locate clear loci of academic power, such as the office of the president and of the provost. These administrators try to exert power; sometimes deans, directors, or other managers who report to them try to resist it. It is also possible to locate committees that have significant power. President Whitmore's Wednesday morning cabinet meeting with vice presidents and directors is one such committee. So is the Building and Grounds Committee (the group most familiar with the political ramifications of completing "the road to nowhere"). It includes the provost, the chief financial officer, the chief operating officer, the vice provost for research and dean of the graduate school, the dean of the College of Liberal Arts and Sciences, the dean of the School of Fine Arts, the vice president for student affairs, the director of Design, Planning, and Construction Management, a special assistant to the provost, and the head of a science department. When faculty members speak about the increasing centralization of power at universities, they generally mean that the president and provost are leaving fewer significant decisions to the occupants of "hives." Instead central administrators, including such groups as the president's Wednesday morning gathering and the Building and Grounds Committee, are setting the parameters for the activities of departments, deans, and colleges. The professors vacillate between claiming and fearing that the supposedly collegial organization of the "academic side" of the university is becoming more like the bureaucratic organization of the "administrative side." Their activities seem to be more rule-governed and to occur in a more hierarchically organized context.

When Provost Wesley arrived, he worked to introduce more uniformity in the rules governing the various schools and colleges and the professors within them. He seemed to follow the mantra of the new managerialism—improve organizational rationality to maximize economy, efficiency, and effectiveness. For instance, noting that different schools and colleges used divergent rules to establish how many years of service (or "credit" toward tenure) an assistant professor might transfer from a previous job at a college or university, he asked his vice provost for academic affairs to introduce a uniform policy. (The vice provost wrote a draft and brought it for approval to the University Senate's Faculty Standards Committee.) By requesting his subordinate to institute a uniform policy, Provost Wesley was using his central position to rationalize a key aspect of academic life.

Seeking uniformity, rationality, and centralization, in his first months Provost Wesley launched initiative after initiative, mainly by appointing a series of task forces. One considered the development, operation, and review of major centers and institutes. A second set considered procedures for establishing a research institute. A third was to establish ways to encourage global citizenship. Because the provost had launched these initiatives, he (and his staff) controlled the selection of task-force members. Professors invited to join such task forces were people respected by the faculty, but they also were people known to be sympathetic to the provost's views about the matter being considered by the task force to which they had been appointed.[10]

Sometimes the provost bypassed the faculty or introduced policies on such short notice that the professors had little time to consider the implications of proposed changes. For example, while a University Senate committee was still considering a revision on the university bylaw concerning professorial leaves of absence, the provost introduced his own preferred wording to the board of trustees. Similarly, after the federal government had fined Wan U for having an illegal policy on research incentive awards, the provost brought the matter to the Council of Deans. From the Council of Deans, the matter was brought to the Wannabe chapter of the American Association of University Professors. (Monetary compensation is a union issue, but the AAUP's executive officer was not familiar with all of the niceties associated with the federal agency's funding of academic research.) Three months after the Council of Deans had acted and several weeks before the board of trustees was to vote on the new policy (it was already on the board's agenda), the issue went to the Senate's Faculty Standards Committee, several of whose members were very informed about the conventions of federal funding agencies.

Some faculty also accused Provost Wesley of failing to "engage in shared governance," when he introduced an "academic restructuring plan" less than a year after moving into his Top Hall office.[11] (One administrator explained to me, "One management theory says that if you're going to make a big change, do it early, soon after you've started the new job.") On the one hand, the plan and its enactment resembled an unexpected clap of thunder. On the other hand, this reorganization is a particularly good example of the gradual growth of centralization: Provosts and presidents had been trying to fold two of these schools for well over a decade, but had failed.

Provost Wesley succeeded. I discuss this case in some detail; by decreasing the power of the deans, the provost increased his own centralized power. In part, Provost Wesley was able to carry out these structural changes because he was an outsider, but some of his predecessors had been professional managers, too. In part, Provost Wesley achieved success by skillfully circumventing the oppositions of professors, deans, and alumni. He also had the support of a powerful chairman of the board of trustees. In this instance, the colleges and departments most affected by Provost Wesley's actions experienced them as an unanticipated thunderstorm, so powerful that it shook branches from trees. Usually, though, Provost Wesley's technique for centralizing power represented the apotheosis of a technique that Wannabe provosts had used since the early 1990s—giving the appearance of shared governance by carefully choosing whom one consults. According to an ex-administrator, the Wan U provosts have had a tendency to ask the opinion of people who agree with them. To describe this practice more technically, they have sought out colleagues and subordinates who would buttress their own legitimacy.[12]

ACADEMIC RESTRUCTURING: THE THUNDERCLAP

Provost Wesley did not consult with the deans or the faculty before folding three schools. Here's the essence of the provost's plan. The College of Continuing Studies was to be downgraded to a division, whose director was to report to the vice provost for education and instruction. Previously its head had reported directly to the provost, as is customary for deans. The School of Allied Health and the School of Human Development and Family Studies were to be dissolved; their departments were to be assigned to other schools and colleges.

Provost Wesley introduced disbanding the schools as the accomplishment of policies that had long been deemed reasonable. Although they did not broadcast their views, many administrators and some professors thought that dissolving the three schools was an appropriate response to their academic failings:

- The dean of the College of Continuing Studies had instituted an online bachelor's and an online master's degree that circumvented the authority of academic departments to approve courses in their disciplines. The academic deans opposed granting online degrees that did not even require any visits to the campus. These deans did not want their units to be compared to online for-profit schools.

- One administrator referred to the School of Allied Health as a "department masquerading as a college." That school had less than twenty faculty members and almost all of its undergraduates were majoring in one department.
- Although the School of Human Development and Family Studies also had a department-sized faculty, its undergraduate teaching load was immense: Over nine hundred students were majors in HDFS. But the School of Human Development and Family Studies could be viewed as an antediluvian remnant of Wannabe's past. Like comparable schools at other universities, it had evolved from a Department of Home Economics, which decades before had offered women their entrée to the state agricultural college.[13]

Provost Wesley was able to dissolve these schools because, as noted, he was indeed a "corporate outsider," a "professional manager" acting with the clear support of Bill Hardway, the (outsider) chairman of the board of trustees who was "more activist" than his predecessors had been. Also he could build on the increasing centralization of power within the university.

Consider Provost Samuel Darning's failed attempt to fold the School of Allied Health and the School of Human Development and Family Studies into other colleges in the early 1990s. He had been acting with the approval of President Oakes, who was an organizational insider, having spent the better part of his career at Wannabe University. Oakes's predecessor, a professional president who eventually left for a first-rank research university, had brought Provost Darning to Wannabe. Darning had made his move on the two schools after receiving the recommendations of a program review committee that had worked for fifteen months to find ways to solve Wan U's serious and seemingly perpetual fiscal problems. (Darning had appointed that committee. Composed of faculty and administrators, the committee had been chaired by the then-dean of the College of Liberal Arts and Sciences.) The University Senate had rejected the committee's recommendations, in part out of loyalty to friends and colleagues who might be fired.[14]

Ultimately, the deans' skillful political battle against Provost Darning's plan preserved the two schools. The deans, especially the dean of human development and family studies, marshaled the schools' supporters to create a hubbub. The *State Capital Record* reported: "After an uproar by students, faculty members, and parents, the schools were saved in the spring [when] the state legislature added $8 million to [Wan U's] budget." Instead, of praising Provost Darning for involving both faculty and administrators in key decisions, the professoriate intensified its opposition to Provost Darning. "A fine scholar and a terrible administrator," "a terrific scientist and a god-awful provost," "a micromanager," professors said. The professors whom I have quoted are sure that their opinion of Provost Darning mattered, but the *State Capital Record* did not print their views. It did state that Darning had lost the support of several trustees. He had been "forced out," the *Record* reported.[15]

Some years and several provosts later, Tyler Johnson, an outsider, also tried to restructure the two schools. According to the *Wannabe Weekly*, he wanted to consolidate the schools of "Pharmacy, Allied Health, Nursing, and Family Studies . . . to increase efficiency and productivity by 'bundling similar administrative programs.'" According to Johnson, "The deans, with input from faculty and staff, will identify cost-saving measures, with all savings being 'directed back into the programs to add needed faculty and improve program quality.'" Parents, students, alumni, and faculty had become accustomed to claiming status as "stakeholders" in university affairs.[16] They protested, though mildly, for although the schools would be consolidated administratively, each one would be conserved academically.[17] Provost Johnson did not send his plan to the University Senate. The restructuring he had proposed was, after all, administrative, not academic. The Senate did not have power over administrative matters.

By 2005, when Provost Wesley announced his plans for the School of Human Development and Family Studies, the School of Allied Health, and the College of Continuing Studies, the proponents of the School of Human Development and Family Studies, including its dean, had become skilled at resisting meaningful (academic) restructuring. Conversely, the central administration knew what kind of opposition to expect and so how to parry it. Provost Wesley gave the affected deans less than twenty-four hours' notice of his intentions. Although he described his plan as "academic restructuring" rather than "administrative restructuring," he did not send it to the University Senate. Rather, bypassing the deans and the faculty, he invoked his central authority. Additionally, the allies of the School of Human Development and Family Studies had to deal with a provost backed by a powerful activist chairman of the board.

Although he had arrived at Wan U after Darning and Oakes had failed in their attempt to eliminate the school, the dean of human development and family studies understood how past deans had successfully foiled past provosts. He did as they had; he publicly complained. He announced publicly that the provost had not spoken with the deans before making his decisions; he had only informed them and their faculties the day before the decisions were revealed. To use the vernacular, members of the schools screamed bloody murder. To use the academic, they accused the provost of not having consulted with the faculty and so with having violated the principles of shared governance and due process. The dean even took out an advertisement in the *State Capital Record* to alert alumni to the provost's action and to request their aid. The central administration countered that this change had been in the works for years. It was not necessary to appoint either a committee or task force, because "the research was done over ten years ago," as a member of the provost's staff explained to me. The *Wannabe Weekly* observed that "the reallocation of programs has been debated for more than fifteen years."

The provost's actions exacerbated emerging conflicts, as the central administration sought to enfold "the academic side" of the university in the bureaucratic organization of the "business side." This provost used principles of the accountability regime to justify the restructuring. He emphasized the positive and spoke the language of scientific administration. The change would help the school, its faculty, and its students. According to *Wannabe Weekly*, "The plan, proposed by Provost Gerald Wesley, will not eliminate any academic programs. It is designed to allow the programs to take advantage of resources and collaborations in their new settings." Provost Wesley invoked the best practices at other research universities. The *Weekly* reported: "'Compared to peer and aspirant institutions, Wan U's many independent schools and colleges have reduced institutional effectiveness and efficiency,' said Wesley." The *Weekly* added, "The restructuring will address the problems of quality control, efficiency, effectiveness, consistency, and stability, but will have no negative impact on programs, faculty, staff, and students." In essence, the central administration was publicly claiming that the restructuring was pertinent to its managerial mission—facilitating such matters as quality, efficiency, consistency, and stability—and so could only improve the professors' academic mission of teaching and doing research. Supposedly, because the central administrators were more familiar with management principles and strategic planning than were the deans and professors, they were the most qualified to make such decisions.[18] That administrative claim to expertise had also developed gradually.

Although Provost Wesley was trying to extend the authority of the "business side" over the "academic side," he was not the first central administrator to claim to have a better understanding of professors' needs than professors had. In the 1990s, when Provost Mike Tremaine had instituted a five-year cycle of program reviews, the provost and deans had used the review to steer weak or eclectic departments in the direction that the provost and deans defined as the academic mainstream.[19] The very notion of instituting external reviews involved making academic departments auditable. After all, the scholars who reviewed a department reported their findings and recommendations to the dean and provost, who used them to negotiate a contract about the future development of a discipline at Wan U. The very term "contract" implied a business-like (rational) agreement that would bring a department in line with the "mission" of the university as a whole. As I discussed in chapter 2, some professors in the social science departments that were being "improved" felt that the administrators were sticking their noses in disciplinary matters, even claiming to know what research the social scientists should be doing and what methods they should use to do it. Provost Wesley was not dictating the sort of research that the faculty in family studies and in allied health should do. However, he was insisting that he understood how to organize the professors' work and that they did not.

Invoking bureaucratic power, Chairman Bill Hardway put the matter more bluntly at the yearly dinner meeting of some trustees, central administrators, and leaders of the University Senate. Chairman Hardway observed that if one of his department heads had taken out an advertisement in an important newspaper to protest a superior's decision, Hardway would have fired him. Although the university was not a Fortune 500 company, as was the corporation that Hardway headed, Hardway emphasized the need for the university to be business-like. ("The university is not a business, but it can be business-like," he reminded trustees at several board meetings.) Professors were to be accountable to administrators; schools were to be accountable to the central administration. Lines of authority were to converge in Top Hall, and the board of trustees was to be the final authority.[20]

To no avail, students and faculty appeared before the board of trustees to argue for the retention of their schools. Bill Hardway criticized their arguments. For instance, when a student said that more than half of public research universities had a School of Family Studies, Hardway told the undergraduate that it was also possible to state that almost half did not. When the undergraduate trustee suggested that more consultations with those affected might have occurred, the board charged the provost to undertake appropriate consultations and report back at the next meeting.

At the board's meeting the following month, Provost Wesley reported that he had participated in seventy-five meetings on the topic, including meetings with the faculty and administrators of all of the schools affected by his decision. He also reported that in consultation with the people affected, he and his staff were working out the details associated with moving both personnel and departments from one school to another. The provost did not review the timing of these meetings and consultations. He did not review whether others had objected to his decisions. Indeed, he did not reveal what anyone had said to him about the restructuring. Ultimately, Provost Wesley followed a procedure he had described to professors when he had interviewed for the job at Wan U: "I will consult others, but then I will do what I think best. I have the responsibility to decide what to do."

Keeping the specifics to himself, Provost Wesley acted as though he had read the work of Michel Foucault: maintaining a monopoly on some kinds of knowledge helped him to solidify his power. When Provost Wesley told the trustees he had engaged in extensive consultation by participating in seventy-five meetings about restructuring, the trustees congratulated Provost Wesley on a job well done. They did not ask about either the content of, or the participants in, the meetings. However, an associate dean sitting near me looked shocked. Members of her college had complained to their dean about the provost's lack of real consultation.

THE DEAN DEBACLE

The centralization of bureaucratic power in Top Hall necessarily decreased the authority of deans to run their colleges as they pleased. Power is, after all, a limited resource; it is not infinitely expandable. If a dean did not like how power was coalescing in Top Hall, he or she could always retire or find another job. Or if a dean chose to contravene the norms of behavior in a bureaucratic hierarchy, the dean could face the possibility of being fired.[21]

At many public research universities, the deans of the schools and colleges report to the provost. They also contest the provost's power, for historically so many institutions of higher education had been a confederation of colleges that many deans have felt free to claim some autonomy. Indeed, at some universities, each dean may have more power over the budget of his or her school than does the university's president. At Harvard University, for instance, almost every school and college sits on "its own tub"; that is, it controls its own income and expenditures. This ability of Harvard's decentralized schools hampers the power of central administrators to dictate policy to the schools, for the central administrators cannot threaten to withhold funds if, say, a dean does not accede to the will of a president (Bradley 2001; Lewis 2006; Keller and Keller 2007).

At Wannabe University, the president and the provost control the budgets of the schools and colleges. That is, they decide the size of each school's budget. The provost hires the deans and presides at the monthly meetings of the Deans Council. He can fire a dean. Using the advice of a review committee, the provost can either reappoint or "not renew" a dean at the end of his five-year appointment.[22] Or a provost (or president) may request a dean's resignation before the dean's term has been completed. As a vice provost explained to me, "We [members of the administration] all serve at the pleasure of the [provost and the] president."

Provost Wesley increased his power, when a year and a half into his tenure at Wannabe University, two-thirds of the deans "disappeared," as one informant put it. Gerald Wesley was responsible for five departures. He folded three schools. He fired two deans, one of whom Provost Johnson had been talked into hiring after what Johnson felt had been an unsatisfactory search. Wesley did not renew a sixth dean after he received a negative review, including negative comments from "his faculty." Two deans accepted better positions elsewhere, and one retired after recovering from a serious illness. Two years before the dean debacle, four deans had been women. After replacements were hired, two women were left standing. Each one headed a school whose graduates entered a "women's field," such as nursing.

Despite the provost's economic and political power over them, the deans seemed to cherish the notion that they could control their schools and colleges and could influence the central administration. They could write negative reviews of the provost when he was up for his five-year review.[23] Just as professors could comment on the reappointment of a dean, even privately visiting the chair of the review committee to do so, deans and professors could also quietly visit the head of a provost's review committee. Because deans could be reviewed by their subordinates, superordinates, and colleagues, some of them took particular care to put on their best face. For example, when several members of the Deans Council wanted the provost to modify one of his plans, each one of them asked "their" professors and department heads to contribute criticisms. At one and the same time, each could identify himself to his subordinates as their spokesperson and could buttress himself from the anger of the provost by noting that these criticisms were bubbling up from the faculty.

Many deans presented themselves to their faculties as powerful figures who stood up to the central administration, when it was in the interest of their faculties for them to do so. These deans liked to present themselves as the ally of the professors. "I told the provost . . . ," Dean Todd Alden was wont to say at meetings with his department heads. "The [central administration] wants to do . . . ," he would report, "but I am resisting" or even "I am refusing . . ."

Central administrators gave a different account of their interactions with these same deans. A former associate vice provost said of one, "He goes back to his faculty and tells them, 'I told the provost that is not acceptable.' But he doesn't do that. He does what the provost tells him to." This ex-administrator continued, "I think just about all of the deans do that. They say that they objected. But they do what they are told." As Wolverton and Gmelch (2002) insist, deans have historically been the mediators between bureaucratic central administrations and departments governed by collegiality. At Wan U, the deans like to be seen as go-betweens, standing up for departmental colleagues, not as obedient bureaucratic functionaries.

At Wannabe University, provosts have fired deans when professors provided them with an irrefutable cause. In at least two instances, faculty viewed those deans as having engaged in egregious behaviors. In one case, a dean was conducting an affair with a female colleague at the home of another colleague. Both of the professors involved in the assignation, the mistress and the keeper of the key, were getting larger discretionary ("merit") raises than their colleagues who had met the ordinary and public criteria for receiving merit raises—publishing articles and books about one's research and receiving grants. A professor gave data about the pattern of raises to the president of the local chapter of the American Association of University Professors. The president visited the provost. The provost visited the dean, and the dean immediately resigned.

In another instance, a dean had done a superb job at raising funds from outside of the university, getting resources from the central administration, hiring "minority professors," building relationships with state corporations, and attracting better students. However, the other deans didn't like him. According to informants, he was a "polarizing figure" who hogged the floor at meetings of the Council of Deans. Well-placed administrators and professors in his school say that he had bragged to the other deans that he was "the best dean," had alienated central administrators by forcefully disagreeing with them in public, and had estranged his own faculty by "getting even" with professors who opposed his plans for the school. For instance, the disaffected professors claimed that he found justification for increasing the teaching load of his critics or he threatened to withhold the resources needed by an alienated department's graduate students if the department did not follow his wishes.[24] The deans had reason to honor the "strong suggestions" of the top central administrators and to be reluctant to buck them.

Reactions to this provost's 2006 two-page version of the academic plan illustrate that reluctance. Supposedly to encourage feedback from both professors and colleges, the provost had visited every school and college to explain an academic plan requested by the board of trustees (and discussed in chapter 8). He had also asked the deans for feedback from their faculty. As characteristic of a mechanistic bureaucracy (Morrill 1995), the deans expressed dissent privately.[25] When he mentioned the policy at the next meeting of the Deans Council, there was relatively little discussion. Instead of speaking publicly, some deans had made appointments to visit the provost to discuss the policy. "With some trepidation, your dean came to discuss that with me," Provost Wesley said with a blush and a smile to an associate dean who asked a question about the 2006 academic plan at a meeting of a University Senate committee to which the provost had been invited.[26]

Some faculty members felt that the retirement or resignation of so many deans had no relationship to the provost's management style. One professor noted that one of the deans was recovering from cancer. Mostly, though, in separate conversations, professors told me: "Well, they were old enough to retire." "It's hard to refuse a better job." "They would have left anyway." "Any provost would have fired that dean. The dean had lost the support of both the senior and the junior faculty. It was inevitable." Although most academics know colleagues who have ignored "job feelers," none of these professors suggested that sometimes people put off retirement or that many people do not entertain "job feelers" if they are happy with their present personal and professional circumstances. A department head repeated his college's scuttlebutt, "For years [the president] knew that these deans were roughly the same age and could retire at about the same time, but no one expected them to retire all at once." A well-placed administrator said, "The provost was responsible for five of the nine deans who left."

Organizationally what counts is that the provost had the opportunity to appoint new deans. He did not have to be organizationally loyal to them—although a provost customarily backs his deans when they are carrying out university policy. However, the new deans would supposedly be organizationally loyal to him. He was to be their boss. He would appoint them. Furthermore, choosing those deans, the provost could seek to "upgrade" the administration. He could hire internationally. He could hire people with larger academic and administrative reputations than the deans whom they replaced. He could (and did) spread that hiring over several years to minimize the disruption of the university. "We have a wonderful opportunity here," Provost Wesley told the board of trustees when he described the deaconal searches. "You heard him," a departing dean said dryly to me. "A wonderful opportunity. Fortuitous." As we spoke, it became clear that the departing dean felt that Provost Wesley had taken the opportunity to "upgrade" the quality of Wannabe's deans and to consolidate power.

LITTLE CAT FEET

Like Carl Sandburg's fog, sometimes centralization "comes on little cat feet." Unlike the fog, it does not move on. Rather administrators plan for centralization to occur gradually; they also plan justifications for its indefinite stay. They are engaging in the *gradual institutionalization of legitimacy*. In essence, when they introduce a new policy or practice that the faculty (or students) do not like, they suggest that the change is not meaningful. Gradually, people accept the new way of doing things; through habituation, it obtains legitimacy (see Berger and Luckmann 1967). Then the administration modifies the policy in a way that gives it a little more power or control. If (or when) the professors or students protest, they tend to complain about the newest change, often in a way that validates the legitimacy of the penultimate change.

For instance, today many professors at research universities take for granted that at the end of every academic year they are supposed to complete forms that quantify their accomplishments: how many undergraduate and graduate students they have taught in which courses, how much scholarship they have completed and how they have disseminated it, how they served the community, the number of committees of which they were a member. In the academic year 2007–2008, this form ran to 108 items and was eight pages long. That year, the form that faculty used to apply for tenure and promotion was fifteen pages; a faculty committee revised it so that it would be easier to use. Although professors debated the wording on some items, no one questioned the existence of these forms. They had attained legitimacy.

Here are some other examples of the gradual institutionalization of legitimacy. In these examples, administrators were very conscious that the fog creeps in on cat feet.

Students had been living in houses near the campus for some years, when absentee landlords began to gobble up more houses and rent them out at $600 a bedroom. (That's the 2006 rate. Almost all of the houses had three or four bedrooms.) As undergraduates will, many held parties, some quite noisy, replete with underage drinking and even, in several instances, with disc jockeys whose not-so-mellow tones blared through Ashton neighborhoods. Working with the town, the central administration wanted to curtail noisy parties, and in 2007 the Division of Student Affairs even established an Office of Off-Campus Services. Its tasks included working to improve the relationships of students living off-campus with their Ashton neighbors. Its powers were limited, mainly because the university did not know which students lived where. It kept track of their "home addresses," not their temporary Ashton locations. "We are trying to establish a way for students to register their off-campus addresses," the director told residents of a neighborhood near campus. "At first, saying where you live off-campus will be voluntary. Then eventually, we'll make it mandatory. After all, most of them will have been giving us their off-campus address."[27]

Central administrators working to establish "student outcomes assessment" seem to have reasoned in a similar way. They introduced an unpopular procedure, and then they proposed to make it more ubiquitous than they had originally claimed. As discussed in chapter 7, the provost's office introduced procedures to gauge how much students were learning, when the regional agency that accredited Wan U required Wan U to do so. They never directly stated that they "believed" in the educational principles associated with the national and regional demand for assessment.

When they addressed faculty committees, members of the provost's staff vacillated in their discussion of the need for assessment procedures. As many professors in the College of Liberal Arts and Sciences complained, they suggested that the provost was asking people to do what had to be done. They said: "The provost didn't take accreditation requirements seriously when he was at another university and it was a major mistake." "It has to be done for reaccreditation." "There's no choice." "The professional schools have to pass periodic accreditation, so do some of the departments [such as psychology] in CLAS [College of Liberal Arts and Sciences], so it's not such a big change." Speaking to a committee of representatives from each department in the College of Liberal Arts and Sciences, all designated to work on assessment procedures for their unit, the assistant vice provost in charge of assessment even said, "We have to do this. The assessment is being done for reaccreditation." The assistant vice provost claimed that assessment had no other purpose. A permanent guest of the committee, he made his comment to the full group, including the group's leader, a social scientist appointed by the dean of CLAS. Several months later, that social scientist said that the provost might use the assessment materials to help him decide how to disperse resources.

> Let's say the English department says that learning Chaucer is essential to English majors. I don't know; maybe learning Chaucer is important to their mission statement and then their students aren't doing well on Chaucer in the annual assessment, and that they want to hire another Chaucer expert. Meanwhile, Urban Studies says it needs to hire [someone to teach a vital subject]. . . . Student assessment will help the provost decide between those competing claims, because it will help him to see how the departments are fulfilling their mission.

"Wait a minute," a humanist immediately objected. "We were told that assessment was only to satisfy accreditation requirements. You said it wouldn't be used to decide who gets lines [permission to hire]." Around the circle of neatly arranged chairs, men and women nodded agreement, displeasure—downright frowns—on their faces. "So what," the social scientist responded. "You have to do assessment anyway."

BEATING BACK THE FOG

Of course, professors do not accept every attempt at the gradual institutionalization of the administration's legitimacy. Rather, the Wan U professoriate invoked a variety of methods to beat back the pressure to accede to centralization.[28] Some of these were more direct than others. I do not know which methods are most common, for there is no way to count the number of administrative decisions that impinge on professors, let alone to take a random sample of all of them. My impression is that most professors preferred forms of indirect resistance. They saw "no reason to create an unnecessary fuss," especially if doing so might foster a reputation as a "troublemaker" or "loose cannon," or even worse invite retribution.

DIRECT METHODS

Sometimes professors used the University Senate, a Senate committee, or the Graduate Faculty Council to resist centralized authority. For instance, although the provost and deans had favored the establishment of research incentive awards, a Senate committee composed mainly of professors successfully contested them. (As discussed in chapter 3, after the federal government had fined Wan U, because a federal agency had deemed the wording of the relevant provisions to be illegal, two central administrators had revised it and eventually the revision wended its way to the Faculty Standards Committee.)

The provost's office took the reworded policy to the Deans Council and to the faculty union. The policy was placed on the agenda of the board of trustees, and then a vice provost introduced it to the Faculty Standards Committee for quick ratification.[29] The committee did not want to act with untimely speed, especially because some of its members were strongly disagreeing with one another. A subcommittee of six people—including a vice provost, two department heads, and three professors—met six times in one month to review the revised policy. Eventually, the subcommittee agreed that the policy was unnecessary, because only five people, all members of the same college, had qualified to receive the award. The subcommittee decided that those five people did not need an additional incentive to apply for large grants and that furthermore it was foolish "to have a policy for less than a handful of people." The primary opponent of the measure had also been against it several years earlier, when the measure had been initially proposed. He prevailed this time because of the "collegiality" of the discussions, the group's ability to convince administrators on the subcommittee, and the willingness of subcommittee members to reason with a recalcitrant member who remained firm in his desire to retain research incentive awards.

Sometimes professors may organize to make frontal attacks on policies they abhor (and on the administrators who suggest those policies). Through 2007, professors in the School of Engineering and in the science departments of the College of Liberal Arts and Sciences had successfully resisted the inclusion of research assistants' tuition in the budgets of grant proposals. As discussed earlier, in the 2004–2005 academic year, they had asked all of the candidates for provost their ideas about this matter, and when the new provost arrived, he discarded the idea of changing the Wan U policy. These groups rallied again, when in 2008 Provost Wesley reintroduced the notion of charging the granting agency for the tuition of graduate students supported by federal grants. This time, the faculty Research Advisory Committee of the graduate school sent an e-mail delineating the grounds of their opposition to the faculty Listserv and asked professors to discuss the plan.[30]

INDIRECT METHODS

Professors also use such indirect methods as *ritual compliance*. Going through the motions, they seem to comply. However, as Birnbaum (2001) explains, they do "as little of what was asked as possible and [find] ways around the rest." Thus, at a Senate committee meeting, a professor expressed pride in his department's ability to evade taking one of the provost's initiatives seriously, while seeming to comply.[31] At another meeting, a department head told his colleagues, "The question is how little can we do so that we look like we are [doing it] and won't have someone in the administration saying they'll do it for us." A year later, an associate professor assigned to provide what the central administration had requested told his colleagues: "I'm trying to figure out how to do this with as little pain as possible. . . . Eventually this initiative is going to collapse under its own weight."

Influenced by the rapid turnover of top central administrators, professors and departments also "waited it out." At a meeting of representatives from the College of Liberal Arts and Sciences, a department head who had spent decades at Wannabe University said: "Provosts come and go. Each one brings his own policies. This may just be a temporary policy. *How long do you think we can put off doing what this [provost] wants us to do?*" (emphasis added). Similarly, speaking to an old friend who had become an administrator, a professor expressed his dislike of one of the provost's policies; he thought his friend would dislike that policy, too. The friend replied, "Let's see how long he stays here."[32] Professors and even administrators "guesstimate" the power and length of tenure of administrators whom they believe to be occupationally mobile. The shorter the time that an outsider is likely to spend at Wan U, the less likely it is that professors need to heed that person.

Sometimes members of a department decided that the group would simply not follow direction, especially if they believed they could do so without suffering any consequences. They might even take pride in their department's lack of compliance with policies that they considered to be "silly" or to be "make-work." One department thought ridiculous the requirement that students consult an advisor before they register for courses. To ensure compliance with this rule, departments were supposed to "lower the bar" on students—to instruct the computer program used for registration to bar students' registration until they had consulted their advisors. Some of the department's members argued that the students were old enough to figure out what courses they wanted and needed to take. A few men even objected, "I'm not their mother." (Although everyone conceded that the central administration would not keep track of which departments were complying and which were not, some departmental faculty objected to the conflation of mothering and advising students.)

In the following paraphrase of an exchange between two professors waiting their turn at their physician's office, a professor from one department identified this procedure as a nuisance, while a professor from another dismissed the notion that one had to follow such rules.

> **Professor 1:** I have two basketball players in my class who are out of town [playing in a tournament]. I had to call our secretary to have their [computerized] bar lifted so they could register [for next semester's classes, also by computer] while they are away.
>
> **Professor 2:** We don't take things like that very seriously in my department. We don't even put the bar down [that prevents students from enrolling without seeing an advisor]. Students can just enroll.

AGREEMENT

Of course, not everyone tries to duck administrative initiatives. Some professors agree with central administrators on some issues. Rather than ignoring the latest plan, acceding to it, or engaging in ritual compliance, some professors may embrace it. Especially when it comes to a plan to "improve" undergraduate instruction, many professors who care about the quality of their own teaching have backed attempts to introduce reforms. "You should hear [a certain professor] talk about how his department devalues teaching," an informant who was enthusiastic about working with undergraduates told me. "He's absolutely adamant that his department devalues teaching." Critical of their departments, such professors may welcome teaching initiatives sponsored by the central administration.

In sum, some professors agree with the central administration. However, resisting authority, other professors may stage direct or indirect attacks. They may turn to either the University Senate and its committees or the Graduate Faculty Council and its committees. They may engage in ritual compliance, or they may just ignore administrative directives. Sometimes, though, when faced with an administrative policy that professors feel doesn't touch their immediate concerns, they may consciously accede to the wishes of the central administration, especially if the administration claims that the issue is vital to the university. Like the administrators who are so busy plotting strategies that they cannot see how they are contributing to significant social change, so too professors pursuing research may not notice how by ignoring new "teaching initiatives" they are facilitating the centralization of administrative power and the enactment of an accountability regime. If they do notice, they may not care.

6

Teaching, Learning, and Rating

Writing in the *Wannabe Weekly* in 1998, Mary Matthews, vice provost for undergraduate education and instruction, reminded the faculty and staff of the university that "President Whitmore and Vice Provost Tremaine have emphasized the importance of undergraduate education at a research university." Like them, she affirmed that what the current education literature identifies as "teaching and learning" (and the faculty simply refer to as "teaching") are vital to a research university. (Teaching refers to an action in which the instructors engage; learning refers to the activity of students. Hence an emphasis on learning implies being "student-centered.")[1]

Vice Provost Matthews's article presaged a spate of heady internal politics, as Matthews asserted bureaucratic supremacy over several other claimants to jurisdiction over aspects of instruction. The column's second sentence is noteworthy. Matthews said: "The Office of Undergraduate Education and Instruction, created to make our commitment [to undergraduate education] visible, is charged with spearheading our efforts toward educational excellence at the undergraduate level and instructional excellence at all levels." With the phrase "charged with spearheading our efforts," the vice provost declared that her office was key to transforming Wannabe University.

As we will see, the undergraduate learning experience figured centrally in the ranking system Wannabe's administrators used to gauge (audit) their standing among national research universities. Simultaneously, by using the phrase "created to make our commitment visible," she invoked the significance of "openness" in a society dedicated to audit. By being "open" or "transparent" (see Strathern 2000; Gawley 2008; Power 1997), one might prove to both friends and enemies that one is what one claims to be and so lay to rest suspicions that one is hiding the truth or behaving in an ignoble manner. That opening paragraph also implied: Even the administrators of a research university realize that education is the institution's raison d'être.[2] As the spring 2006 draft of Wan U's mission statement announced:

> We create and disseminate knowledge by means of scholarly and creative achieve-
> ments, graduate and professional education, and outreach. Through our focus on
> teaching and learning, the University helps every student grow intellectually and
> become a contributing member of the state, national, and world communities.
> Through research, teaching, service, and outreach, we embrace diversity and cul-
> tivate leadership, integrity, and engaged citizenship in our students, faculty, staff,
> and alumni.

TEACHING VS. RESEARCH

Although teaching lies at the core of all undergraduate institutions, professors at research universities, such as Wannabe University, tend to downplay
the importance of teaching and emphasize the value of research to their
jobs, while today central administrators insistently state that "teaching and
learning" are crucial to the university's mission. In the 1960s, both professors and administrators commonly identified a research university as
a "community of scholars." Today administrators are wont to explain that
professors are "lifelong learners" and that both professors and undergraduates belong to a "community of learners." Indeed, the contemporary jargon
would foist that identity on the university itself: "A university is a community of learners."[3]

It is probably an exaggeration to say that professors and academic departments do not take the contemporary slogans very seriously. However, there
are many professors who view them as so much gobbledygook not even
worthy of resistance. When slogans about "teaching and learning" were
mentioned at a meeting I observed, several men pursed their lips as though
they were sucking a lemon, for many professors at Wannabe University
seem to feel that teaching is a secondary activity. At a research university,
they were happy to affirm, "research counts." For most professors, the quality and quantity of a person's research is a source of professional prestige,
just as the quality and quantity of the scholarship published by members of
a department or of a university affect the group's collective prestige.[4]

Consider the attendance when in late 2006 and early 2007 the Provost's
Task Force on Teaching, Learning, and Assessment held four lunchtime forums to discuss a report calling for some significant changes: the auditorium was almost empty. At each meeting, there were fewer than thirty people scattered around the room, and a goodly number of them, perhaps half,
were members of the task force. I would be inflating participation were I to

say that 10 percent of the faculty members on the Ashton campus attended the forums. Most members of the task force came to more than one forum, and some of the "regular professors" in the audience included several people who had attended more than one meeting. At the very most, forty professors who were not on the task force came to hear about the group's recommendations. This pattern of attendance was not unusual. A middle manager who was involved in undergraduate instruction and had been on committees about undergraduate education confirmed, "I've been at lots of meetings where the committee wanted to discuss their recommendations with the faculty. But when you looked around the room, the only people there seemed to be the people on the committee."

The professors attending the Forums of Teaching, Learning, and Assessment were presumably people who cared about teaching (or teaching and learning). They complained that other professors did not take teaching seriously. Insistently, they echoed the task force's call that the university should institute a "culture that values teaching excellence." By appealing for the creation of such a culture, they necessarily affirmed that it did not then exist. Of course, here and there in some seemingly isolated pockets, a few professors and departments take what they call "teaching" more seriously than others. Also, whether one looks at professional schools or "more academic" colleges, almost every department includes professors who insist that "teaching matters." "Teaching is part of our job," some say. "Good teaching should count for merit raises," others argue. But even as they give lip service to the importance of teaching, many professors demur. The reason some faculty members tenaciously and defensively say that "good teaching *should* matter" is that being a good teacher, even an excellent teacher, doesn't count for much. When discussing the report of the Task Force on Teaching, Learning, and Assessment, a member of a University Senate committee noted, "We all know who Wannabe's top researchers are. But we don't know the names of its top teachers."

Research universities inscribe the importance of research (as opposed to teaching) in common practices. Although professors at research universities are required to spend less time in the classroom than are professors at other sorts of undergraduate institutions, Wannabe University's bylaws stress the importance of *both* research and teaching to tenure and promotion. However, again and again professors report that assistant professors who are "superior researchers" and "weak teachers" receive promotions and tenure, whereas those who are superior teachers and weak researchers do not. At a public meeting, the head of Wannabe University's Institute for Teaching and Learning expressed his dismay that when awarding tenure and promotions to professors, departments and schools do not even consider "the scholarship about teaching and learning" to be "real scholarship." (Speaking about that scholarship, he used its acronym, "SATL," and so affirmed that those engaged in such work consider it so important that they have given it a special moniker.) Members of the Task Force on Teaching, Learning, and Assessment also insisted that department heads and merit committees discount articles and books about teaching when they award merit raises. Indeed, at meetings of the University Senate's Faculty Standards Committee, members readily explained that when setting the formula used to calculate merit raises, their departments had decided to weigh research more than teaching and had also assigned scholarship about teaching and learning to the tangential category "teaching," not to the prized classification, "research."[5]

The pattern of granting tenure and promotions at Wannabe University resembles the pattern at American research universities (Lewis 1975, 1996). Both the determination of academic merit and the operation of the academic job markets are all about the quantity and quality of published research (Lewis 1996). As Lionel Lewis explains, at research universities, when it comes to getting jobs and keeping jobs, good teaching—even exceptional teaching—is of "marginal worth." As he puts it, "Those who work hard at teaching and approach it with idealistic devotion are entrapped. If [their] scholarship dwindles [their] marketplace value becomes nil. In effect, those whose sole focus is on teaching become hostages to the institution where they work" (1996: 144). They are not mobile. They cannot find another academic job. Especially if they have enjoyed the experience of serving on university committees and have garnered a reputation as a sensible and sensitive leader, some of them might flirt with becoming administrators in order to develop some career mobility.[6] But when first tackling administrative tasks, they are still shackled to their current institution. "I'm at a crossroads now," said a humanist who had been an associate professor for well over a decade and who had briefly served as an associate dean. "I have to decide whether I really want to be an administrator." She had been elected to so many powerful and sensitive Senate committees (including its Executive Committee) and subsequently been appointed to so many university committees (including key search committees) that she was on an eleven-month (administrative) salary rather than a nine-month (professorial) salary. Only after having been officially deemed an administrator and having succeeded at her assigned tasks could she hope to find a "higher" administrative job at some "lesser institution." Only then would she join the ranks of the mobile corporate administrators discussed in chapter 4.

Strategically, the professoriate's emphasis on scholarship means that the central administration would face less faculty resistance and downright opposition if it were to consolidate its power on matters pertaining to "teaching and learning" than if it were to impose its authority on research. Because so many individual professors are caught up in the importance of their own research, the faculty as a collectivity sometimes let slide by "reforms" that affect teaching. I do not mean to imply that all professors care about research more than teaching. Yet even though professors at research universities report that they devote the largest block of their time to teaching, "publishing professors," even those who care about teaching, are aware that their activities in the classroom are peripheral to their careers (Lewis 1996). At Wannabe University, "non-publishing professors" who do not seek such quasi-administrative posts as associate department head, know that they have little influence on the central administration. Administrators rarely appoint them to key college and university committees. (Some department heads are an exception to this rule and are appointed to lots of committees. Although they may no longer publish, their departments have high standing in their disciplines, because their members publish a lot and receive many grants.)[7]

Often publishing faculty are not oriented toward the Wannabe administration, for (merit raises and salary aside) they are rewarded for scholarship by the recognition of professional colleagues located around the country and sometimes abroad. External recognition may bring internal rewards. The comments of a scientist's wife, who was herself an academic, illustrate the faculty's tendency to value external rewards. She proudly told a friend that when external reviewers reported about her husband John's department, they said how lucky Wannabe was to have him on its faculty. On another occasion, she noted that when they were younger, several men in John's department had competed with one another for external recognition and so for the internal goodies that external recognition might sometimes bring, including merit raises.

Committed to the supremacy of research universities over liberal arts colleges, many members of the "publishing faculty" resent central administrators who push them to devote more time to their undergraduate students.[8] Several professors in the same department mentioned a meeting in 2000 when their department head announced one of Mary Matthews's new goals: Before graduation, every undergraduate should have been enrolled in at least one reasonably sized class in their major subject taught by a senior professor. Some people agreed with Matthews's proposal; others did not. "What does she think this is? A liberal arts college?" an ambitious man had complained. "It would be great if we could find her a job at a good liberal arts college," someone else had suggested. A third professor, who had not published recently, had objected, "But every undergraduate should have a

professor who knows them well enough to write a letter of recommendation." Perhaps thinking about her own undergraduate career, a publishing
professor had asked, "If every undergraduate doesn't have a course with a
full-time faculty member, who will write their recommendations for graduate school? You need more than a letter from a teaching assistant to get in"
to a good graduate department or professional school.

According to several accounts of that meeting, no one specifically mentioned the possibility that the faculty had a responsibility to students who
would graduate from Wan U and would then look for a job. Nor did anyone mention the clauses in Wan U's mid-nineties mission statement that
proclaimed Wan U's responsibility to its students: "We will be a center for
intellectual pursuits offering the citizens of [the state], the nation, and the
world the highest quality educational services. . . . The University will focus
its efforts on ensuring that the student experience fosters the transmission
of knowledge and inspires intellectual curiosity in each student." Given the
professoriate's emphasis on research, it would be naive to have expected
them to have done so. To hear many tell it, a research university is about
just that—research.

RATING RESEARCH UNIVERSITIES

There is some irony to the current emphasis on teaching and learning. For
the past few decades, universities across the United States have gauged their
public standing—have subjected themselves to external audit—by submit-
ting requested data to the editors of the annual edition of "America's Best
Colleges" published by *U.S. News & World Report.* To climb those rankings,
Wannabe University, like every other research university, must address issues involving undergraduate education. Although the items the magazine
uses for rating research universities and liberal arts colleges are not identical, both formulas pay little explicit attention to either the quality or quantity of faculty research. (The only item of potential relevance to research
is how administrators at comparable universities view the reputations of
specific institutions.) The magazine's editors explain:

> The indicators we use to capture academic quality fall into seven categories: as-
> sessment by administrators at peer institutions, retention of students, faculty
> resources, student selectivity, financial resources, alumni giving . . . [and] "grad-
> uation rate performance." The indicators include input measures that reflect a
> school's student body, its faculty, and its financial resources, along with output
> measures that signal how well the institution does its job of educating students.
> (2008 ed.: 77, 78)

Whether these indicators measure what the magazine claims is another matter.[9] What counts is that in the process of chasing a good ranking, colleges and universities transform themselves to conform to the indices that *U.S. News & World Report* employs. The process is similar to how law schools respond to their rankings of law schools. As Espeland and Sauder (2007: 333) report: "Rankings evoke self-fulfilling prophecies that gradually transform law schools into entities that conform more closely to the criteria used to construct rankings . . . commensuration [the process of attributing meaning to measurement] changes the form and circulation of information and how people attend to it." In part, that reification of the meaning of rankings occurs because a high ranking increases both applications (Monks and Ehrenberg 1999; Stevens 2007) and the admissions "yield rate" (the percentage of applicants admitted who actually enroll).[10] A higher rating may attract more in-state students and so decrease the dreaded "brain drain." Like winning football and basketball teams, it might also induce more high-paying out-of-state students to apply.[11] If a high rating also results in a higher out-of-state yield rate, the resulting gross tuition is a valued revenue stream. Indeed, in order to increase their income, some universities are increasing the percentage of out-of-state applicants whom they accept. As I noted in chapter 2, in the late 1990s Wannabe University had increased its student body to increase resources, including gross revenue. (A decade later, when demographers predicted fewer graduates from the state's high schools, the admissions staff was working to establish relationships with high school guidance counselors in western and southwestern states. If those accepted attended Wan U in sufficient numbers, they might not only feed the yield rate, but also establish a stream of applicants who would pay higher tuition.)[12]

In part, the rankings affect colleges and universities by encouraging them to change their practices in order to achieve a better score on the indices that *U.S. News & World Report* uses, for the rankings are seductive. They seem to provide a path to elite status; at least, according to informants, that is what top central administrators supposed when, in the mid-1990s, they decided to "transform" Wannabe University by "improving" its ranking in the magazine's annual report. Attentive to the magazine's indicators, around the country colleges and universities are introducing programs to help new students adjust more easily to higher education. Intended to increase retention rates, Wannabe University identifies these one-credit classes as its "First-Year Experience Program."[13] They might also be called a "First-Year Retention Rate Program" or even a "Higher Graduation Rate Program," since a higher retention rate from the first to the second year of college translates into a higher graduate rate. An increased retention rate also has other financial ramifications. It may decrease the spending needed to recruit applications, and so it is a sound investment. As Wan U's vice provost for enrollment management told a *State Capital Record* reporter in 2006:

> When you recruit a student to attend your university, you want to see students be successful. Also you want to make sure students can graduate. . . . Retention rates are important. They not only help students succeed, but they help polish the university's reputation, because those rates are factored into the university's ranking in the annual *U.S. News & World Report* best-schools reports. It also makes sense on the business end for the university to protect the investment made to recruit the student in the first place. It costs [Wan U] $680 to recruit a student. . . .[14]

To put it somewhat differently, the *U.S. News & World Report* indicators bellow: Stress teaching and learning! They advise: Initiate changes in precisely those areas that research-oriented faculty are likely to ignore. Chatting about changing teaching policies, a Wannabe middle manager affirmed: "Sometimes the faculty don't even notice [that there's been a meaningful change]." Because professors who don't notice (or don't care) are ignoring educational initiatives or are engaging in ritual compliance, even Wannabe's middle managers understand that the central administration has an opportunity to step in and to change the structure of undergraduate education. Asked about some of their activities, these middle managers saw themselves as following the directions of their bosses in the central administration. To them, their mission was clear: to improve retention and graduation rates. By improving Wan U's performance on the *U.S. News & World Report* indicators associated with undergraduate education, the central administration placed itself in what is commonly called a "win-win situation."

Because they help central administrators to develop strategies for transformation, the *U.S. News & World Report* indicators seem superior to other measures of the quality of universities. Indeed, other measures contain indicators that are more difficult for central administrators to manipulate since they fall into areas that professors claim to be their own turf. Consider three other common measures.

- Membership in the elite American Association of Universities (AAU) is a somewhat different indicator of worthiness. It is a dichotomous measure: a research university belongs to the group or does not. Founded in 1900 by fourteen doctorate-granting institutions, the AAU currently has sixty members from the United States and two from Canada. Membership is by invitation only. When deciding whether to invite a doctorate-granting institution to be evaluated for membership, the AAU uses criteria similar to those of TheCenter (see below). It introduces more qualitative criteria to reach a final decision. Membership in the AAU is "a big deal."[15]

- The Lombardi Program on Measuring University Performance of the University of Florida (also called TheCenter) ranks research universities by such measures as the dollar amount of its federal grants, the number of faculty members who have been invited to join such groups as the National Academy of Sciences, as well as by the number of doctoral degrees it awards yearly and the number of postdoctoral fellows whom it supports. These measures are available from the U.S. Department of Education and are related to those used by the National Research Council.

- The National Research Council, the research arm of the National Academy of Sciences, provides another set of ratings. It conducts decennial evaluations of Ph.D.-granting departments and ranks them by discipline. Research universities, departments, and professors take these rankings very seriously. For instance, in 2005 a central administrator favored eliminating the doctoral program in a specific science. He noted that the science department was not even among the top 100 doctoral programs in its discipline. "The NRC doesn't even rank below 100," he told me. He added that the department teaches a lot of undergraduates in its required general education course, but it does not garner "significant grants." Its members are not at the forefront of "cutting edge" research. The department, the vice provost summed up, "is a bad investment." It "will never be productive." To emphasize his strong feelings, he reiterated, "It's not even in the top 100 departments [in its field as] ranked by NRC, but the department at Neighboring State University is."

Professors strive to work in a highly ranked department; its luster shines on them. When a colleague leaves for another position, they comment on the rank of her new department. Departments mention their NRC ranking when they recruit both faculty colleagues and graduate students. So do deans. Indeed, one dean even checked the NRC rank of departments that had successfully recruited Wan U professors. When the competing department was "better" than a Wan U department *and* the departing professors had a more prestigious appointment, the dean was wont to explain: "We simply couldn't match that."[16]

Starting as early as 2002, the dean of the Wannabe Graduate School assiduously worked with departments so that they could put their best foot forward when the NRC gathered data to construct new rankings that were expected to be published in 2008. He encouraged one department to redefine itself as a "doctoral program" and to accept only those who on their application for graduate study stated they wanted to earn a Ph.D. The change enabled two well-published professors to be called members of the doctoral faculty and so enhanced how the department presented itself for NRC review.[17] That dean used e-mail to ask all faculty to respond to questions associated with the NRC review. He also had the questions that the NRC asked posted on a website so that professors could become familiar with them. But despite this massive effort, the dean knew that he could not easily increase some variables about which the NRC inquired, such as the dollar amount of the faculty's research awards and professors' reputations in their fields.

From the point of view of strategizing to improve a rating, the *U.S. News & World Report* rankings offer the best possibilities. It is easier for central administrators to manage the enrollment and to manipulate class size than to increase the total value of the faculty's research grants and contracts by many millions of dollars or to hire members of either the National Academy of Sciences or the National Academy of Engineering.[18] Furthermore, the other measures I have reviewed may not appeal to such important publics as politicians, parents, and potential students. Parents and students may care more about an institution's student-teacher ratio and average class size than about how professors spend their non-teaching time. Besides, one cannot buy a copy of either the Lombardi or the NRC ratings in the bookstore at the mall. And even many professors have never heard of the American Association of Universities, a dean reminded me when we discussed the quality of research at Wan U.

One can purchase *U.S. News & World Report* at the mall. One can also easily download its annual edition of "America's Best Colleges." At a research university as at a liberal arts college, improving how one scores on its indicators about undergraduate education is simply good business.

BUTTING HEADS OVER PORTFOLIOS

In the mid-1990s, then-provost Mike Tremaine brought in a slew of new subordinates who might help Wannabe University climb to a higher rung in the *U.S. News & World Report* rankings. In 1996 he hired a new dean of the College of Liberal Arts and Sciences (CLAS). Two years later he brought in an associate provost for enrollment management and a new vice provost for undergraduate education and instruction. Mary Matthews, the vice provost for undergraduate education, had been an associate vice president at an eastern research university. Victor Steibel, the expert on enrollment, had arrived from a western research university. (He was to become a political star, especially after he became "good friends" with President James Whitmore and was rapidly promoted to vice provost.) Todd Alden, the new dean of the College of Liberal Arts and Sciences, had been at a research university in the Midwest.

The three newcomers were to butt heads over which instructional function belonged in which administrator's portfolio. Sometimes the two vice provosts were also to disagree about which task should come first, rearing the chicken or laying the egg. Both a central middle manager and a college administrator explained the problem that these three people faced. Should Victor Steibel, the vice provost for enrollment management, recruit a higher percentage of high school valedictorians and salutatorians before Mary Matthews, the vice provost for undergraduate education and instruction, beefed up the Honors Program, or vice versa? And what about the undergraduates participating in the Honors Program housed in the College of Liberal Arts and Sciences? Were they to be transferred to a program supervised by Mary Matthews's minions, or were they to remain Dean Todd Alden's responsibility?

Some tasks did not involve a choice. The provost, the president, and the trustees had agreed to follow the consultants' advice and to "grow the enrollment." The strategic question was how to do it and how to accommodate the academic and social needs of more students. Decisions about how to manage admissions fell to enrollment czar Victor Steibel and his staff.[19] But he was not the only powerful administrator who had a marked interest in the size of the undergraduate body. One well-placed administrator estimated that if the student body increased by 30 percent, the number of students taking courses in the College of Liberal Arts and Sciences increased by 60 percent, since almost all students take thirty credits of general education courses in CLAS and some schools require their students to take additional CLAS courses.

There is some variation in the number of CLAS credits that undergraduates are required to take. General education requirements vary by college; the requirements for a bachelor of science degree from the School of Engineering are not identical to those for the bachelor of fine arts degree. Also, in 1998 students had to complete a certain number of credits in CLAS before they could even apply to the schools of Business, Education, Allied Health, Pharmacy, and Family Studies. (Students in nursing were admitted straight from high school, but they too were required to take specific CLAS courses.) More students also created a crunch on such other academic services as advising, not even to discuss the strain on residential services.

The central administration, including Tremaine and Matthews, worked to placate the deans and professors, who feared larger classes. Matthews spoke about "excess capacity." "The university has excess capacity. . . . There are available seats in many courses," she reassured them. Many professors did not believe that claim. One humanist recalled a meeting in 1997, when she sat between a friend in pharmacy and another in family studies. "We joked that [the pharmacist] would teach family studies," for there were lots of seats in pharmacy and almost none in family studies. In addition to maintaining that there was excess capacity, the central administration had assured the deans that if they could show "need," they would get "more lines"; in other words, that they would be permitted to hire more professors, each of whom occupied a line in the budget. One college administrator bitterly recalled that those lines did not appear and even scornfully suggested that Matthews's estimate of "excess capacity" had been based on data that she had requested from the Office of Institutional Research and that she had hastily calculated on the proverbial back of an envelope.

Other than affirming that the university had "excess capacity" and so could absorb more students, no one discussed the financial implications with the faculty. Nonetheless, many professors assumed that because hiring faculty is costly (salaries and associated fringe benefits are the largest expense at educational institutions), administrators chose to increase the size of the student body before expanding the faculty. They thought their numbers would eventually increase. However, the administrators' actions put a decided strain on the professors—enough of a strain for a few professors to complain among themselves that the professional managers were imposing on them. A CLAS faculty committee that had convened on another matter managed to get hold of sufficient budget figures to make the rough and possibly erroneous calculation that spending in their college had decreased roughly 10 percent per student.[20]

Additional strains on course size also resulted from the expansion of professional programs. The university "grew" both its School of Business and its School of Pharmacy. The expansion of the School of Pharmacy was two-pronged. First, instead of requiring 120 credits for a bachelor's degree, it "upgraded" its program to a doctorate of pharmacy that required 196 credits (and thus absorbed some of the "excess [seat] capacity" in pharmacy). It also increased by a third the size of an entering class, thus doubling the class size of such courses as genetics, which were required for the pharmacy degree.

Increasing enrollment without increasing the size of the faculty affected all sorts of classes. Social scientists who had once taught required introductory courses of 85 students found themselves teaching the same course materials to as many as 300 students. To accommodate more students, class size was increased even in courses excluded from the general education curriculum. As the "bulge passed through the snake," as President Whitmore described the impact of the increased enrollment on the university, students really struggled to gain admissions to courses required as part of the general education curriculum. Some students found they had to attend summer school to gain admission to required courses. A few weeks before a spring semester several years into the enrollment hike, 1,000 freshmen had still not been able to find seats in enough courses. (Seniors have first choice, then juniors, and so forth. The number of credits a student has accumulated sets his or her place in the registration line.) When students cannot register for required courses, they cannot "finish in four" years. They may take five or even six years to be graduate. (With the approval of the board of trustees, the vice provost for enrollment had instituted a program to encourage undergraduates to "Finish in Four.")[21]

Class size affects pedagogy. A scientist complained about the increased size of a biology class: grading exams for larger classes was so labor-intensive that the scientist had to change the kinds of exams administered. Previously her final exams had included problems to solve, and students were to show how they solved each problem. However, correcting those answers was too labor-intensive to assure that grades would be ready in time for graduation. (At the end of spring semester, grades are due within seventy-two hours so that students can know whether they have accumulated enough credits to graduate.) Since her department did not have funds for more teaching assistants to grade papers, the kind of final exam questions that she asked would have to change. One social science course, in which both class discussions and writing assignments are thought to facilitate learning, increased in size from 30 to 80 students, and so its instructors stopped assigning papers.[22] A dean explained that he didn't care so much about the classes that increased from 100 to 300 students; one teaches a class of 100 and a class of 300 in pretty much the same way, he said. But he was concerned about some classes that grew from 30 to 80 students. The 80 students did not have as much of a chance to discuss course material in class, and since professors frequently dropped the requirement that they write term papers, they were not getting the experience of formally presenting their ideas.

To be fair, sometimes large class size may have improved pedagogy. For example, when his classes were "on the small side," students flocked to take courses from a well-known poet. He had a terrific sense of humor and treated students with respect. Students found it difficult to get a seat in his courses. Indeed, students so esteemed this professor that they still had problems registering for his course once the university's enrollment expanded and his classes became larger. Comparing how he treated large and small classes, this poet explained that sometimes when he had not "really prepared" a class, he would hold a class discussion. He had, of course, done all of the reading. He also knew what topics had excited students in previous years. Those "sort of off-the-cuff" discussions made for an involving class. When the poet's classes grew larger, he always prepared, for the poet found it more it more difficult to generate a good discussion in the larger class. Maybe, he felt, it was better for the students that he always had to have his classes carefully planned.

Administrators had to cope with the problems presented by larger classes. To decrease class size and the student-faculty ratio reported to *U.S. News & World Report*, they had to figure out how to hire more instructors without spending too much money. Other research universities had hired more part-time instructors (adjuncts), as well as more full-time instructors on temporary (non-tenure) lines. Provost Tyler Johnson and Dean Todd Alden planned a similar solution—but one with a key difference. They inaugurated a new category of full-time faculty: the "postdoctoral teaching fellow" or "faculty in residence." Twenty doctoral teaching fellows would join the staff, mainly in the College of Liberal Arts and Sciences. They would teach three courses a semester and would not serve on committees. Nor would they be expected to do research. Contingent faculty with contracts of one, two, or three years, these people supposedly differed from faculty who wandered from one visiting job to another, because they would be enrolled in special courses in teaching methods and would be mentored by tenured professors who excelled at teaching.

At one meeting where he described the new program, Provost Johnson made clear references to how other research universities were exploiting contingent faculty labor (and so implicitly affirmed the idea that organizations draw on the practices of others in their organizational field). He explained that when he and Dean Alden had designed the program, they promised that they would not exploit contingent faculty labor. Provost Johnson hoped that after a few years at Wan U, these fellows would get good jobs teaching at liberal arts colleges.[23]

Expansion of the undergraduate enrollment affected more than class size. For instance, it affected student advising and such enrichment programs as the honors curriculum and the individually designed major. (If Wannabe University did not have a major in, say, criminology, a student could construct an academic program in criminology with appropriate faculty approvals and supervision.) Mary Matthews felt that such programs fell into her bailiwick, undergraduate education; but inasmuch as they affected retention and graduate rates, Victor Steibel cared about them too, and Dean Alden rightfully noted that 85 percent of the students who had designed their own major were registered in the College of Liberal Arts and Sciences.

Ideally, these three administrators would become a team, working together to accomplish tasks that helped Wannabe University. Each of them reported to the provost; each was ambitious to better the university (and maybe also themselves). They seemed to be bureaucratic equals. However, several of them were often at loggerheads. Some administrators blamed Mary Matthews, whom the faculty had also energetically criticized (see chapter 5). Even while noting that the administration of Wannabe University is a very difficult work environment for women, at least two middle managers who worked with Matthews told me she was very bright, had terrific ideas, and was difficult. One described her as "flying too close to the sun," when, in her enthusiasm for her ideas, she forgot that other people also had an interest in the items in her portfolio. Mixing metaphors, this informant added that she "tried to roll right over them." Another informant described her as "polarizing: she walked into a room and there were two sides, hers and everyone else's." One fellow criticized her working style: "Maybe her decisions were too quick. She hired [someone after talking to him] for seven or eight minutes."[24]

Ultimately, of course, the person at the head of a bureaucracy is responsible for his underlings. If squabbles are interfering with the accomplishment of tasks and the people who report to him are struggling with one another for power rather than working as a team, a leader is supposed to broker the peace—or even command it. Provost Tremaine left Wan U in 1999; Matthews, in 2001; Provost Johnson, in 2004. In 2007 many men who were happy to point to Mary Matthews's failings seemed blind to either Mike Tremaine's or Tyler Johnson's failure to impose at least a pretense of harmony among the vice provosts and the deans. Of course, both Mike Tremaine and Tyler Johnson may have been happy for Matthews to be blamed for any discord among key administrators. Both men had a clear ambition to move up and on (as a few administrators and a few professors remarked at the time). Indeed, Provost Tremaine left to be a university president a few years after he had hired Matthews, Steibel, and Alden. Matthews had departed for a promotion at a liberal arts college by the academic year 2000–2001, while Steibel flourished and Alden endured until he retired in 2008.[25]

Administrators who are perpetually looking for a job at a better university (or a better job at a comparable university) may be happy for their subordinates to take the blame. When people from another university telephone their disciplinary colleagues to check on a president or provost being considered for a top job at their university, an administrator wants to "smell like a rose." (On his administrative résumé, Mike Tremaine lists many of his subordinates' activities.) After Provost Tremaine left Wannabe University, even the officers of the local chapter of the American Association of University Professors claimed that he had overspent. According to the sometimes accurate and sometimes faulty faculty rumor mill, Tremaine had promised academic departments more monies than were in the budget so that when friends from other universities checked on him, the Wan U professoriate would sing his praises. Also, in some organizations, subordinates may routinely take the blame for wrongdoing, so that their boss will be vindicated. Just as former presidential staffers have claimed that a particular president of the United States let others take the fall for him, some people who had left Wannabe University asserted that several once-powerful administrators had been fired for either a president's or a provost's failings.[26] Additionally, a retired Wan U administrator advised me: "I've worked with many presidents and many provosts and not just here. A lot of the presidents wanted people to like them and for the provost to be the bad guy. They might routinely pass the buck."

What counts structurally is that the central administrators felt that Wan U had to improve its performance on some of the *U.S. News & World Report* indicators. They convinced others of that need and managed to ride that perceived need to an expanded role in undergraduate education, including curricular affairs. Either at the insistence of Provost Tremaine or with his help, Vice Provost Matthews managed to expand the central administration's involvement in teaching and learning. Wan U built "the BUE"—the Building for Undergraduate Education. It filled the BUE with an expanded Honors Program, an expanded program for individualized majors, an expanded advising program, the First-Year Experience Program, the Institute for Student Success, and a beefed-up Institute for Teaching and Learning. In some instances, an assistant or associate vice provost for undergraduate education and instruction assumed the authority once held by a faculty member, as was the case for the head of the Honors Program. In some cases, the chain of command changed. The head of a program reported to a central administrator rather than to a dean, as occurred in the programs for individualized and interdisciplinary majors. A program absorbed units; the Writing Center left the auspices of the English department for the Institute for Teaching and Learning, much as technical support for classroom audiovisual equipment left Facilities Operations for the ITL. Office space in the BUE became scarce.

"I know that many faculty walk past here and resent us," a middle manager in the BUE said. "They think that we have a lot of people who are not doing anything." The middle manager is right. Many professors and some administrators from the schools and colleges do resent the occupants of the BUE. An associate dean told me, "They built the BUE and put all that stuff in there. Each director of something or other has an assistant director and then an administrative assistant as well. Have you seen data on whether salary and fringe benefits for staff is taking up a larger share of the budget?"

For the faculty, at least, the building is symbolic of the administration's increasing power over both the curriculum and the faculty. "I go to all of these meetings at the BUE," said a professor active in undergraduate matters. "You should hear them. Empire builders. Now they're complaining that we [professors] don't know how to advise students, and they're designing a system to evaluate us as advisors. They wouldn't dream of letting us evaluate them, and you know as well as I do, that lots of undergraduates complain about them."

A high-placed informant in one of the university's schools put it differently:

> [The central administration] complains that we do a bad job at something like advising, and then they throw all of this money at it, more than we can. And they put it in the BUE, while we're limping along with [inferior space and few staff members]. And then they say, "See. We can do a better job at advising than you can." Well, they threw more money at it [than we have], and also the faculty has many more things to do.

Accustomed to watching university politics, some professors and administrators blame individuals as political actors for the centralization of educational and even curricular tasks. According to an informant, "The head of the enrichment program is an empire-builder" who does not cooperate well with others. A professor said of a different administrator, "We've had a lot of people in that job who were difficult and claimed more and more stuff for their portfolio." A school administrator said of a central administrator, "He thinks that whatever job he's in is the center of the university."

In 2007 both faculty and administrators of the schools and colleges still complained about the structural incursions into the curriculum that Vice Provost Mary Matthews had initiated. A well-placed informant noted that the small one-credit freshman-year experience courses had been designed to help Wan U flourish in the *U.S. News & World Report* ratings, which gave special credit for classes with less than twenty students. But he asked, "Who is deciding on these [one-credit] first-year experience courses?" He continued:

> The faculty is supposed to set the curriculum—within budgetary limits—and teach it. All kinds of staff people are teaching first-year experience courses. One of the secretaries [in the school] even taught one. I can't decide whether it's a compliment or ambition. Maybe they want to do what we do, teach. But they have full-time jobs. If they have so little to do that they think they can teach— even topics they're not qualified to teach—give them more work to do.[27]

He continued, "Now a central administrator even wants to give a course on how to write a check and balance your checkbook." (These topics were to be covered in provisional sections of a one-credit course called "Senior-Year Experience" proposed by a vice provost, taught by graduate students in a higher-education program, and approved by the Interdisciplinary Courses and Curriculum Committee that Vice Provost Jeanne Sharpe had appointed and that is discussed below.) When *U.S. News & World Report* presents data about the size of Wannabe's classes, these one-credit courses, limited to nineteen students like the one-credit first-year experience courses, count the same as three-credit courses taught by full-time professors.

INCREASING THE CENTRAL CONTROL OF TEACHING

Just as President Ned Oakes and Provost Samuel Darning's ill-fated attempt to eliminate the School of Human Development and Family Studies and the School of Allied Health had eased the way for Provost Gerald Wesley to fold those units, so too Vice Provost Mary Matthews's activities eased the way for Vice Provost Jeanne Sharpe's incursion into faculty affairs as she obeyed her "marching orders" from the provost.[28] At the very least, the BUE was a fully occupied reality, whose middle managers were ambitious for more responsibility. They did not worry when programs designed to "feed" the ratings produced more incursions onto professorial authority. A professor protested when central administrators in charge of programs housed in the BUE decided to "open up" to anyone a humanities course that had three seats available, but had been designed for students in that humanities major. "A minor example" of interference in the curriculum, a dean said.

Vice Provost Jeanne Sharpe provided a more serious example when, with the approval of the appropriate Senate committee, she established a committee to approve interdisciplinary courses and appointed one person from each of several colleges to serve on the committee. The Senate resolution that established the committee did not mandate that she consult deans when she decided who would represent a college, and she did not do so. As a result, according to one committee member, the professors probably didn't feel that they were representing their schools. "I did not feel I was representing the college," one told me, "and I don't think that [George] did either." Four administrators reporting to her were also voting members of the committee. "I would not mind if they were non-voting members," the same professor told me.

Sharpe's Interdisciplinary Courses and Curriculum Committee approved upper-level courses. It was not required to submit them to the individual colleges and schools, which determined which upper-division courses[29] warranted credit toward graduating with a degree from that college, so it did not. In protest, the Courses and Curriculum Committee of the College of Liberal Arts and Sciences refused to grant credit toward graduation for an upper-division course that had not been approved by some school's relevant committee and passed a motion to that effect. Insisting on the right of the faculty to set the curriculum, the head of that committee explained, "I placed a warning shot across the [ship's] bow." In response, Sharpe called a meeting of the heads of curriculum committees and the associate deans for instruction from the various schools and colleges. At the meeting, the representatives of the schools and colleges affirmed that the Courses and Curriculum Committee of one school needed to have approved a course in order for that course to count toward a student's graduation from any of the schools. The School of Fine Arts might approve a course taken by a student in the School of Business and vice versa, but the vice provost's committee could not be the only authority to decide whether an interdisciplinary course met curricular standards. According to several people who attended that meeting, Sharpe seemed surprised when the group agreed that the vice provost's committee had violated the rule that "the faculty sets the curriculum." As a result of that meeting, the central administration worked to restructure the Interdisciplinary Courses and Curriculum Committee and so implicitly recognized that the deans and faculty of the schools had at least some authority over the curriculum.[30]

However, sometimes the faculty had little or no choice about arrangements involving what or how the students learned. A prime example of the limits based on the faculty's responsibility for undergraduate education is the process governing the institution of "student outcomes assessment," a practice increasingly found at American colleges and universities since it was encouraged by President George W. Bush's Department of Education. At Wan U, student outcomes assessment was part of a general push to make professors accountable for the quality of their teaching.

7

Carrots, Sticks, and Accountability

Provost Wesley sent an e-mail about assessment and accountability to all faculty before the start of fall semester 2006—after groups had begun to work on developing "student outcomes assessment," but before the Provost's Task Force on Teaching, Learning, and Assessment had begun to meet.

"Assessment," it said, "is a word that is bandied about frequently in higher-education circles these days, to the point where it is losing its true meaning and is becoming a catch-all phrase or piece of academic jargon." In that introductory statement, Provost Wesley (or his amanuensis)[1] added, "Assessment, though, is not at all mysterious, and we do it often in our daily lives without labeling it. Assessment is the process of setting goals, measuring our success at achieving them, and then reflecting about necessary changes before beginning the cycle once again." Assessment, the e-mail implied, is intrinsic to the American lifestyle; we live by projecting our lives onto business plans or maybe just computer programs that tally our debits and assets.

When he decided who would be responsible for assessment, Provost Wesley had divided the responsibility for different sorts of activities. As I will explain later in this chapter, universities were being coerced by governments (see DiMaggio and Powell 1991: 67). National political forces were demanding that all institutions of higher education evaluate what are called "student outcomes." Accordingly, Provost Wesley deemed the assessment of student learning outcomes to be so important that he funded a special assistant vice provost for assessment to guide it into existence.[2] That fellow reported to Jeanne Sharpe, the vice provost for education and instruction. Additionally, Dr. Wesley had formed the Provost's Task Force on Teaching, Learning, and Assessment, a group of sixteen faculty and administrators, which was to design ways to assess instructors. Since the 1970s at Wan U as elsewhere, students had been evaluating faculty through questionnaires, now officiously called SETIs, or Student Evaluation of Teacher Instruments. Using the education literature about SETIs, yet another committee had previously reported that the Wan U instrument was flawed. Also, the provost's charge to his new task force implied that Wannabe University's SETI did not provide enough information about instructors' performances to permit a reliable audit of their teaching and to hold them accountable for their performance when they were considered for promotion or tenure.[3]

FACULTY ACCOUNTABILITY: ALL STICKS, NO CARROTS

Provost Wesley had directed the Task Force on Teaching, Learning, and Assessment to "(1) enhance the quality of teaching and learning at the undergraduate and graduate levels; (2) offer opportunities for professional development for faculty; (3) develop assessment tools to inform and improve classroom instruction; and (4) ensure that quality of teaching will be a strong consideration, along with research, in reappointment, promotion, tenure, and merit, as mandated in the bylaws." In essence, the provost had ordered the group to make plans for the "workforce development" of the faculty and to find ways to assess how well these workers had learned their new tasks. Participation in workforce development would be optional; no one would tell a professor that she *must* receive training. However, the assessment of teaching would be mandatory. Vice Provost Sharpe set out to enact the provost's charge.

There are many ways to direct people to make themselves auditable and accountable. Perhaps because the central administration specified that it would not make any extra resources available with which to accomplish either student outcomes assessment or the assessment of instructors, the central administration tried to appeal to the pride that the faculty might feel in a job well done. At the first of four forums designated for discussion of its draft report, Vice Provost Sharpe rose from a table on the right of the stage of the 175-seat wood-paneled auditorium, walked stage left to the lectern, and welcomed the twenty-five or so people in the audience. (They included members of the task force.) As co-chair of the Provost's Task Force on Teaching, Learning, and Assessment, she quickly appealed to pride in scholarship and affirmed her belief that teaching and scholarship are complementary activities. To paraphrase: Excellent teaching and excellent scholarship go hand in hand. We want to find ways to encourage the faculty to value teaching. She continued, "We are a data-based institution. We have lots of ways to measure research, but we don't [currently] have satisfactory ways to measure the quality of teaching." As her co-chair, an associate dean of education, explained in a PowerPoint slide:

At a research extensive university, *research is the coin of the realm*; however, the great universities achieve that stature because of their superiority in both teaching and research. Teaching, like research, is of paramount importance at Wannabe University and the university community is striving toward a culture that celebrates and supports superior achievement in both areas.

Vice Provost Sharpe understood that many professors did not share her concern with either the quality of instruction on the Wan U campuses or finding valid and reliable indicators of the quality of teaching. As she said on another occasion:

I do know that many faculty (not all, by any means) take any stress on undergraduate education as a threat to research and graduate education because they operate under the assumption that it's a zero-sum game and that a person could not do a good job at all three (which we know by many examples is not true at Wan U).[4]

The university had to find a way to convince those professors that good teaching—even the effort necessary to achieve outstanding teaching—does not detract from the ability to do excellent research and also that it is acceptable, perhaps even desirable, to measure the quality of teaching. As she stood on the podium, Sharpe affirmed that it would be difficult to get some people to buy into the importance of teaching: "Changing an organization's culture is a slow process. It takes time."

Comments of the professors in the audience indicated that Vice Provost Sharpe and the task force might have underestimated just how much time it would take to accomplish culture change. For instance, one professor said that some people do an equally good job of teaching and research, but sometimes concentrating on one comes at the expense of the other. He insisted, "Presumably the young people we are hiring are very high-level scholars. This document places a burden on them." He insisted, "There are lots of ways of making a good teacher. . . . [This way] puts a burden on the junior faculty by putting all of their teaching methods under a microscope. It is quite chilling." He added, "The university always said that research comes first and teaching comes second. . . . Harvard can survive a good number of mediocre teachers, but not a good number of mediocre scholars. We are not good enough to sacrifice scholarship."

A few of the professors in attendance told one another that the essence of the task force's report was to redefine the administration's involvement in a central professorial task—teaching. They noted that the report implied that teaching was too important to leave solely under the aegis of the professoriate. The administration would find ways to help professors do a better job teaching, but it would judge them as well. As the report explained, the university "need[s] to address ways to support instructors in their teaching and to consider methods to evaluate teaching, both formative [for the instructor's benefit alone] and summative. . . ." Although a sentence in the report noted that some professors were splendid teachers even though they did not use the new technologies increasingly available in the Wan U classrooms, "support" for instructors included pedagogical training provided by the Institute for Teaching and Learning with a stress on the new technologies.[5] The report emphasized that the university would equip every classroom on every campus with the new technologies and would also provide training in their use.

The task force was also recommending that departments agree to monitor (audit) the quality of their instructors' work as teachers and also that professors collect certain kinds of data to make auditable the quality of their work in the classroom, lecture hall, or lab. A variety of methods were to accomplish the evaluation of professor's accomplishment as teachers, including "summative" evaluation by peers. "Summative" evaluation referred to senior professors observing a junior colleague in a series of classroom visits; these would be used to help judge whether an instructor should be awarded tenure or promotion. Training in how to observe the quality of an instructor's pedagogical techniques would be available from the Institute for Teaching and Learning. The report also recommended the use of "teaching portfolios" to gather evidence of an instructor's pedagogic skill and so to help assess his fitness for tenure and promotion. The portfolios might include the syllabi prepared for courses, student projects, and even student papers—materials the instructor supposedly "has on hand so that it does not require a special effort to collect them," the vice provost explained.

Again professors in the audience demurred. An engineer argued that "having to maintain a teaching portfolio will intensify the competition among assistant professors and there will be a lot of one-upmanship. . . . This will make more work for the faculty. It will take a lot of time to make portfolios and to observe teaching." One particularly angry professor belonged to a department that had received so many research grants that it had to hire yet another administrative assistant to process the paperwork. He vociferously objected to classroom observations. He feared that down the road observations by departmental colleagues might be replaced by observations by "experts in teaching," whom he viewed as "not qualified" to assess the information being conveyed and so how it was conveyed. He also questioned who was qualified to assess a portfolio. Would a committee have to send a teaching portfolio to an expert in a subfield, much as it would send a professor's publications to an expert to learn how much they had contributed to specialized knowledge?

To calm some people attending the forum, the co-chairs reminded everyone that the task force's recommendations were just that—recommendations. To become official policy, they needed approval from the University Senate, the trustees, and (through contract negotiations) the Wan U chapter of the American Association of University Professors. If the new procedural rules became policy, they would have consequences. Thus, the head of a subcommittee of the task force explained at another forum, if new rules were to be approved and a department were not to follow then, it would be "opting out of the tenure process." Its assistant professors could not receive promotion and tenure; its associate professors could not receive a promotion either.

The wheels of change are indeed slow and cumbersome at American universities. Several months after the four forums, the provost sent a slightly amended version of the talk force's recommendations to the University Senate for approval. That group's Executive Committee sent it to both its Faculty Standards Committee and its Scholastic Standards Committee, which established a joint subcommittee to review the task force's recommendations and the provost's comments on them.

At a meeting of the Faculty Standards Committee, a vice provost explained the new policies as an attempt to ease the administration's chore of making judgments about the faculty. Although that vice provost did not use either the term "audit" or the word "accountability," other central administrations did stress accountability. For instance, at the first task-force forum, the vice provost for education and instruction explained that administrators were having a hard time interpreting the colleges' and schools' recommendations for tenure and promotion. (Deans presented their recommendations to the panel, which included the provost and his "academic vice provosts"; to wit, the vice provost for education and instruction, the vice provost for administration, the vice provost for research and dean of the graduate school, and the vice provost for multiculturalism and international affairs.) She expanded: When sitting to decide whether someone should receive tenure or promotion, the provost's panel had very little information about the quality of an instructor's teaching. Repeating herself, she said, "We don't have enough data, and we are an institution based on evidence." The university forms they consulted requested a statement about the candidate's "teaching philosophy." It also requested copies of students' quantitative evaluations of the instructor's courses, as well as their average score. According to another vice provost, these were "not adequate data" about teaching. "We might be looking at two people with similar research records, but one is said to be a good teacher and the other, not. And all we have are numbers about teaching. And we don't know what the difference is between a 7.3 and a 7.7 or an 8.2 and an 8.5."[6] Both vice provosts were saying that the central administration not only cared about assessing the quality of teaching, but also about fulfilling its own direct obligation to the board of trustees and its indirect duty to the state, for official universities policies stressed the importance of teaching. Professors were accountable for their job performance. Departments were accountable for evaluating them, and the university was also accountable to others.

Accountability for teaching, some argued, was even implicit in a university's mission. As noted earlier, in the late twentieth century, inspired by business practices, universities had adopted mission statements. Those of public research universities customarily emphasized how they serve a state by educating students who contribute to its economy. Thus, Wan U's current mission statement announced: "Through our focus on teaching and learning, the University helps every student grow intellectually and become a contributing member of the state, national, and world communities. . . . [W]e promote the health and well-being of [the state's] citizens through enhancing the social, economic, cultural, and natural environments of the state and beyond." Such enhancement also entails teaching undergraduates; public universities engage in "workforce development" to assist the state.[7]

As Vice Provost Sharpe well knew, Wannabe University's strategic plan emphasized the importance of teaching. The first goal of the strategic plan even suggested that a favorable learning environment is a precondition of scholarship: Wan U aims to "provide a challenging and supportive learning environment that fosters achievement and intellectual interaction among undergraduates, graduate students and faculty members and promotes excellence in research, scholarship and artistic creativity."

The bylaws of Wannabe University stressed teaching too. Indeed, they announced that teaching is central to a professor's job:

> A University exists for the twofold purpose of teaching and research—the dissemination of knowledge and the extension of the boundaries of the known. Though it must have buildings and equipment, wise administrators, and earnest and intelligent students, it is obvious that its purpose cannot be accomplished unless its teachers are without exception competent, and in as many cases as possible, distinguished to a greater or lesser degree. . . .

Furthermore, an article of the bylaws that has often been cited at meetings of the Senate's Faculty Standards Committee (and sometimes even in departmental discussions of promotion and tenure) identified skillful teaching as a necessary (but not sufficient) qualification for tenure and promotion:

> Tenure and promotion in the professorial ranks will be granted only to persons of outstanding achievement. Specific evidence of superior performance in scholarship and in teaching is of primary importance. As a minimum standard for tenure and/or promotion there must be evidence of strong performance in both scholarship and teaching and superior achievement in at least one of these areas. . . .

Speaking for the task force, Vice Provost Sharpe was invoking these carefully honed policies. They were providing "good organizational reasons" (Garfinkle 1967) to change how professors approached teaching and kept records about their job performance. Although no one used the terms "auditable" or "accountable," ultimately the administration's claim to be implementing existing written policies had become a tool for strengthening an accountability regime. That is, as (scientific) administration strengthens accountability and auditing within the organization that it manages, it becomes easier for external auditors to be efficient. (Later in this chapter, I will consider the power of such external auditors as regional accrediting agencies and the federal government.)

The central administration was not so naive as to believe that the changes it proposed could be easily enacted. It had to cope with faculty responses to its proposed policies, especially those of the Senate committees assigned to review them. Some professors complained that they could not identify the carrots included in the task force's report. "This report doesn't say why people should spend more time trying to become better teachers, at least it doesn't mention [real] rewards," said a member of the small subcommittee asked to evaluate the task force's report. "It doesn't offer any carrots—just sticks," he added. "If you aren't a good teacher, you won't get tenure. If you have tenure and you don't do a good job teaching, who knows? If they do good work [research], they [poor teachers] are not even being swatted with a medium-sized stick. No one [with tenure] is going to get fired for being a bad teacher." In the memo of conveyance that accompanied their report to the two larger committees from whom they had been drawn, the subcommittee's members observed that the plan was "all sticks, but no carrots." It suggested creating rewards for teaching, such as the distinguished teaching professorships found at some top-notch public research universities that are members of the American Association of Universities.

Other faculty had decided that the administration was impinging on professors' ability to control their own jobs. They had reacted to the central administration's good organizational reasons as though they were a direct expression of "relations of ruling"—"forms of consciousness and organization that are objectified in the sense that they are constituted externally to particularly people and places" (Smith 2005: 13). Asked why he had attended the task force's forums, Professor Thyme, a senior member of his department, explained, ". . . because of a clause in the report that implied that [the head of the Institute for Teaching and Learning] would hire people and send them into classrooms to observe and evaluate faculty teaching." He added that such a practice would mean "people who knew absolutely nothing about [my field] might wind up evaluating what I taught."

The draft report actually recommended "peer review." The institute would train faculty to evaluate one another. An assistant professor found that recommendation sound. "How," she asked, "do you judge someone's teaching if you don't watch them teach?" Others felt that peer reviews were not a good evaluative tool. Two people who had taught at the City University of New York had attended the first faculty forum of the Task Force on Teaching, Learning, and Assessment. At both forum and committee meetings, one reported that his CUNY department had found peer review to be worthless. If the person being observed had advance notice, she rehearsed and turned in an impeccable performance. So his department had decided to send observers in unannounced. That procedure didn't work either. Often when an assistant professor walked into his classroom and found an observer in the corner chair in the last row, he got so nervous that he blew the peer review.

Although Professor Thyme had never taught at CUNY, he recalled the comments of the other professor who had once taught there. She had reported how departments could use teaching observations to discredit people. She had spoken about a department at City University, where the personnel committee customarily sent a colleague known to make very harsh judgments to observe the classroom skills of assistant professors so that it "would have something negative in the [person's] file if the personnel committee didn't want to give [that person] tenure."

Hearing this statement, at least one member of the task force had protested. Such travesties would not occur, explained a member of the task force who also had a position of authority at the Institute for Teaching and Learning. She and her colleagues at the institute would train the observers to evaluate *pedagogical techniques, not content.* Because they were properly trained, they would be objective. And because the data gathered during the observation of classroom teaching would be based on proper training, it would have the imprimatur of authority. In essence, this member of the Institute for Teaching and Learning was claiming that professionals in her field were necessarily objective. Tautologically, they were professional because they were objective, and objective because they were professional (see Abbott 1988). Objectivity could be viewed as a ritual that both confirmed and affirmed professional status (cf. Tuchman 1978: 82–103).

The explanation offered by the expert on teaching in higher education did not satisfy either Professor Thyme or some other senior professors. For Thyme, the issue of the interrelationship between the content of a class and the best way to prompt students to engage themselves with the class materials remained an issue of professional and disciplinary expertise. "There are clear standards in each discipline for scholarship, but not for evaluating teaching," he said. He noted that the disciplines were not to develop their own criteria for good teaching, but were to be trained in observational techniques by the Institute for Teaching and Learning. He added, "It doesn't say that because there are no clear standards within disciplines that the disciplines need to develop their own criteria. The [paragraph] assumes there is a universal standard of teaching, even though [no one assumes] that there is a universal standard for research across all disciplines."

Several weeks later three professors captured Thyme's concern, as they chatted while waiting for the beginning of a Senate committee meeting. As Thyme had done, they resisted the notion of auditing. The problem, as one man saw it, was that even within an academic discipline, one person might not have sufficient expertise to evaluate another's explanations to students. Specialization within disciplines is so exquisitely honed that departments had to consult outside experts to evaluate the quality of a candidate's publications when he or she applied for tenure or promotion. Why was the evaluation of teaching any different?[8] If an instructor did not assign a standard textbook, but rather created a syllabus based on scholarly articles, who was qualified to judge whether she had included the most important items? Furthermore, these professors agreed, the administration acknowledged the clear division of expertise characteristic of academic departments. Only experts in a candidate's area who also worked at a top department at a good research university were supposed to evaluate the publications of Wan U professors being considered for tenure or promotion. Given this recognition of expertise, how were the faculty to evaluate teaching? Did the faculty know enough about one another's areas to judge one other's teaching? Could one evaluate pedagogy without an appreciation of the content that the instructor was asking the students to learn? Some professors said yes to this series of questions; others said no.

The answers to these questions are probably immaterial. What matters theoretically is that some professors raised these questions and that some professors equated proper evaluation with expertise in a disciplinary specialty. Their conversation about how they should be audited—if they must be audited—emphasized the very specialized expertise that had qualified them for their jobs and that they believed to be personified in administrative attitudes toward research and scholarship in academic specialties. As they saw it, central administrators, deans, and department heads all emphasized the importance of research specialties, especially at a wannabe university seeking to upgrade it research reputation.

Here's how a powerful Wannabe administrator had explained to me how one "upgraded" a university's research profile, its professors' "productivity,"[9] and, especially, the total dollar amount of the research grants and contracts that the university gleaned in one year: "You hire people in fields [specialties] where there is a lot of money [to be raised through grants and contracts] or where interest in funding is quickly emerging. If the person doesn't get a grant within three years, you fire him." Earlier, a different high-level administrator had advised me that one could learn which areas were "cutting edge" and so were likely to attract federal funding. In some fields, this administrator added, department heads gather at the discipline's annual national meeting and discuss, among other things, federal granting priorities. This administrator also insisted that the best way to improve a university was to hire professors who worked in those specific areas. Neither administrator suggested that pedagogy was pertinent to such hiring decisions, though some experts on teaching techniques believe that there is some association between such techniques and specific content.[10]

The task force was also running into the problem of professionals' insistence on defining their rights and responsibilities—the nature of their work. It can be quite difficult to convince people who see themselves as professionals to make themselves auditable. Professionals do not willingly cede authority over their own work (Abbott 1988; Freidson 2001). Medical boards are not quick to revoke medical licenses; nor are lawyers wont to banish members from the bar. Also, when several professions claim the right to do the same task (or the same sort of tasks), their practitioners enthusiastically claim and defend what they define as their turf, including the right to regulate their own peers. The disputes among psychiatrists, psychologists, and social workers—all of whom claim the right to engage in talk therapy—are a classic example of such professional conflicts (Bucher and Stelling 1977).

Some central administrators understood that some faculty would resist becoming more auditable and that others would not care about easing the ability of the central administration to fulfill its own policies. Members of the central administration also knew that to accomplish change, one had to engage people. Often conflict bespeaks engagement. As the assistant vice provost for assessment said in another context: "I am told that it is a good thing for you to argue [with me and each other]. . . . It means you are taking this seriously" (cf. Eckel and Kezar 2003).

THE LIMIT OF IMITATION

Earlier I noted that when educational institutions engage in branding, they may imitate one another. The very notion of "best practices" that universities have adopted from the business world implies that one surveys one's field, visits exemplary firms (or colleges), and copies practices that seem both most productive and most suitable to one's own organization. For instance, when it proposed to create a structure to coordinate scholarship, education, and outreach about the environment, the second draft of Wan U's 2008 academic plan recommended surveying such structures at other universities and adapting the structure most suited to conditions at Wannabe U.[11] Similarly, in the early 1990s to improve its academic counseling services to student athletes, an assistant vice provost had educated himself about the programs at other research universities and adapted one of them to Wan U conditions. Indeed, when I had observed to a middle manager that I had noticed that administrators copied practices that they had learned about at professional meetings, he asked very defensively, "What's wrong with that?"

Imitation can also protect against the "liability of newness" (Stinchcombe 1965: 148). When new organizations emerge or older organizations seek to institute new procedures, they risk failure. As Stinchcombe (1965: 148) explained decades ago, "The process of inventing new roles, the determination of their mutual relations and of structuring the field of rewards and sanctions so as to get maximum performance, have high costs in time, worry, conflict, and temporary inefficiency." To risk failure when the annual budget of a university is almost $1.5 billion a year (as is that of Wannabe University) is truly to put it in jeopardy.

However, imitation has limitations. Although imitation enables adaptation to an organizational field, it may not address the elements *outside* of universities that either affect or even cause a problem and over which the university has no control. For example, "best practices" used to market professors' inventions can help a research university that is trying to survive the decreased state funding associated with neo-liberalism and, some say, globalization. To increase revenue streams, Wan U and research universities can copy one another's practices within the limits set by law and, perhaps, honor. But no university or subset of universities can either abolish neo-liberalism or eradicate globalization. An individual university or group of research universities can only do its best to adapt and survive.

Similarly, no one research university (or subset of research universities) can elevate the status of undergraduate teaching to the status that both professors and universities accord research. As we have seen, the low status of undergraduate teaching relative to research has developed not only from the reward system *within* universities, but also from factors *external* to universities, such as the status system of academic professions. As Lionel Lewis (1996) pointed out, a research university will not be able to enhance the status of teaching simply by offering punishments and rewards, because the priority that both the university *and* academic disciplines accord research marginalizes the status of teaching undergraduates. To change faculty attitudes toward teaching and to get professors to make themselves more auditable will require more than carrots and sticks.

STICKS AND CUDGELS

The associate dean of the School of Education, also the co-chair of the Task Force on Teaching, Learning, and Assessment, reminded his audience that university policy was not the only reason to infuse teaching with more positive value and to evaluate instructors. There was an even better political reason: acceding to the power of the federal government. Margaret Spellings, secretary of education, was demanding accountability. As one of the associate dean's PowerPoint slides announced: "Today, assessment and accreditation issues are part of the fabric of university life. . . . In addition to accreditation concerns, state and federal initiatives (e.g., the Spellings Report) expect institutions of higher education to be accountable for effective teaching and improved student learning." I watched a few people nod their heads in affirmation as the associate dean said "accreditation" and "the Spellings Report." (The report was written by the Commission on the Future of Higher Education, which in 2005 U.S. Secretary of Education Margaret Spellings had charged to help develop a comprehensive national strategy for postsecondary education, exploring such issues as access, affordability, and higher education's role in reversing America's declining competitiveness in the world economy.) Both the federal government and the accreditation agencies carried a big stick external to the university; each was a force with which every research university must comply. But one stick, that of the federal Department of Education, had more innate power than the other.

THE HIERARCHY OF STICKS

The federal government does not have *direct* power over colleges and universities, but it exercises indirect power in so many ways that it is a coercive power. Federal agencies have policies governing how universities can spend the indirect funds associated with grants and contracts. They mandate that all researchers be trained in ethical practices and that a university board review the methods of science and social science research to ensure that they meet ethical standards. They forbid discrimination against minorities and women. And when a college or university contravenes federal regulations, the government agency may fine it millions of dollars or even cancel all of its federal grants and contracts, if, for example, its facilities for experimental animals did not meet established standards. (Wannabe University had received such a fine in the not-so-distant past.)

The federal government also has *indirect* power over how institutions of higher education teach students. It exercises this power through accreditation agencies. There are six large regional agencies, such as the Western Association of Schools and Colleges and the North Central Association of Colleges and Schools, and many smaller ones. Colleges and universities are members of the associations that accredit them. The U.S. Department of Education assigns to these and to other approved accreditation agencies the task of determining whether a particular institution meets standards that qualify its students to receive federal loans and grants. Suppose that the regional accrediting agency that reviews Wannabe University declared that Wan U did not meet its standards; then students at Wan U would not be permitted to receive federal loans and grants to attend Wan U. In all likelihood, Wan U (and many other institutions) would go out of business. An accrediting agency holds a big stick over the institutions of higher education for which it is responsible.

The Department of Education holds an even bigger stick over the accrediting agencies. It wields a veritable cudgel. It can refuse to certify them or it can certify them for a limited period. As the *Chronicle of Higher Education* reminded on November 24, 2006: "The Education Department reviews accreditors every five years, an occasion the agency often uses to persuade or cajole them to make changes in the way they operate. Without the resulting recognition, accreditors lose an important part of their utility to institutions: Students are eligible for federal aid only if their institutions are approved by recognized accreditors" (Bollag 2006b). And the Department of Higher Education has refused accreditation to agencies, though not the most powerful ones.[12] Guided by its National Advisory Committee on Institutional Quality and Integrity, since 2005 it has insisted that accrediting agencies require both periodic external assessment of academic programs and the development of systematic means to understand how and what students are learning and to use the evidence obtained to improve the academic program. In sum, it has wielded the cudgel of student outcomes assessment. The potential power of that cudgel helps to explain why the provost's office had hired an assistant vice provost just to manage student outcomes assessment. That man was working with multiple committees, some within colleges and schools, some across them, to institute the first steps toward student outcomes assessment before the Regional Accreditation Agency (RAA) sent its representatives to learn whether Wannabe University had met the RAA's standards.

A standard about academic programs included a concern with student outcomes assessment. It stated that

> the institution [should] use . . . a variety of quantitative and qualitative methods to understand the experiences and learning outcomes of its students. . . . The institution [should] devote . . . appropriate attention to ensuring that its methods of understanding student learning are trustworthy and provide information useful in the continuing improvement of programs and services for students.

It even told educational institutions to discuss its assessment of course goals and objectives, general education goals and objectives, assessment of programs and of student learning in the jargon of corporate strategic planning. One planned. One defined missions, goals, objectives, and the metrics used to assess them. One initiated; one assessed; one revised the objective; one improved; and one assessed again. One gathered data. One engaged in "scientific management." One believed in CQM (continuous quality management).[13] The provost's e-mail about the crucial role of assessment in everyday life seemed to echo Wan U's regional accrediting agency.

Ultimately, management's monitoring of internal goals and objectives and perpetual systemic self-correction become an audit of management itself (see Power 1997). When an organization audits its own processes, it alters what the external auditor must do.

> Instead of painstaking documentation of the whole system of transaction controls, the auditor tends to now focus on *key* controls and particular risks. . . . Organizations set policies and design procedures for implementing and measuring performance in relation to these policies. Results are fed back into the system in the form of reports, comparisons, etc. and remedial corrective action is taken where necessary. . . . The internal control system is a form of structured self-observation. (Power 1997: 82, 83)

Power argues that such an internal control system becomes the measure of management because auditing "is a product in its own right." It is an "internal monitoring mechanism which is part of the system and which feeds back results into systemic and operational matters," and thus is "an external process of reporting on and validating the quality of the management system" (84).

Since the central administrators of Wan U wanted to receive a sterling report (as it indeed did), a committee appointed by the provost worked for several years to produce a "self-study" indicating how well the university had met the standards of the Regional Accreditation Agency. Like the delineation of standards, the executive summary of that "self-examination" spoke in an officious voice: "The institution is committed to assessment and is moving to make existing assessment efforts more systematic while at the same time embarking on new initiatives to strengthen student-learning outcomes assessment as part of its overall approach to institutional effectiveness." As required, Wan U reported the steps it was taking to institute assessment, including "by the end of academic year 2006–2007, all departments will have developed means of measuring the learning outcomes of their undergraduate majors, as well as complete assessment plans," and "in the academic year 2007–2008, actual assessment, data collection, and reporting will take place." Wan U even explained to its RAA how the administration was modifying the faculty's attitudes toward its courses:

> The University has also initiated several efforts that will improve the effectiveness of course delivery and the curricula of majors and concentrations. Current efforts to renumber courses into four rather than two undergraduate levels, along with efforts to articulate learning outcomes for courses and majors and concentrations, will lead faculty to think in terms of student learning rather than teaching, and lead to more majors and concentrations exhibiting structured course sequencing with senior capstone experiences. Students and faculty alike will be more aware of learning goals and therefore more likely to achieve them.

In essence, this statement implies: The administration is leading the faculty to abandon its claim to professional expertise. It is devising methods for them to learn the importance of goals, objectives, and a particular kind of assessment of students.[14] Through audit, the central administration is (to use Eckel and Kezar's [2003] metaphor) "taking the reins."

KOWTOWING TO THE CUDGEL

A faculty's preexisting experience with accreditation boards affected a school's or department's attitude toward accreditation and assessment. Although a university is only reaccredited every ten years, some schools face separate accreditation panels on a more regular basis. For instance, the Accreditation Board for Engineering and Technology (ABET) visits the

School of Engineering every six years. Some departments such as journalism, physical therapy, and communication disorders also face accreditors periodically. Schools and departments that faced routine reaccreditation were more likely to accept the desire of Wannabe University's central administration to institute both assessments of faculty and assessments of student-learning outcomes. Some of them, such as the communications department, already sent observers to faculty classrooms. Accrediting agencies mandated that others, such as journalism, engage in student outcomes assessment.

The professors in schools or departments that did not face routine accreditation by an outside agency were more likely to make a fuss than professors whose schools or departments routinely faced accreditation, but there were clear exceptions to this rule. The head of one department that was routinely accredited seemed to mind increased university control over the professors in his department, and he did not want to increase his supervision of them. He argued that a lack of resources made some activities impossible. He opposed the preparation of teaching portfolios ("too much work, especially for people who do not yet have tenure"), peer observations ("if I were to assign an observer to every class taught by an assistant professor, I would need more than thirty observers every semester"), and student outcomes assessment ("professors give grades").

The head of another routinely accredited department sat quietly in meetings of the College of Liberal Arts and Sciences' departmental "assessment liaisons" until the leader of that group slipped and said the provost might distribute resources according to how a department fared when it administered student outcomes assessment. Suddenly that department head looked very angry, indeed. Someone sitting near me mumbled, "No college kid left behind," a clear reference to President George W. Bush's policy "No Child Left Behind," which used tests of students to allocate resources to schools. I heard professors mumbling, "No college kid left behind," more than once or twice.

On the other hand, at a meeting of a University Senate committee, a former department head who had instituted summative peer observations reacted as though he had been personally insulted when a professor noted that such observations might not be objective. He turned red in the face and spoke quite loudly, "I would never do that!" The person whom his department had sent to the meetings of departmental "assessment liaisons" sat quietly through most of that group's discussions and let other liaisons argue with the group's leader, an associate dean, and the assistant vice provost for assessment who attended these monthly meetings. What's significant about the institution of student outcomes assessment is that neither professors nor departments had a choice about *whether* their department would engage in assessing student learning, but only *how* it would do so. No matter how much they resisted being audited, they were told to make themselves accountable.

Meetings discussing student outcomes assessment were initially very heated affairs. Professors insisted that they already assessed their students: they graded papers and exams; they wrote comments; they gave course grades. Group leaders invoked the cudgel: The University must institute such assessments; the Regional Accreditation Agency required them. They added that the provost also thought assessment to be a good idea, but never explained why—beyond referring to the memo quoted at the start of this chapter.

At one meeting, tempers flared. The assistant vice provost for assessment, the dean-appointed leader of the CLAS committee of liaisons, and the head of the General Education Oversight Committee (GEOC) visited a meeting of the GEOC social science subcommittee. Opposed to assessment, an agricultural economist decided to play dumb. After winking at a colleague, he said softly, politely, modestly, and with a friendly yet serious half smile, "I don't understand. I grade my students." He refused to understand the explanation that assessment is different from grading. He echoed a colleague who wanted to do a "real social science study," one that had a "good research design" and involved before-and-after measures of how much students knew about specific topics. He refused to understand that no one was asking for a study with a good research design. He refused to understand that student outcomes assessment was intended to assess how well a department planned and executed the goals of its curriculum, not the potentially idiosyncratic grades of an individual professor. At one moment, this professor was insistent, at another, confused. He was so quietly impossible that finally the assistant vice provost blew up: "If you don't do student outcomes assessment, there won't be any social science requirements in the general education curriculum." (One subcommittee member was aghast at the economist's behavior; another had trouble not laughing.)

Student outcomes assessment did not disappear. On separate occasions two professors, who were politically active and respected by both their colleagues and administrators, explained to me that the seemingly idiosyncratic policies of Wannabe University's corporate administrators would not simply fade away. They had each independently learned that many of the new policies were not idiosyncratic at all. In a discussion of student outcomes assessment, one noted, "I really objected to student outcomes assessment, but then I called friends in my field, who chair departments around the country. . . . They are instituting [that policy] at their schools, too." A professor active in her national organization said, "It's happening everywhere." Some new faculty also brought the news that Wan U was instituting practices that had been in effect at their last job.

Here's how one of them explained student outcomes assessment:

> They [administrators] were working on introducing student outcomes assessment at my last university. It's like the students are being processed the way you process hot dogs. You take raw material and you put it on an assembly line. You check for defective hot dogs. Almost all of the hot dogs are good. When one is defective, you ask how to change the process. You don't try to figure out what went wrong with the raw materials you were assembling. Not with this kind of continuous quality control.

As did other members of the faculty, he felt that

> student outcomes assessment means you're really assessing the professors and the departments, not the students, because you assume that the students . . . must be qualified to learn, just like you assume that the supplier delivered good parts for you to assemble. If [the students] don't come to class or don't do their work, it's not their fault. It's our process. It's not about input; it's all about quality control on the assembly line.

This analogy to the processing of food—or electronics or cars or clothing—also implies that administrators control aspects of the curriculum, for assembly lines are not self-constituting phenomena. Historically and today, owners and managers, not workers, designed and established assembly lines or paid others to do so.

The assembly lines control more than the product as the product's components move from one worker's station to the next. They control the workers, too. Checking to see whether the faculty are processing students properly, student outcomes assessment makes the faculty accountable to the institution and the institution accountable to the accreditation agency and the agency accountable to the National Advisory Committee on Institutional Quality and Integrity, and that committee is accountable to the U.S. Department of Education and its cudgel.

Provost Wesley and the other provosts of public research universities in the region were very conscious of that chain of accountability. At one meeting, the leader of the group of departmental assessment liaisons revealed that Provost Wesley had recently met with those other provosts. They talked about how to do student outcomes assessment for general education courses, he said. They noted that their gen. ed. requirements were similar and it would certainly be convenient if they designed an assessment tool that all of them could use. But then they decided it was a bad idea. The Department of Education might jump on the bandwagon of common or standard testing. The group leader reported: The provosts feared that assessment could turn into "No Student Left Behind." "Did you read in the *Chronicle* [*of Education*] what Margaret Spellings said this week?" an associate dean then asked. "We better do something before she does it for us," a departmental liaison observed. Even cooperating, the regional universities could not dispel the external threat. Comments within departments echoed that sentiment. Professors reported that their colleagues had agreed, "We better figure out how to do this before they [the administration] do this for us." The liaison for a humanities department reported to the Liaisons Committee, "My department had a serious discussion of [student outcomes assessment]. We feel it is an example of the worst kind of 1950s educational research, but we'll do it for you."

BEING STUDENT-CENTERED AND CARING

Ultimately, some professors argued this version of professorial accountability and responsibility is not about education as traditionally defined—education as *ex ducere*, "to lead out" or "to guide out." Rather, it simultaneously commodifies education and transforms it into training. As Stephen Brint (2002) points out, although public research universities have not abandoned the liberal arts, they have increasingly stressed the practical arts. As a result, a primary task of universities has become pleasing consumers—students and their parents—and so making themselves accountable to them. Those paying (or borrowing) to get an expensive college education want to know that they can use what a student has learned—or at least the diploma and grades the student earned—to get a job.

One sees this sort of emphasis on commodification, consumerism, and accountability elsewhere in university towns. I think of student apartment complexes that attract renters by advertising that every unit features a flat TV screen and an Xbox. Those ads resonate with student unions that resemble shopping malls and echo university viewbooks that highlight recreational facilities where students can work out, meet, and make friends.[15] The university is appealing to the informed consumer, who is also at the heart of the Department of Education's notion that comparative data on student outcomes assessment will help students and parents decide which institution of higher education will give them the biggest bang for their buck. But what if education is not about informed consumption?

Many professors readily admit that some of their colleagues are lousy teachers; some do not even hand out a syllabus for their courses. (One associate dean asked the Senate's Student Welfare Committee to correct such travesties. He noted that his son attended a public university that had a Student Bill of Rights.) But, they insisted, the way that Wannabe University discussed its emphasis on students conflated student learning with student life; that is, it did not distinguish between intellectual activity and other sorts of activity.[16]

For instance, the main page of the university's website stressed what the university made available to its students—what the student was purchasing—without specific references to education. A series of sentences crawled below a slide show of pictures of Wan U. The first sentence, "Wan U is a student-centered institution that prepares graduates for the road ahead," accompanied a picture of the main pedestrian mall on campus. With other "Points of Pride," it formed a boastful paragraph: "State-of-the-art facilities grace every Wan U campus. Wan U's distinguished library is the top public research library in the region. The faculty are student mentors and world-renowned scholars. Dorm life is active and fun. Wan U is . . . enhancing its campuses with state monies. Wan U stands among the top public universities in the nation. Ninety-two percent of recent graduates are either employed or are in graduate or professional school. Division I in NCAA sports, Wan U is filled with all-star student athletes and fans. Wan U is a school of choice among the nation's most talented students." The slogan on the web page of the vision of student affairs was more succinct: "One Division. Multiple Services. Students First."

The website of the Instructional Design Department of the Institute for Teaching and Learning addressed itself to faculty; but without discussing education, it too spoke of being student-centered. It preached the management jargon of goals and objectives. "If you know your course's goals and objectives [subject matter deemed important for student learners], we'll help you find ways of using technology to engage your students or even non-technological ways of doing so—if you want to ask us." It explained that it uses

> a student-centered learning approach as a vehicle for [faculty] to learn about instructional design. While the redesigned course is often the goal of the faculty, our goal is the process. Faculty who have undergone this process—in addition to having a redesigned course that addresses evolving pedagogical issues such as student-centered learning, multiple learning styles, information literacy and responsible inclusion of technology—possess the instructional design skills necessary to maintain any changes to their courses. They can then transfer these skills to other courses for which they are responsible.

All of a faculty member's courses can then be student-centered.[17]

This emphasis on student-centeredness and student engagement in classes conflates learning and style. Giving advice to faculty on how to involve undergraduates in course material when they are teaching large courses, the head of the Institute for Teaching and Learning stressed techniques that might help students to pay attention and to believe that you care about them. Here are some of his suggestions, as reported in the *Wannabe Weekly*:

> It always amuses students when you show early pictures of yourself. It's one of the ways I start to get involved with the class, irrespective of size.
>
> Small talk builds the relationship between professors and students. . . . Greet students and make them feel it's an individual experience. Chat with people in the aisles. If they see you doing that, they'll be more inclined to talk to you.
>
> Use humor. . . . If the class is particularly long, add a bit of humor every 20 minutes. It gets students' attention, and helps them return to concentrating.
>
> Explain to students that you will not be able to get to know all of their names, but you will try.

A professor reported how he had instituted another bit of advice he had received from a member of the Institute for Teaching and Learning. It, too, was intended to make students realize that "I care about them."

> Every week I put questionnaires on the desks of ten students, different areas of the classroom each week. The questionnaire asks how they think the class is going and if they have any improvements to suggest. Then I act on the suggestions. Some students said I had too many items on a PowerPoint slide and others wanted more detail. So I've changed what I do: Now the slides I use in class have less detail, and the slides I post on the class website have more detail. . . . My student ratings have gone way up: 9.8 [out of a possible 10].

Some professors argue that this approach is "cynical." "It's not about teaching; it's about looking like you care about the students," a social scientist said.[18]

Like much else in contemporary life, the emphasis is on appearances. I observed a small class in which the instructor claimed that a new central administrator was trying to do something about student partying and drinking "because he cares about students and drinking is dangerous." A young woman immediately spoke up: "They [administrators] don't care about us," she insisted. "They just want to give the appearance of caring. They don't care about us at all."[19]

8

Plans and Priorities

The town of Ashton was developing a "vision statement" so that its policy makers and administrators could plan for the future. On a snowy Saturday in December 2007, more than sixty town residents gathered in the cafeteria of the middle school to assess the town's needs. They included at least four professors, a few retired professors, two Wan U administrators, and two retired administrators, including the mayor, who had once held a central post at Wannabe University.

One of the two active administrators was new to the community. He had arrived in the 2007 fall semester with Wan U's new president, Richard (Rick) Daniels.[1] As often occurs when people who work at Wan U gather in a non-university setting, some gossiped about happenings at the university—the search for new deans, the problems posed by students renting houses in neighborhoods around town, what the new president was like.

As President Rick Daniels's assistant and the mayor discussed town-gown relationships during President James Whitmore's administration, an imprudent professor butt into the conversation. He announced, "My students say that the administration doesn't care about the students; it just wants to give the appearance of caring." President Daniels's assistant gave an immediate response: "That's what we found when we got here, but we're going to change that." Then the mayor reprised statements she had made before the eavesdropper had joined the conversation: "I still say that President Whitmore was right for what had to be done then, and President Daniels is right for what has to be done now."

President Daniels was supposed to consolidate what President Whitmore had achieved. President Whitmore had transformed Wannabe University. He had raised monies, accumulated "Points of Pride," and pushed Wan U ten notches up the *U.S. News & World Report* rankings; he had established Wan U as a national presence, not a mere regional university. On several occasions during his first months in office, President Daniels recalled how he had viewed Wannabe University, while provost of a public university that was ranked higher than Wan U. "Of course I knew about Wan U," he joked. "I could see it moving up when I looked in my rearview mirror." President Daniels was supposed to accelerate the growth of Wan U's academic reputation (including its research grants and contracts), help to increase the university's stature as it jostled with competing national and international institutions for position in the academic game, and lead it into the exalted realm of the Association of American Universities. He was also supposed to heal relationships with some constituencies who seemed to feel that Whitmore had ignored them—especially the faculty and the undergraduates. The search committee hoped that Daniels, an accomplished scholar and a man who enjoyed being around students, would become a presence on campus.

Consolidation implies continuity. President Daniels was not supposed to transform Wannabe University. He was not to accomplish "deep" and "pervasive" change—the definition of transformational change in the higher-education literature (see Eckel and Kezar 2003) and the task to which President Whitmore had devoted his tenure. He was to help Wan U "take the next step." Whitmore's administration had inflicted wounds as it had done "what had to be done." ("You have to break a few eggs to make an omelet.") Daniels was supposed to heal them. His assigned task of making Wannabe University even stronger expressed an early finding in the organizational literature: Although there are exceptions, as a rule university presidents are "constrained" by so many factors that there is "a lack of a relationship between institutional functioning and presidential succession" in higher-education institutions[2] (Birnbaum 1989: 132). To be sure, universities may compete to hire the exceptions, much as corporations do. In the case of some universities, "the acts of an individual president appear to have a profound effect on levels of institutional functioning" (132), just as some heads of corporations successfully define themselves as the source of their organization's "transformation." The histories of prominent colleges and universities are replete with praise for a special president (see, e.g., Keller 2004; Gittelman 2004), who through the sheer power of personality and past executive accomplishments exercised heroic leadership, much as that mythic and dynamic corporate leader might do (Khurana 2002).

Presidents have the responsibility of responding to a hostile and coercive external environment; those with significantly less authority may initiate other institutional changes so long as they stay within the values of the new managerialism by increasing economy, efficiency, and effectiveness. Middle managers bring news of new ideas from the meetings of their professional associations. They suggest implementing procedures that have "worked" elsewhere.[3] Deans and central administrators argue for the incorporation of "best practices" developed at other institutions. Indeed, they may become so infatuated with others' best practices that they might not even realize when they or their predecessors have "invented" a best practice. As others copy their best practices, they may even seek to abandon it so that they can copy others' methods. At Wan U, the slogan of best practices had become so pervasive that I often heard professors use the term in committee and Senate meetings.

Professors at Wan U claim that although there was "presidential continuity" during President Whitmore's eleven-year term of office, there was significant discontinuity at the administrative level that had direct responsibility for faculty affairs. As universities conformed to the corporate model, deans and provosts were to come and go. During President Whitmore's eleven years as president, four different men had been the chief academic officer and provost. Ignoring the insider who twice served as acting provost and was twice spurned for a permanent appointment to that job,[4] some faculty members noted that each of the three outsider provosts introduced policies that seemed to contradict those of his predecessors. Provost Mike Tremaine (and Vice Provost Mary Matthews) emphasized the importance of undergraduate instruction. Tyler Johnson had stressed the importance of "research, especially funded research." Gerald Wesley gave weight to "outreach"—service to the state and its citizens, what at least one professor preferred to call "public engagement."[5] By highlighting different and competing aspects of professors' jobs, each provost demonstrated that change within organizations is not only the result of coercion, imitation, and professional norms. It also results from individual agency—actions including interventions that are intended to initiate change and (often) to put an individual's stamp on an organization. Each provost had tried to leave his own mark. Each had designed a mission statement and a strategic plan. (Each plan was sufficiently distinctive for a dean to tell me, "We follow the 1995 [Tremaine] plan, the one with the red cover.") As one faculty expert in organizations observed, by the time Provost Wesley had arrived at Wan U, earlier provosts had made an impact. Putting himself in Wesley's shoes, he suggested, "You want to be able to show that you've done something. You want to be able to say more than I carried out the initiatives of the guy before me. . . . Wesley has to do something to make a mark on Wan U if he intends to move on to a better job."[6]

Speaking with one another, the faculty listed the provosts' accomplishments, shortcomings, and political skills. Buying stamps at the Ashton post office, I heard professors mumbling that Mike Tremaine had overspent his budget just before resigning from Wan U. At a local supermarket, faculty chatted about the antipathy between Provost Tyler Johnson and Dean Todd Alden. The *Wannabe Weekly* listed each man's successes when each resigned to assume a presidency elsewhere. Tyler Johnson's "accomplishments at the University include developing the framework for an Academic Plan, a document that will serve as a roadmap for the University's academic priorities, capital projects, and the allocation of resources for the next decade." Mike Tremaine "strengthened undergraduate education through dynamic new approaches to orientation, advising, the first-year experience, the Honors Program, instructional quality, and living and learning arrangements. The student body . . . increased in number, in diversity, and in quality." Some professors privately noted that when Tremaine's administration proposed "dynamic new approaches" to undergraduate education and engendered fervent professorial discontent, Tremaine gave Mary Matthews the credit for those programs, while accepting credit for popular accomplishments, including an increase in private fund-raising.[7] They explained that Tremaine had been both ambitious and politically skilled.

For the faculty, the swift replacement of one provost by another mandated cautious actions. Earlier, I discussed one factor that both professors and departments considered: Why follow the newest policy of the newest provost when he might leave soon? Maybe if an academic department stalls long enough, it will never have to make the change. There was another consideration as well: Protect oneself and one's department. Why bother to "talk truth to power"? According to the faculty, if the provosts didn't want to hear the truth, they might "get even." Keeping one's views to oneself would be advantageous in both the short and the long run. One would be in a better position while the current provost was in office and so better off when the next provost arrived.[8] To get on, some professors and middle managers seemed never to express an opinion in a public meeting, although they might have scheduled a private meeting to say what they thought, as is the practice in a mechanistic bureaucracy (Morrill 1995). For example, when one dean was being evaluated for reappointment, several professors from different departments privately visited the head of the reappointment committee to express their reservations. Other professors seemed to butter up whomever was in power and to avoid anyone in even temporary disgrace. For instance, at many receptions, both faculty and middle managers went out of their way to greet the director of athletics, who was a regular at President Whitmore's Wednesday morning staff meeting. However, at a reception for an incoming central administrator that was held just after an editorial in the *State Capital Record* criticized the director of athletics, few people greeted him. He almost seemed to be invisible.

The professors' behavior resembled that of the upper-level and middle managers especially when it came to greeting the director of athletics during his temporary "disgrace" and when it came to speaking "truth to power." Indeed, the professors behaved *as though* they were members of a mechanistic bureaucracy (see Morrill 1995), not (tenured) professionals with significant job security. Why? One social scientist, who was old enough to remember the 1960s but too young to retire, mused:

> My guess is that the corporate university breeds a corporate mentality among the faculty, squelching the free exchange of ideas and criticism that once characterized universities. Deans and provosts used to be accustomed, even inured, to fairly strong attacks upon their decisions, and they learned (maybe painfully) that they *had* to listen to their faculty. In the corporate university there is a sense of futility of complaint and a sense of danger in doing so.

He added:

> The sense of futility arises from the top-down nature of decision making, which begins with the board of trustees. . . . The sense of danger arises from the competitiveness that a corporate culture breeds. Rewards are given and sanctions imposed based upon criteria that the faculty have not set. Moreover, we have little idea how they can be assessed. . . . The corporate culture creates a zero-sum game, with winners and losers on all matters.

The public behavior of professors indicated that they wished to protect both themselves and their departments. Anticipating a meeting where faculty might be expected to criticize the second (public) draft of the Provost's 2008 academic plan, an informant asked:

> So if a [geographer], say me, speaks up about how the academic plan does not take account of the fact that we are unable to offer enough classes to enable students to graduate on time and we are unable to staff our gen. ed. courses with faculty members, although faculty staffing is part of the design by GEOC [the General Education Oversight Committee], I risk endangering the department. Would I get sufficient support from other departments to make us safe, especially from the departments that are now in current favor with the provost? Would anybody from [one of the biology departments] dare support my position?

If nobody does, the geographer is endangering both himself and his colleagues.

Before the advent of academic freedom, professors may have been cautious in expressing their opinions (see O'Neil 1999). During the 1960s and early 1970s, in some universities, colleges, and departments, speaking one's mind was a norm. Today, universities are sinking into the corporate culture; many professors do not say what they think. When professors speak their mind, especially when they "speak truth to power," they are making news.

CUMULATIVE PRESSURE, UNCLEAR PRIORITIES

Successive provosts and a changing university structure placed increasing and shifting demands on the professoriate. As one policy succeeded another, the latest sometimes seemed to contradict the last. For instance, twice in 2003, when the central administration was reorganizing itself, the board of trustees modified regulations about who had the authority to sign off on checks of specific dollar amounts.[9]

Central administrators intended many of these practices and policies to help Wannabe University survive and even flourish in the competitive and demanding atmosphere of contemporary higher education. Although they may not have intended to do so, they also introduced practices associated with an accountability regime. They not only made more demands on the faculty; they also introduced more supervision and regulation of professorial tasks, akin to the institution of student outcomes assessment discussed in chapter 7.

PRESSURE TO DO EVERYTHING

Some professors said that although sometimes they could not tell which policy took priority in which situation, they did know that they experienced the *cumulative* demands of the provosts as intense pressure. These cumulative demands had transformed Wannabe University into a greedy institution—a place where the organizational culture emphasized both a long workday and a long workweek (see Coser 1974). For instance, Dean Todd Alden worked long and late and dismissed people who did not do so as "lazy." Working long hours had become part of the campus culture; so had converting that extra effort into "results." Professors advised one another about the experiences on their end of campus. "If you think that the people in the humanities feel pressure," one professor announced to another in the supermarket, "you should see what it's like in the sciences." Some professors even complained to a provost in a polite and understated way.

Here's one example: Every month Provost Tyler Johnson invited professors to his home for a brief late-afternoon gathering. Because, as he explained, he wanted to get to know the faculty, he had each person say "a little something" about their work. Now and then, Johnson introduced a faculty member with praise, as he did when calling on the hardworking chair of a particular committee to "say a few words." With thanks, the professor noted that the faculty seemed to be working harder and harder. Each taught more students (as a result of Mike Tremaine's expansion of the undergraduate body); each was expected to publish more and to receive more grants (as a result of Johnson's emphasis on research). The committee he headed demanded a lot of time, too. The man specified that he didn't mean to complain, but he had less time to see his family. His work was absorbing his life.[10]

Sometimes rather than complaining *to* a provost about the unrealistic expectations placed on faculty, professors complained *about* the provost who expressed them. A 2008 draft of Provost Wesley's academic plan prompted so much anger about both insufficient resources and managerial style that it was withdrawn. President Daniels and his chief of staff rewrote it. Nonetheless, the provisions of Wesley's rejected draft and the faculty's reactions to them are telling. For instance, one professor announced to his colleagues: "There are only twenty-four hours in a day. How are people supposed to do more research, more teaching, and more outreach?" In a long memo distributed through e-mail, a department head in the sciences criticized the plan for saying, "Do more of everything," without providing additional resources:

> In the sections dealing with improving undergraduate and graduate education, the basic message appears to be "Do more of everything"—teach more undergraduates in smaller classes, admit better students, admit more community college students, double the number of honors students, produce more Ph.D.s in a shorter time, triple the number of postdocs on campus, etc. In the absence of a clear commitment of significant new resources, many of these goals are incompatible with the other things we are supposed to do more of—publish more books and papers, serve on more editorial boards, participate in more professional societies, get more grants.

He insisted that expecting more "results" without providing more resources was not sensible:

> . . . It is not reasonable to expect faculty members to write more books if they are in departments with computers from the early 1990s and sharing printers. It is not reasonable to propose a program in Environmental Toxicology if we lack adequate facilities for housing and caring for aquatic animals. It is not reasonable to double the number of honors students doing research without a major increase in money to support such research. It is not reasonable to expect Ph.D. students to complete their degrees in less time if we are falling behind our peer institutions in graduate fellowships and summer support for graduate students.

The faculty's critical attitude was exacerbated by Provost Wesley's managerial style and by the rapid turnover in provosts. At some other universities that have successfully "transformed themselves," the administration and the professoriate had a history of trusting one another (Keller 2004). At others, administrators have exercised "collaborative leadership." Eckel and Kezar (2003: 70) say that when higher-education institutions want to transform themselves, "collaboration entails empowerment—more than advisory, but real decision-making authority. Unless individuals are deeply involved in the formation, decisions, approval, and implementation, there is little hope that the campus will be transformed." Collaboration requires the faculty to "buy in."

At Wan U, the provosts' managerial style exacerbated the faculty's feeling of being pressured and so intensified resistance to some plans, especially Provost Wesley's academic plan. Rather, a professor who had received a campus award for service to the university wrote in an e-mail circulated among professors in several schools:

> The common denominator here is lip service to the faculty, but no serious attention paid to the faculty's ideas, expertise, talents, or voice. The Catch-22 is this: The [wasted] time the faculty spent on developing the academic plan [by attending special colloquia to which some of them including this fellow had been invited], and now spends on trying (I believe, ultimately in vain) to correct this almost pernicious document, is time faculty might have spent on teaching and research—teaching, I might add, an increasing number of students, the teaching of whom was—surprise!—not planned for when they were admitted. . . . We are become *voces clamantes in deserto*.[11]

In another e-mail, he added:

> . . . the point remains: a document affecting faculty had little real faculty input. Revising that same document in no way alleviates or ameliorates the situation, except to the extent revising is a tacit admission of error. But the situation exists, and will continue to exist until the faculty, individually, as small units, and as larger ones, are not only involved directly in an academic plan (and are listened to, as the environmental subcommittee was not) but are given the resources to carry it out. And these resources are not to be taken from Peter to support Paul. . . . No 1% from linguistics to support a grant-getting position in nanotechnology. Ex post facto lip service won't work. And neither will academic cannibalism.

Several professors reiterated an observation I had previously heard from other informants. "Wesley has a habit of consulting with a few people—

different people on different issues—and then calling meetings to say what he is going to do. And then he says that he consulted people because he called the meetings."[12] One man experienced in administration announced to me: "Consultation is more than talking at people whom you have gathered in a room." Another man said, "At the meeting [with the faculty about the academic plan] Gerald said he wants to get the plan to next month's meeting of the board of trustees. He has a habit of presenting plans and saying there is no time for either the faculty or the Senate to discuss them because he promised to get it [the plan] to the board of trustees."

Professors expressed both annoyance and downright anger about the academic plan and the time available for discussion. Many were annoyed that the provost had not left enough time to engage in "meaningful consultation" with the professoriate. In an e-mail to members of a powerful committee on which he served, a powerful department head wrote: "The justification for the time line is a 'deadline' to present the plan to the BOT [board of trustees]. Yes, well, who set this deadline, and who agreed to this deadline? Not faculty members . . ." They were irate about the demands being made on them. Of the two provocations, they cared most about the infringement on their own self-interest. Talking with me, professors from many different schools expressed anger about how the plan ignored their advice, while making demands on them without providing the resources with which to meet those demands. A social scientist, who had previously been careful to avoid discussing campus politics with me lest he be quoted, described the reaction to the draft of Provost Wesley's academic plan: "There's an uproar all over campus. It's worse than when Wesley folded the three schools. Then people said, 'Okay. I don't like what he did. But it doesn't affect me.' Now it [the academic plan] affects everyone, and everyone is complaining." As another person observed, "Even the scientists are protesting that Provost Wesley's academic plan gives short shrift to the fine arts, the humanities, and the social sciences." As a department head in the sciences had observed in his widely distributed e-mail:

> Large areas of the academic enterprise at the university, particularly in the social sciences, the humanities, and the fine arts, seem to play little role in this plan, or are relegated to odd positions like contributing to workforce development. Even the physical sciences are not particularly well represented because of the heavy focus on environmental and biomedical issues. This almost ensures a lack of enthusiasm among many members of the University community for implementing the plan.

Not all of the responses of the professoriate revolved around callous self-interest and the lack of consultation. Some people also invoked principles. The head of a science department wrote in another long and well-circulated e-mail: "Instead of beginning the Preamble by saying 'we must redouble our efforts,' there should be a clear statement of what exactly a university, and Wannabe University in particular, is supposed to be and how we hope to get there." "What is your vision of a university?" a professor had asked Provost Wesley at the faculty and staff meeting to discuss the provost's academic plan. The provost had not understood the query; he had interpreted it as questioning his commitment to public education. As a middle manager observed:

> His passion was aroused by [the] question and probably his anger, too; essentially he responded with a statement of why he should be taken as a man of goodwill with respect to the future of a land-grant institution. However, the pressure exerted by legislative hearings and encounters with the board of trustees were also evident in his emphasis on the need for an academic plan and rationales for more university funding bids like "workforce development" (i.e., "things they want to hear").

"The people I work with say the plan doesn't have a vision," the middle manager confided.

THIS YEAR'S PRIORITIES

With or without resources, professors found the pressure to be everything to everyone confusing, especially because each succeeding provost stressed a different part of the faculty's job. As a few professors told one another (and me) privately, each new provost sought to make himself distinctive from his predecessors—and so possibly more marketable when he applied for the next senior administrative job. With some circumlocution, here's how Chet Muller, a powerful department head, explained the problem to Gerald Wesley when this provost visited a Senate committee meeting:[13]

> When Mary Matthews was here [as vice provost for undergraduate education and instruction], everything was about teaching. She made it clear that she wanted changes in teaching, that teaching was a really important part of our job. Then she left and [her boss] Provost Tremaine left and Provost Tyler Johnson arrived, and all we heard was research, research, research. Now you're here and you keep saying service, outreach to the state. We'd like to cooperate, but what are we supposed to be doing? It [the administrative message to us about our duties] keeps changing. . . .

To understand Professor Muller's subsequent statements, one must understand an unhappy duty that academics take for granted as part of their professional responsibilities: sometimes they fire their own colleagues, whom they discuss as "the young people up for tenure." Deans and central administrators may overrule their decisions; however, individual professors, department heads, and departments as a collective also know that deans and provosts judge them by how they vote on colleagues' qualifications for tenure ("tenure cases").[14] The decision "not to grant tenure" by failing to renew someone's contract in their sixth year of service is difficult precisely because the juniors and seniors have worked together for so long. They have argued and made up; they have lunched; they have listened to one another's questions at colloquia. They may know each others' children and spouses. The senior professors may also remember how tense they felt when they were up for tenure, and often they know that they cannot offer sufficient reassurance to help a candidate for tenure to calm down. Even as senior professors sit in judgment over junior professors, one informant explained, "Some part of them sympathizes with the juniors. It's almost like when they say what the juniors should be doing now, the seniors are reflecting on what was expected of them when they were up for tenure and also what's expected of them now that they have tenure." When tenured professors talk with one another, their junior colleagues symbolize where the seniors have been and where they are now.

Thus, Professor Muller continued, defining the responsibilities of professors is particularly important when dealing with assistant professors who are trying to earn tenure in their jobs. And, he specified, the problem of defining responsibilities is particularly acute for young professors whose appointments vary from the norm. Professor Muller cited arrangements that belong to specific locations within the academic matrix system, namely, jobs that give people two "supervisors" (such as a department head, a program director, or a regional administrator) instead of one:

> How are we supposed to judge the tenure of joint appointments and of the people at the regional campuses? They get asked to do more service [outreach] than other assistant professors. [My department] give[s] a bachelor's degree at one of the regional campuses, so we asked our junior colleagues who teach there to establish a disciplinary presence. [Each of them had replaced a just-retired senior professor.] They did a good job of that. They did such a good job that they didn't have enough time for their scholarship. We tried to create conditions that would help them out, but we cannot duplicate the working conditions at the main campus.

Professor Muller announced: "I don't want to hire [people for the regional campuses anymore]. I don't like feeling that we're not being fair to them."[15]

THE CONSEQUENCES OF STRUCTURAL CONFUSION

Structural confusion about job responsibilities creates political and bu-reaucratic problems in a complex organization undergoing increased centralization. At the very least, it creates a tension between the central bureaucratic authority and the units claiming some decentralized respon-sibilities for personnel decisions, such as the schools and colleges and their constituent departments. The central administration may implement poli-cies that instruct departments to make specific sorts of decisions. For in-stance, Provost Johnson mandated departments to design central policies governing "professional responsibilities," his website provided a template on which departments could base their document, and he expected depart-ments to enforce that policy. Essentially the professional responsibilities document provided that if a department head felt that a professor was not doing enough productive research (publishing, getting grants, or both), the department head could assign that professor additional teaching or service responsibilities.

Wannabe University was not the only higher-education institution to introduce a method of auditing professors' "post-tenure production." After negotiation with the local chapter of the American Association of University Professors, a public research university relatively near to Wan U had intro-duced periodic "post-tenure review" of all professors. At a state university where Provost Wesley had served as dean, each department had designed procedures to determine whether a professor was a slacker. Wesley had overseen the preparation of documents delineating both the faculty's pro-fessional responsibilities and the consequences for "faculty who displayed chronic low achievement." In that university's department of mathematics, the professor could either accept the assignment of additional work or initi-ate an appeal through what amounts to a "mini-trial" in which someone's colleagues serve as the jury.

The central administration also defined other ways for a department or a department head to assign differential responsibilities to its members. Provost Wesley insisted that, with the approval of the central administra-tion, a department might specify that one professor should concentrate on teaching, another on research, and a third on outreach—even though each person has an appointment in, say, the department of animal science. Pro-vost Wesley told the Senate's Faculty Standards Committee that he favored placing these specifications in letters of appointment to the professoriate and that his office would review all of the hiring letters for new faculty. (Provost Johnson had begun reviewing all hiring letters after some depart-ment heads and deans had included expensive specifications in these let-ters without making sure that there would be sufficient funds. For instance, they might promise a laboratory without knowing about the availability of monies to furnish it.) Indeed, at a public research university where Provost Wesley had served as dean, the provost signs every appointment letter.

Chet Muller disagreed with customized letters of appointment. As he saw it, "individualized" responsibilities create problems for departments. Although academics don't like to think of their departments as members of a complex bureaucracy, the departments are indeed part of complex organizations with clear bureaucratic components. Bureaucracies supposedly abhor individualization; the classic definitions of bureaucracy all insist that bureaucratic organization entails the application of the same rules to everyone. To engage in tautology, that's why they're called rules. Defining individualized responsibilities for professors decreases the ability of colleagues to tell one another (and themselves) that they apply and have always applied the same set of rules to everyone—that, for instance, they denied someone tenure because "we had no choice." Because slightly different rules apply to each person, individualizing responsibilities diminishes the claim of both a department and its department head to treat everyone in the same way and to have always done so.

Chet Muller felt that a department head who used "different rules for different colleagues" would lose credibility (and power) when dealing with his colleagues. In a bureaucracy supposedly based on meritocracy, "different strokes for different folks" also aggravates existing conflicts and introduces new ones. Rather than "measuring" himself against a norm, a professor may start to "audit" his career against those of his colleagues. To be sure, some professors probably engage in that sort of competitive self-monitoring now. But, some professors argued, *personalized* letters of appointment encourage and so probably exacerbate personal competition, as well as a dedication to one's career as opposed to loyalty to a particular university.

"DIVERSITY" AS PRIORITY

The march of provosts created pressure and confusion about professorial duties, some faculty opposition to administrative plans, and even ambiguities about Wan U's mission. One point of special tension was Wan U's responsibility to educate the state's citizens from a variety of backgrounds and to expose all students to diversity so that they could flourish in a changing country and a shrinking world. From Provost Mike Tremaine (1996) to Provost Gerald Wesley (2009), the central administration established inconsistent policies toward diversity. Sometimes it lauded education for a changing nation. Sometimes it did not. Sometimes it expressed its commitment to educating for diversity, even as its actions fell short.

ORGANIZATIONAL AMBIVALENCE

When it came to educating students to live in an ever-more diverse country, Wan U seemed stricken with "organizational ambivalence"—allegiance to what its leaders perceived to be conflicting, even non-compatible goals.[16] On the one hand, university leaders expressed their desire to admit more students of color and to hire more professors from underrepresented minorities. On the other hand, some of them emphasized the importance of merit (defined as grades and SAT scores for students and scholarship for faculty) and behaved as though they thought that hiring a diverse faculty was incompatible with "hiring the very best."

The vice provost for enrollment management captured this ambivalence when in fall 2007 he delivered his annual report on undergraduate enrollment to the University Senate. A senator had asked him about the enrollment of underrepresented minorities. "Higher education has changed," he answered.

> It is no longer defined as a public good; now it is a private good so we have a dual mission. The state wants us to educate the best and the brightest, and we are doing that. We are enrolling more valedictorians and salutatorians. The SATs of each entering class are going up. But the state has also given us the responsibility to educate first-generation college students and low-income students.[17]

In context, "first-generation" and "low-income" were euphemisms for "minority."

But which minority? As at many other institutions of higher education around the country, Wannabe University enrolls many Asian Americans. Although Asian Americans constitute only 2 percent of the state's population, they are almost 10 percent of Wan U's undergraduates.[18] The grades, class standing, and SATs of Asian American applicants tend to be higher than those of other minorities, such as African Americans and Latinos. Thus, there are many Asian Americans in the Honors Program, but almost no African Americans and Hispanics. The parents of many of these Asian American students are professionals who were educated abroad.

The parents of many African American and Hispanic students are also college-educated, but these students are still more likely to be the first in their families to attend college. They are the "first-generation college students" to whom Vice Provost Victor Steibel referred. Although African Americans and Latinos are almost 20 percent of the state's population, together they are roughly 10 percent of Wan U's enrollment. Many of the African American and Latino students are very qualified to attend Wan U. Many live in the suburbs, sometimes in segregated suburban neighborhoods. I

suspect that if one compared the "typical" records for Asian American, Latino, African American, and white applicants, the typical Asian American
would be more likely to qualify as "the best and the brightest."[19]

Although a senator had essentially asked Vice Provost Steibel how much
Asian Americans contribute to the "good scores" and high retention rates
of minorities, Steibel did not answer that question. Nor did he give a direct
answer when another professor asked him how he "balanced" the university's seemingly conflicting goals—to enroll both "the best and the brightest"
and "the first-generation college student." To be sure, these two categories
are not necessarily dichotomous, but this observation begs the question.
Rather, the pattern—which members of which group are most likely to
fall into which category—captures the conflict between Wan U's two enrollment missions. The institution is fraught with organizational ambivalence.[20] That ambivalence is embedded in the history of diversity initiatives
during James Whitmore's presidency.

SOME HISTORY

In the mid-1990s, the then-chair of the board of trustees, President Whitmore, and Provost Tremaine all identified "multiculturalism and diversity"
as essential to the mission of the university. The three men had believed
that the university had a responsibility to help all students prepare for an
ever-more diverse society; indeed, that task was a responsibility to both the
state and the nation. The demographic trend was clear: People of different backgrounds would increasingly work together as both the country and
the labor force became more diversified. In 1998 they established an Office of Multiculturalism and Diversity, appointed Professor Kevin Wilson
as vice provost for multiculturalism, and gave him an independent budget
and suite of offices. The new office included four academic units and five
non-academic units.[21] Although no one had planned this outcome, each
academic unit had a non-academic counterpart. Thus, the Office of Multiculturalism included a Women's Center, founded in 1972, and a Women's
Studies Program, founded in 1974. Although not intentional, such duality
supposedly helped to create "synergy" and cooperation. (In 2006 there was
talk of an Institute for LBGT [Lesbian Bisexual Gay Transsexual] Studies.)
As an institution, the university separated the students' academic and social
lives. Colleges and schools were strictly academic. The vice president for
student affairs was in charge of the students' residential life, health, career services, and risk management, to name but a few of the categories on
his website. Part of the same administrative unit, the cultural centers and
academic programs devoted to inequality supposedly addressed the whole
student.

In its first ten years, the Office of Multiculturalism and Diversity expanded in a way that seemed to indicate some recognition of its importance. A new chairman of the board, Mike Sugarman, was interested in emphasizing diversity in undergraduate education, because doing so "would help business" as corporations' employees, including their managers, would increasingly come from a variety of ethnic groups (including racialized ethnicities). Vice Provost Kevin Wilson was instructed to design a diversity plan and to make a report to the board of trustees about Wan U's progress toward its implementation. The Office of International Affairs became a unit within a renamed Office of Multiculturalism and International Affairs. Most first-rate research universities do not house international affairs and diversity together. As a 2008 committee reported, "After benchmarking our peer institutions, it was clear that a centralized organization dedicated to international education was the norm." It is probable that the Office of International Affairs was joined to the Office of Multicultural Affairs because at roughly that time the university had decided not to invest appreciable monies in international undergraduate education. Victor Steibel, the vice provost for enrollment management, had informed a committee chaired by the dean of the School of Business that he simply did not have the resources with which to tackle international education. However, the expansion of Kevin Wilson's portfolio also suggested that his superiors had confidence in his work.

Vice Provost Wilson seems to have had powerful allies; but, as we have seen, at universities people come and go. Sugarman felt strongly enough about diversity to give Wilson his private phone number. Although Wilson was not a member of the Wednesday morning group, he seemed to enjoy President Whitmore's favor. Sometimes Wilson's allies could not protect the Office of Multiculturalism from attack, especially factional disputes within the professoriate. For instance, at one point, some women who were active in the Women's Studies Program approached the dean of the College of Liberal Arts and Sciences to transfer their program from the Office of Multiculturalism and Diversity to his college. Forthrightly, Dean Todd Alden told Wilson that these women had seen him. Both men understood that including a popular major in one's portfolio was attractive, but having responsibility for a minor, such as Asian American studies, was an economic drain.[22]

At times Vice Provost Wilson seemed to feel that President Whitmore "would not let" the Office of Multiculturalism be dismantled. However, he was sufficiently politically astute to ward off attacks, sometimes before they happened. For instance, a reporter for a conservative newspaper told Wilson that he had been assigned to write about the cultural centers as a waste of money and was putting off doing the story, but could not do so indefinitely. Wilson constituted external review panels to evaluate the cultural centers so that experts from other universities could demonstrate how they "contributed to the mission of the university." The panels' very positive reports were a form of political protection from both internal and external threats.

The importance of diversity to the board of trustees, President Whitmore, and Provost Tremaine was also implicit in the Wan U vision statement approved in 1995 as part of the university's strategic plan. It included: "[Wannabe University] will be perceived and acknowledged as the outstanding public university in the nation—a world-class university. . . . It will be a *diverse* community where the highest moral and ethical values will prevail with a dual purpose, an inward focus on learning and an outward focus on service" (emphasis added). In April 2006, to comply with the requirements of its Regional Accreditation Agency, the board of trustees approved a new mission statement. It mentioned Wan U's "dedication to excellence demonstrated through national and international recognition," but it did not mention diversity. Board Chair Mike Sugarman had felt that it was vital to encourage diversity. He had asked Vice Provost Wilson to report to the board. When his term was over, Sugarman had explained, "The more we talked about diversity, the more people realized that it is important to me." James Whitmore had understood Sugarman's concern so well that he even asked Wilson to deliver a report every six months. Wilson had thought that interval was too short; it's hard to see progress in six months. Chair Bill Hardway did not ask Wilson to report to the board, but he permitted him to do so.

I do not think that the omission of the word "diversity" from the 2006 mission statement was intentional. The head of the committee that wrote the mission statement supported the work of the vice provost for multiculturalism, but the issue of diversity did not have the same salience for her as it did for people of color. (The word "diversity" was added several months later after both staff and faculty objected that some successful programs aiding both Wannabe University students and minority residents of a nearby city could be eliminated if the university did not recognize diversity as part of its mission.)

Issues of racialized ethnicity, gender, or sexual orientation rarely have as much salience to observers as they do to the people who experience discrimination based on that identity. Also, as a few Wan U students have reminded me, sometimes white people "feel awkward about bringing up questions of race." They seem fearful that they will say the wrong thing and be criticized as racists. Two African American middle managers seemed to make a similar point. They noted that often they were the only people of color at meetings and that white people tended to avoid issues of race and racism in their presence. "It's not malicious," they told me. "Maybe they don't know what to say, so they wait for one of us to say something. Then, maybe, if one of us had said something about race, one of them will say something about diversity." But usually, one continued, "white people don't bring those questions up." That failure of, say, white heterosexual males to introduce issues of racism, sexism, or homophobia may mean that some questions are never addressed, especially if people of color, gay people, and women have such small numbers in an organization that they are being "very careful about picking their battles." The need to make choices applies to members of the board of trustees as well as to middle managers. It was particularly salient to the approval of the mission statement that failed to mention diversity.

One spring afternoon in 2006 I observed the black members of the board of trustees "picking their battle." They were few in number, for there were relatively few women, African Americans, or Hispanics on the Wan U Board of Trustees. With one exception, the heads of all of the major trustee committees were white men. (A black man headed the powerful Committee on Academic Affairs.) Since the seats for trustees were arranged around a U-shaped table with the heads of the most powerful committees sitting at the head of the table, the women and all but one of the people of color sat along the legs of the U. No one commented on this arrangement publicly.[23] One woman who was a trustee confided to me her concern that the governor seemed to be ignoring "diversity" and mostly appointing "white men."[24]

At that meeting, board members failed to notice that the mission statement did not include the word "diversity." However, they asked Vice Provost Wilson pointed questions about the report on multiculturalism that he was presenting to them. The questions of African American members of the board seemed so orchestrated that I wondered whether Vice Provost Wilson had set the questions up. (When I asked him about coordination, he changed the topic.) The African American trustees reminded their white colleagues of possibilities that might otherwise have been ignored. Here's the first of these exchanges as noted in the board's minutes:

> [The trustee] acknowledged the process of athletic recruitment in which [coaches] are able to recruit the best in their athletic disciplines. He wondered if some of those strategies could be utilized to achieve diversity on the faculty. The data show that the numbers are better than they were but the absolute number started out pretty low. . . . He wondered if Vice Provost Wilson could comment

on how to implement some of the athletic strategies into faculty recruitment. Vice Provost Wilson responded that one of the advantages that programs such as Athletics has is funding or resources. . . . [A] number of other institutions have reserved funding for recruitment, which is becoming increasingly necessary to be competitive in attracting the best and the brightest. Vice Provost Wilson said that it was also important for us to recognize that we need to seek those who are in the pipeline, which also takes resources.

Wilson noted that several years earlier the University of Michigan had raised $15 million to recruit faculty from underrepresented minorities. He added that Harvard has set aside $50 million for this task, and (according to the minutes) Yale University was raising a "sizeable sum." Furthermore, it noted: "Vice Provost Wilson was not suggesting that the University is in a position to set aside $15 or $50 million, but he noted that having a much more focused, systematic approach to this process may make a difference" in building a multicultural faculty and staff.

Wilson's answer was politically interesting because the attitudes of the provost toward recruiting faculty from underrepresented minorities had shifted when one provost left and a new one arrived. Provost Johnson was friendly with Vice Provost Wilson, but he had refused to permit colleges and schools to set "hiring goals" for women and underrepresented minorities. "Too much like quotas," he had explained. On the other hand, Provost Wesley's staff did not initially include the word "diversity" in its mission statement, but Wesley did approve of hiring goals.

Other incidents also expressed this organizational ambivalence. By 2006, the second year of Provost Wesley's tenure at Wan U, members of the provost's office engaged in actions that seemed to devalue the Office of Multiculturalism and International Affairs. At the annual spring dinner meeting of the trustees with the Executive Committee of the University Senate and some key administrators, someone brought up a question about the retention and graduation rates of underrepresented minorities. Vice Provost for Education and Instruction Jeanne Sharpe noted that many of the programs that she supervised (including the tutoring and peer assistance programs in the BUE) were directly addressing those rates and were responsible for improving them. Vice Provost for Enrollment Victor Steibel, who also served on the board of directors of the African American Cultural Center, demurred. "The cultural centers have been doing it [working on these issues] longer and they do it better," he informed the group.[25]

Vice Provost Wilson's office did not see an influx of monies to recruit African American and Latino faculty and to hire more women in the sciences. Instead, he staved off attempts to dismantle his office. When Provost

Wesley restructured the schools of Family Studies, Allied Health, and Continuing Studies, he had also proposed removing international programs from Wilson's purview. After someone whom he apparently trusted told him that the people of color on the faculty and the staff would never forget or forgive him, he had not done so.[26]

However, Wesley made the same proposal as part of the draft academic plan that he presented in 2008. Then he explained that he was going to create another vice provost. The new administrator would be in charge of international programs, continuing education, outreach, and regional campuses—"everything that's underfunded," one associate dean observed after the meeting. ("The Grand Poobah of the Underfunded," the perennial faculty wag laughed later.) Yet a few weeks before, when the board of trustees had approved a major in African American studies, Provost Wesley had informed the *State Capital Record*: "Diversity is a big thing for us. It's going to be a prominent piece of our academic plan." Two months later, the forty-five-page draft of Provost Wesley's academic plan did not discuss diversity in a systematic way. Rather, it scattered references to diversity here and there.[27] At roughly the same time, the American Council on Education was organizing its third small-group meeting to recommend that institutions think about encouraging the articulation of education for multiculturalism and diversity with education for internationalism (see Olson, Evans, and Shoenberg 2007). A university senator with some power confided that combining offices of diversity and offices of international affairs seems to be emerging as a "best practice." From that perspective, Wan U might be viewed as a leader in an emerging practice, but the current best practice assigns "diversity and multiculturalism" to one office and "international study" to another. As provost of a conformist university striving to be among the best but not yet one of the very best, Gerald Wesley appears to be throwing his weight (and money) toward studying abroad, attracting out-of-state students, and recruiting international students. Internationalism seemed to be a fashionable fad circa 2005–2008, as suggested by the title of books in the online bookstore of the American Council on Education.[28] Equally important, demographic patterns have also made internationalism attractive, for the central administrators anticipate a decrease in the number of high school graduates in the region. Attracting out-of-state students, including international students, would fill those anticipated empty classroom seats with undergraduates who pay out-of-state tuition. In this instance, conformity to the "internationalism fad" might produce a revenue stream.

Perhaps Provost Wesley's vacillation was also an attempt to please his superiors. "I should think he learned something from his last job," a professor with friends at Respectable Research U said. "He has to know how necessary it is to please the president." President Daniels, like President Whitmore, favored "planning for diversity." President Daniels even used politically correct language. At meetings he called Bill Hardway "Mr. Chair," not "Mr. Chairman." He was the first person at Wannabe University *not* to refer to the head of the board of trustees as the "chair*man*." Although it was politically wise for Provost Wesley to give at least lip service to diversity, he also had personal convictions about this matter. He felt that it was extremely important that a college education should be accessible to the students of the state. Attending a luncheon at the African American Cultural Center, he had discussed with the students his experiences as the first person in his family to attend college and had also shared some of the travails of his sister, who despite learning disabilities, became a librarian. Provost Wesley's personal experiences—his attendance at a public university, his experiences at Respectable Research University—contributed to the initiatives Provost Wesley introduced and to his choice not to support other programs. However, what matters sociologically is the organizational ambivalence about diversity—the problem of priorities. If one assumed that priorities conflicted, which priority mattered more?[29]

As the years passed and one provost replaced another, priorities shifted. Not every change was prompted by organizational ambivalence. The Wan U provosts and presidents clearly cared about public higher education. Each one of them had attended a public university. Those who are currently presidents of other colleges or universities work at public institutions. Well-meaning, these provosts and presidents have faced daunting tasks as they sought to transform Wannabe U. They have coped with diminishing public funds. They have had to please governors, legislators, and trustees. They have had to manage the slow-moving behemoth that is academia—with colleges and deans all of whom wanted something from them, professors oriented toward their own professional lives as opposed to the welfare of the university, athletic boosters, the Ashton town council, students—with, in short, the myriad of characters who, following current business practice, are called "stakeholders" (as opposed to interested parties).

At the same time, the presidents and provosts set out to make a life for themselves and their families. As participants in the new and active labor market for university administrators, each had wanted to make his mark in order to keep his job or to have the chance to move on. They did not intend to contribute to the gradual legitimation of an accountability regime.

9

Making Professors Accountable

A "business-like" concern permeated President Rick Daniels's initial formal presentations to the professoriate. Daniels began one of his first appearances at the University Senate by saying, "There are three ways for a university to break even: Earn more, raise more, and spend less." Two months later he implied that like President Whitmore, he valued the conversion of scholarship into profit: "The legislature has been very generous with us," he told the Senate. "They have given us funds to support our Eminent Scientists Program [to hire several eminent scientists in fields that might produce a revenue stream] and to support our Center for Entrepreneurship."

On another occasion, President Daniels stressed the need to find new revenue streams. "I will always be frank with you," he responded to a question raised at a faculty forum on a draft of the 2008 academic plan.

> I have heard all of the arguments for and against charging graduate student tuition to granting agencies [at the two other public research universities where I had significant administrative responsibilities]. You are making arguments that I have heard before, and I have made up my mind. To move ahead, we simply have to find money to hire more professors. . . .[1]

President Daniels added that charging tuition to grants was also good for business in another way: "When one of the universities [where I served as a senior administrator] started charging graduate tuition to grants, it moved up eight places in the rankings."[2]

Until the late twentieth century, earning money had not been a time-honored "core value" of American higher education.[3] Rather, as Nannerl Keohane reminds (2006: 60, 61), since the late nineteenth century, American research universities have combined elements of four different ideals: the primacy of research (as stressed in early nineteenth-century German universities), the crucial importance of teaching to train the mind and to shape future leaders (as emphasized at Oxford and Cambridge universities), the deep appreciation of the liberal and fine arts as a source of enriching one's life (as expressed in the mid-nineteenth-century idea of the "great traditions of Western civilization"), and the extraordinary utility of practical knowledge to alleviate daily problems (as embodied in the Morrill Act of 1862 and "foreshadowed by Franklin and Jefferson, who asserted the practical importance of knowledge 'in the nation's service'").

Today the mastery of practical knowledge in the nation's service is becoming synonymous with registering patents, incubating start-up companies, and "growing" revenue streams; professors receive rewards for engaging in these activities. In the 1960s, '70s, and '80s, many "pure" university scientists had implicitly looked down on their corporate colleagues, when they had explained how academic jobs differed from corporate research. They had cited the distinction between articles and patents, and added that professors published their findings in academic journals listed on their curriculum vitae; scientists who worked for corporations recorded their patents on their résumés. Also, as they saw it, "published work" was available for public use and so could advance science; whereas "patented work" might halt scientific progress by ensuring that only the patent-holder had access to a discovery. Professors found the distinction between open and closed access to information so significant that as late as the 1990s, "corporate scientists" with lots of patents had trouble translating their achievements into academic jobs.[4] As universities have become more corporatized, the meaning of holding patents changed. Today at least one Wannabe social scientist lists his patents on his curriculum vitae and so announces that he is an economic asset to his academic employer. He is participating in, even feeding, Wannabe's market ethos.

THE KNOWLEDGE BUSINESS

Although the literature on the marketing of higher education discusses such aspects of university business plans as enrollment management and budgeting, it emphasizes the transformation of research into a commodity (e.g., Kirp et al. 2003; Washburn 2005). By stressing the commodification of research, the literature stresses the directions in which research universities are *trying* to move, for few research universities are earning a *significant* portion of their budget from patented faculty inventions.[5] Such income has been a relatively minor part of Wannabe University's auxiliary revenue.

Instead, at Wan U the public expression of the market ethos has highlighted service to the state. The central administration of Wannabe University has been particularly clear that the governor and the legislature were very interested in lines of research that might promote the development of both the state's industries and "workforce," especially the training of citizens to enter key occupations where there is an existing or anticipated shortage of workers. When they spoke at President Daniels's inauguration, the state's governor, trustee head Bill Hardway, and the new president all addressed the need to align university research with state priorities. Some deans have also cared about these matters. Both the law school and the business school have programs to meet the needs of a white-collar industry whose profitable activities are of particular economic concern to the state.

Although Wannabe's central administrators as well as the deans of the law school and the business school would probably cringe at the comparison, in this specific sense higher education at research universities resembles the training activities of community colleges: both serve the needs of the state (Brint and Karabel 1989, 1991). The faculty despised this comparison. In late 2007, after Provost Wesley explained to the faculty of the College of Liberal Arts and Sciences that programs educating needed workers would have funding priority, one senior professor condemned the provost to his colleagues by saying that the provost was treating Wannabe University as though it were a community college. For the provost and president, such service was a political reality. At President Daniels's inauguration, the governor even emphasized how the development of Wannabe's graduate programs was a service to the state. He said that he appreciated the university's contribution "to our economy and, yes, to our quality of life." Additionally, he praised President Daniels's commitment to improving graduate education, suggesting that doing so would "improve Wannabe's research capacity." The governor was very clear that research capacity could translate into corporate dollars, jobs, and taxes.

The central administration of Wannabe University was also very conscious of the potential link among research capacity, research income, and graduate education. In one of his first talks to the University Senate, President Rick Daniels explained that for the university to improve its national ranking, it had to increase research activity and improve its graduate programs. An improved national ranking would be an economic asset in several ways. As we have seen, it attracts "quality undergraduates." It also attracts graduate students interested in doing research with specific professors who have active (read "funded") research agendas. Additionally, it attracts faculty, who want to be associated with a top department at a top university, for a highly ranked department can provide capable graduate assistants, excellent facilities (such as labs, equipment, and libraries), and intellectually stimulating colleagues. All of these factors are interrelated.

Faculty research and scholarship help to increase a university's "research capacity." In a never-ending cycle, research capacity begets research. Together research and research capacity beget reputation; reputation begets excellent students and faculty, who of course beget more research and an increasing research capacity. Both beget the university's ability to attract still more research grants and contracts. To invoke an old cliché, "nothing succeeds like success."[6]

President Daniels, Provost Wesley, and the then–vice provost for research recognized this never-ending cycle in 2008, when they addressed the University Senate about the potential of Wannabe's graduate programs. Each man used the word "investment." Each said, "We have to invest wisely"; that is, the university must put money into departments that are "good enough" to elbow their way into the top twenty graduate programs in their disciplines. They also warned the faculty that to succeed, Wan U had to fold both inferior and mediocre graduate programs. As they saw it, since these programs were incapable of achieving the improvements that would make Wannabe University stand out from competing research university brands, they were a waste of scarce resources. To be blunt, they were a waste of money better invested elsewhere. I will return to the question of how one decides which graduate programs are "good enough" and which are either inferior or mediocre.

There are known ways ("best practices") to accomplish the goals of improving research and scholarship in programs that one has decided "to grow." For instance, one can hire faculty in specialties that are well-funded or are emerging as fungible. Earlier I noted that several deans and vice provosts had reminded me of this option.[7] It was also included in one of the first rewrites of the 2008 academic plan. Also, as a vice provost had informed me in 2005, to funnel monies where they will "do the most good . . . to build good graduate programs," one may have to eliminate others. The monies spent on a barely successful program in geology may be transferred to a promising program in sociology. That option, included in several drafts of the 2008 academic plan, was not popular with the faculty.

Although some faculty reviled the notion of "taking from Peter to pay Paul," by 2008 the Wannabe professoriate had lost the power to decide some of the university's important intellectual directions—at least when those directions had clear associations with probable revenue streams. As a dean reminded me, the faculty is responsible for the academic affairs of a research university. However, he emphasized, especially when backed by the board of trustees, who are legally responsible for the university, *the administration may intervene in academic affairs if or when academic matters have implications for the economic well-being of the university.* "Taking from Peter to pay Paul"—requesting that every academic department rescind

1 percent of its academic budget for redistribution by the central administration—might further strengthen the departments that were most capable
of recruiting and graduating excellent students, attracting large grants, and
building research capacity; in short, being of practical service to the state.
The identification of the departments that "deserve" either more or less
funding necessarily entails decisions about academic and intellectual priorities. The provost, president, and board of trustees were to make those
decisions, not the faculty.

Finally, President Daniels had another proposal for improving the graduate school. He suggested that Wannabe University might try a different way
of "managing the graduate enrollment." As he put it:

> Wannabe University's management of undergraduate enrollments is probably
> the biggest success story in many years. . . . It is the one thing if anything that
> has put us on the map. Something can be learned from that and can be applied to
> the graduate school. We need a data-mining office. We know an amazing amount
> about our undergraduates, but not about our graduate students. Actual graduate
> admissions are handled locally [in departments], but there are things that can be
> done to assist that [local] process.

He added: "It's a risk. Applying lessons from undergraduate enrollment to
graduate enrollment is a risk. Other universities don't do it like that."

As Stinchcombe explained, organizations want to avoid "the liability of
newness" (1965: 148). Complex organizations avoid risk; they suffer from
a tendency toward "structural inertia" (Hannan and Freeman 1989: 66; cf.
1977). One reason for that inertia is "internal politics. . . . Even weak resistance can greatly slow processes of change" (Hannan and Freeman 1989:
66). From an administrative point of view, one task that university administrators face when they seek to introduce change is to overcome faculty
resistance. Generally, they may find it easier to push recalcitrant professors to accept a best practice that has been benchmarked at other research
universities than to convince them to take a risk. Accordingly, when trying
to convince scientists and engineers that charging the tuition of graduate
assistants to research grants would have a positive outcome, Rick Daniels
invoked best practices. Agreeing to an anticipated motion to establish a task
force on the graduate-tuition issue, President Daniels told the Senate that
all but two of the top twenty-five public research universities charge graduate tuition to grants. By implication, President Daniels was asking why
these professors thought that their assessment of the situation was correct
and all of those other leading universities were wrong.[8]

The problem of risk was also germane to President Daniels's desire to
"mine data." When President Daniels spoke about instituting a new way to

"mine data" about graduate students, he was encouraging the faculty to support the risk that he was willing to take. By citing Wannabe's past success in managing its enrollment, President Daniels was essentially saying that the risk was not as grave as it seemed—at least not at Wannabe, which had a history of successfully managing the undergraduate enrollment.[9] Stating that the new office would not interfere with concrete graduate admissions, he was also placating professors who feared that administrators might interfere with graduate admissions. (At the University Senate, several professors asked whether the president wanted to centralize graduate admission.) Indeed, President Daniels seemed to be saying that the administration was offering "to help," not to hamper.

Some of the professors listening to the new president may have wondered whether the "help" of the central administration might generate unwanted guidelines for departments to apply as they made their decisions about graduate admissions. After all, President Daniels had strong views about who should be admitted to graduate programs. "I don't understand why any department would want to admit a graduate student whom it was not willing to fund," he told the University Senate. (Generally, the graduate students in academic departments serve apprenticeships in research or teaching to earn their keep. The graduate students in professional schools usually pay tuition.) Even if a professor agreed with President Daniels that unfunded graduate students are undesirable, she would probably resent a presidential guideline forbidding the practice.[10]

Not all guidelines and preferences that originate on high in the bureaucracy become mandates for action, but many do. Sometimes those "mandates" seem silly. In the 1980s, a Wannabe president admired the beauty of the region's rocks, and suddenly boulders sprouted around the campus landscape. Other preferences may produce meaningful directives, including a demand that deans, department heads, and professors audit themselves or accede to auditing by others. As we shall see, the processes of auditing and accountability are central to the acts of defining a "good" graduate student and a "good" department. Those definitions can also affect organizational risk. By drawing on the professoriate's own criteria for excellence, the central administrators decrease the probability of faculty objections to their notions of what is "good."

MORE AUDITING AND MEASURING

Auditing and accountability are not interchangeable exercises. Not all auditing involves accountability; nor is all auditing coercive. Wanting to know what members of a class have understood, an instructor can give a surprise quiz without incorporating the resulting scores in students' grades. The quiz is a mere audit. Were the professor to include the grades earned on this quiz in his calculations of the grade for the course, the professor would be imposing accountability. Some forms of audit scream of consequences and so of accountability. A letter from the Internal Revenue Service to a taxpayer who engaged in creative accounting can strike fear in the heart of the recipient, just as it may scare an honest taxpayer with lousy records or a careful record-keeper who has a particularly auditable job, such as novelist. Similarly, even if they accept their institution's criteria for granting tenure and even if their publications are copious and first rate and their teaching skills are incomparable by their institution's standards, some assistant professors are a study in fear as they await that audit called a tenure review. That audit involves accountability: if one doesn't receive tenure, one loses one's job. Because they were experienced at performing audits and at being audited, when they were facing an audit of all graduate departments, many professors understood that even though they might agree with the criteria being used to audit the quality of their graduate students, their departments, and even their own academic worthiness, they might not like the audit's outcome.

To some faculty, the development of data about the quality of graduate programs seemed a straightforward extension of the central administration's devotion to "data-based" management. The provost and his vice provosts respected data so much that they even identified it as a "lever of change." In chapter 7, I discussed how, to facilitate decisions about tenure and promotion, the central administration wanted additional data about the quality of professors' teaching. Recall that Jeanne Sharpe had told a faculty forum, "We are a data-based institution. We have lots of ways to measure research, but we don't have satisfactory ways to measure the quality of teaching." By collecting data about the quality of an instructor's work in the classroom, the provost hoped to introduce a "culture that celebrates and supports superior achievement in both" teaching and research.

Similarly, the provost and his vice provosts understood that even the categories used to classify data may be agents of change. As described in chapter 7, Wan U's administrators had affirmed that the selection of categories can lead to redefinition of a situation, when its self-study for reaccreditation noted, "Current efforts to renumber courses into four rather than two undergraduate levels, along with efforts to articulate learning outcomes for courses and majors and concentrations, will lead faculty to think in terms of student learning rather than teaching." There are additional indications that central administrators viewed the definition of categories as guides to action.

Consider two examples. After explaining to the University Senate that the new academic plan would eliminate some graduate programs to increase the support of others, Provost Wesley introduced Lloyd Hawthorne, then the vice provost for research and dean of the graduate school, to "explain the metrics" developed to gauge quality. Also, when President Daniels proposed establishing a vice president for enrollment management, he suggested that the new vice president should have authority over the existing Office of Institutional Research.[11] Explaining that he doesn't have time to supervise that office properly, he reasoned that placing the research office in the unit that would manage undergraduate and graduate enrollment was logical, since the Office of Institutional Research was already "mining data" pertinent to enrollment. In both instances, the data constituted an audit, an examination, and verification of a condition. Provost Wesley wanted to use metrics to cut programs. President Daniels wanted to use metrics to shape enrollment. Both associated the collection and analysis of these data with decisions to take actions. Thus these audits had consequences. They would make departments accountable for their achievements (or lack of them). Since all of the graduate departments were being forced to participate in these audits, they were a form of "coercive accountability" (Shore and Wright 2000).

To be sure, the faculty accepted as valid the criteria that Dean Hawthorne had developed to judge the quality of graduate departments. All were items that faculty discussed among themselves as indicators of quality; that is, as accomplishments for which professors and departments should strive. Put somewhat differently, all were items that professors and departments cited when they audited themselves to determine where their department stood in their discipline. These items included the number and quality of faculty publications as well as the college or university from which accepted doctoral applicants had received their undergraduate degrees,[12] how applicants had scored on GRE exams, how long graduate students took to earn their degrees, and where they got their first jobs.[13]

Even a measure that some scientists wanted to add is an indicator that faculty and departments use when they audit themselves. "Aren't you going to take grant activity into account?" a bench scientist asked, when neither the president, the provost, nor the dean of the graduate school specifically mentioned that indicator of academic success. For the scientists, taking account of grant activity as well as the indicators that Dean Hawthorne had mentioned "just" involves recognition of the way things are, "just" as the parents of college applicants are "just" trying to make rational decisions when they consult *U.S. News & World Report* to help their children make choices about college applications and admissions. The professors' failure to question whether and how these measures and activities are appropriate and conversely the professor's introduction of another variable—grant activity—expresses how very much the administration's activity appears to be an expression of common sense. How else would one proceed? The professors' reactions also captured how very much they take for granted the right of the administration to use these indicators to audit them, to hold them accountable, and to plan the future intellectual tradition of the university. *These indicators are themselves extensions of existing auditing and accountability criteria*—although professors tend not to think of them that way.

The planned audit of the quality of the graduate departments also seems so commonsensical, because it is an extension of other audits. For instance, the reaccreditation of departments, colleges, and universities involves audits that contribute to an accountability regime. So, too, does the periodic assessment of departments achieved by obtaining external reviews. These are supposed to reveal both the quality of a department and its long-term and short-term needs. Indeed, one might view Lloyd Hawthorne's and Gerald Wesley's audit of the graduate programs as an extension of Wannabe's policy of systematic external reviews.

EXTERNAL REVIEWS

In an external review, a department produces an extensive self-study, which is sent to a panel of external visitors and one internal professor, all of whom the dean selects in conjunction with the department under review. The report includes information about graduate students—where they come from, how long they stay, where they go. It also presents such indicators of the "quality" of faculty as the recent grants and publications of the department's members. It explains requirements for the undergraduate major and for graduate degrees. The review team visits and interviews a program's leaders and its faculty. Its members may choose to speak with both undergraduate and graduate students.

An external review is an exercise in accountability with implications for action. At Wannabe University, as at many other research universities, the report of the review team is the basis for a contract signed by the provost, the appropriate dean, and the department. In the past, it specified how each party would contribute to strengthening the department.

The new conditions being introduced under President Daniels's imprimatur implied that eliminating a department had also become an attractive administrative option. President Daniels was not the first administrator to introduce that possibility. Several years before President Daniels and Provost Wesley mentioned eliminating programs to the University Senate, Dean Todd Alden of the College of Liberal Arts and Sciences had folded a department. When discussing his decision before the board of trustees, in a solemn voice the dean had both stressed how difficult he had found his decision and justified it by providing a summary of the latest external review. The board's minutes reported, "Given the concerns raised by the external evaluation, [Dean Alden] could not support the costs associated with replacing faculty and staff who retired and resigned, nor bring the Department up to full capacity." At the time, President Whitmore had "re-iterated that the decision [to fold that department was] . . . consistent with what the board has charged the administration, which is to identify those areas of high student demand, excellence or the potential to achieve excellence and national standing, and to reallocate resources to those ends. In addition, the university must also keep in mind our mission to the state's economy." Now, though, the central administration would also conduct its own *internal audits* to reallocate resources.

Earlier I reported that Provost Wesley had been dissatisfied with the external review process. At a meeting with other provosts of public research universities in the region, the provosts had agreed that sections of the typical external review were so predictable as to be useless. Almost every review concluded that with additional resources, especially new faculty lines, the department under consideration could become one of the top departments in the country. The provosts felt that so many summaries making essentially the same claim were an offense against common sense. Not every department could shine; not every professor is a potential star. The provosts needed to know which professors and departments deserved serious "encouragement."[14]

Just as one could hold departments accountable for their activities, so too one could mandate that professors become responsible for their own actions—or for their lack of them. At research universities around the country, central administrators also introduced more *individual accountability*. They transformed what had once been a system of requesting a merit raise into a system of proving that one had fulfilled one's *professional responsibilities*.

MERIT FORMS

Most American professors do not understand annual merit reports as a form of accountability.[15] At Wannabe University there are two kinds of annual forms. Professors submit one form to their department so that an elected committee can decided who "merits" a raise. (Each academic department determines how it will score the forms. The department head then submits the suggested raises to the appropriate dean for ratification.) The other form originates in the provost's office. Combined with the forms of every professor in an academic department, it becomes the basis of a departmental report to the dean, the dean's report to the provost, and the university's report to the State Board of Higher Education. At the provost's level, it helps to determine college and department budgets.

Supposedly, the process of writing the budget is transparent. So many achievements should translate into so many dollars. Gawley (2008) points out that transparency is a euphemism for "selective concealment and instrumental disclosure." For instance, the head of one unit in the Division of Student Affairs told me that she managed an inflated budget. The vice president for student affairs had tucked some other group's expenses into her unit's budget. She reminded Provost Tyler Johnson of this arrangement whenever it was her turn to appear at the annual budget hearing. In another division, a high-level manager had cobbled together the funds to establish an office by pooling monies from here and there. When the office's middle manager needed more funds to accomplish a requested expansion, he had first to learn the sources of his office's funds. Deans may also engage in creative accounting. Although professors may know that their own department has a private bank account to meet unexpected needs,[16] they rarely get to observe the intricacies of budgetary processes, let alone the budgetary ingenuity that appears to be inherent in the "transparent" workings of the bureaucratic hierarchy. What they do see is that their annual merit report has consequences for their future activities.

I want to highlight for a moment two aspects of the departmental merit report—the parts that specify the quantity and location of a professor's scholarship and the quality and size of a professor's classes, advisement load, and involvement with graduate students. Provost Johnson had created the template for a "Policy on Faculty Professional Responsibilities" to be enacted by each academic department. As reviewed in chapter 3, it specified that if a professor was a shirker (if he did not publish enough scholarship or apply for a sufficient number of grants), he must be assigned additional teaching or administrative duties. That is, each professor was responsible for carrying her share of the collective load and if the merit report to her department indicated that she had not done so, she would be held accountable.

Post-tenure review is another variation on this theme. After negotiation with the local chapter of the American Association of University Professors, a public research university relatively near to Wan U had introduced periodic post-tenure review of all professors. Every few years, they would have to demonstrate that their productivity levels (scholarship and teaching) indicated that they were pulling their share of the weight. Even when professors recognized that they were being subjected to additional controls—that is, to an accountability regime—some took pride in how well they passed the test. "Some people thought I would have a problem with the post-tenure review," I heard one professor from that university say at a party. "But they complimented me on my achievements." The fellow smiled as he listed off all of the work he had turned out in the past few years. So proud of their ability to excel at tests, professors may not question the right of their superiors to audit and hold them accountable. I will examine professorial compliance in chapter 10.

THE ACCOUNTABILITY REGIME IN BRITISH UNIVERSITIES

British universities already have in place many of the auditing and accountability techniques that Wannabe University has been considering. That centralized national system may give hints of some of the consequences of making higher education more accountable. Some British professors claim that along with decreased salaries and budgets, their accountability regime is destroying higher education. Fewer people are becoming professors. They also claim that auditing techniques are transforming education into training. Some aspects of the British system may predict where American universities are going.

The British government has had an invasive interest in the quality of teaching and research in higher education since at least 1979, when Margaret Thatcher set out to "reform" the British system of higher education by getting rid of the "rotten apples." Britain experimented with a variety of auditing and accountability techniques. As consistent with current policy, repeated poor showings on mandated audits could decrease funding and even result in closure.

The British Quality Assurance Agency was established in 1997 to audit colleges and departments in a five-year cycle. It contracts with what it terms "the main higher education funding bodies," such as the British Higher Education Funding Council, in order "to safeguard the public interest in sound standards of higher education qualifications, and to encourage continuous improvement in the management of the quality of higher education."[17] Does a university follow "good practices"? Does it maintain suitable academic standards? The Quality Assurance Agency breaks these concerns up into manageable bites and provides higher-education funding bodies with guidelines about how those bites should be supervised.

The British audit is more invasive than its American counterpart. A visiting team of "specialists" not only examines the sorts of documents that an American university prepares for an accreditation agency; it also conducts interviews to learn whether the "internal Code of Practice for Quality Assurance (Taught Programmes) . . . engages . . . in its entirety . . . with the Code of practice for the assurance of academic quality and standards in higher education, published by the [Quality Assurance Agency] and The Framework for higher education qualifications in England, Wales, and Northern Ireland."[18] As the Quality Assurance Agency explains on its website, attention to academic departments is meant to "ensure the equality of student experience and assessment across the University as a whole." Supposedly, attention to universities promotes the equality of the student experience and assessment across the country. To achieve that uniformity, the team that the agency sends to colleges and universities checks the syllabi of courses to learn whether goals and expected outcomes are clearly defined. Team members visit classes to determine whether they are well taught and make appropriate use of technologies available through the Unit for the Enhancement of Teaching and Learning. According to at least one British sociologist, training on how to be a teacher includes learning how to make oneself subject to audit (Evans 2004: 66). The visiting team also examines "student progression and achievement," "student support and guidance," and "learning resources."[19] In essence, the Quality Assurance Agency orders departments and colleges to audit themselves on specified dimensions so that it can perform a *secondary audit* to ascertain whether the departments and colleges conform to the national standards that the QAA has defined (see Power 1997). The activities of the Quality Assurance Agency escalate centralization and also rationalize education as a consumer product.

Audit and accountability are intimately tied to the market logic. The Quality Assurance Agency implements the market logic by posting every university's and every department's scores so that students and their parents can invest in the education that will best prepare the students for their chosen jobs (providing, of course, that the college or university admits them).[20] These procedures supposedly help a student to determine which is the better investment, an education in accountancy at the University of Edinburgh—where the quality of teaching and learning, the quality of student progression, and the quality of resources are all "commendable"—or one at Bradford College, where these items are "approved, but." What if a student is not qualified for admission to the University of Edinburgh? Should she take a degree in building and surveying? Bradford's record in that program is "commendable." Such devotion to market logic promotes centralization, since the definition of quality is a centralized definition, much as an American consumer determines the trade-in value of a car by consulting a centralized source, *Kelley Blue Book*. Should the canny consumer buy a gas-guzzler that holds up well in front-end collisions or a small-car that gets many miles to the gallon, does badly in collisions, but holds its value at trade-in time?

This system also supports a kind of "hyper-instrumental rationality." Following Ritzer (1993, 1998, 2000), sociologists have come to call this sort of rationality McDonaldization. Ritzer argues that the development of instrumental rationality inherent in the new market logic (re)produces an emphasis on efficiency, calculability, predictability, and control, and that each increase in efficiency, calculability, predictability, and control produces yet more efficiency, calculability, predictability, and control. Ultimately, the escalation of this cycle increases what Ritzer (1993) has termed the "the irrationality of rationality."

The British have embraced this concept and connected it with application of the audit culture to universities (see the essays in Hayes and Wynyard 2006), for they understand themselves to be attacked by a government that distrusts both universities and educators even as it claims to be working toward mass higher education. Here are two examples of irrationality in the British system of accountability. Richard Gombrich (2000) told a Japanese audience the tale about how an auditor assessed a tutorial session. Responding to a student's idea, the tutor pulled a book off his shelf and recommended it to the student. The auditor criticized the tutor because the book was not included in the syllabus. Others (e.g., Evans 2004; cf. Gombrich 2000) complain that former tax collectors have served as university auditors. More generally, British academics decry the new emphasis on training as opposed to education as an indicator of irrationality.

The British system also audits individual productivity. It emphasizes scholarship, and poor scholarship affects individual and group funding. At specified intervals or a rotating basis, every professor is supposed to submit the scholarship she has completed since the last reporting period (generally four or five years).[21] These data become the basis of the Research Assessment Exercise—where teams of scholars in a discipline rank others' work on a three-point scale. The top rank indicates that the scholarship is internationally important. The rankings themselves have promoted sarcasm. Evans (2004) suggests that scholarship is ranked "in terms of national, international, and presumably inter-galactic importance; recent proposals suggest the award of stars to each academic, so that we can emerge with one, two, or three stars" (Evans 2004: 119–20). With some irony, the late Natalie Allon used to apply a similar system of ranking to well-known academics, though she arrayed them as soap opera stars, other television stars, Hollywood stars, and Emmy or Oscar winners. Evans sounds more biting than Allon. She writes that the Research Assessment Exercise "makes circus monkeys out of academics, in that it demands performance in a certain ritual of behaviour and the organization of all behaviour toward the pattern of that ritual" (120). Rules and their outcomes mutually constitute one another.

As true of its American counterparts, the promotion and tenure system and annual merit reports, this centralized system of audit and accountability has an impact on the development of knowledge. Although in Britain disciplinary panels get to define standards, the system encourages research on some topics but not others; publication in some journals but not others. It may also discourage innovation. As the late Marshall McLuhan once noted, by the time that academics set up a large meting to discuss an innovative idea, that idea isn't innovative anymore.

OMENS AND REMINISCENCES

To some Americans, the British system augurs what could happen here. In President George W. Bush's second term, Secretary of Education Margaret Spellings raised questions about academic accountability, consumer value, and student outcomes assessment. She argued that universities must be accountable to the public and suggested that national student outcomes assessment would help consumers to evaluate the educations sold at different institutions. Her notions of how to achieve these goals seemed reminiscent of the British model.

Ironically, at Wannabe University some of the people working to institute student outcomes assessment (as Wan U's Regional Accreditation Agency had mandated) were not familiar with British practices. For instance, at a meeting of the Faculty Standards Committee, a professor of education asked whether there are data indicating the impact of student outcomes assessments on teaching and learning. Responding, both the vice provost for education and instruction and the assistant vice provost in charge of assessment had noted that the practice is too new for anyone to have done good research on that question. Similarly, when a faculty member who had taught in England mentioned the Research Assessment Exercise in front of the vice provost for administration, that central administrator seemed to find the practice shocking. In charge of codifying some aspects of Wannabe's assessment of faculty, he had kept track of what Americans were calling "best practices" as opposed to what the British identified as "good practice." Seemingly unaware of British practices, these central administrators must be ignorant of what British faculty thought about both the Research Assessment Exercise and Quality Assurance Assessment.

Although some Americans may not be aware of current British practices, many British academics seem aware of what's going on in the United States. Some British scholars even remind us that Ritzer (1993) applied his concept "McDonaldization" to American higher education. Here's how the British sociologist Frank Furedi (2002: 49, 50) summarizes Ritzer's application of McDonaldization to American higher education. *Efficiency* "is evident in the proliferation of computer graded assessments and the adoption of textbooks and accompanying multi-choice questions assignments"; *calculability* is found in "the increasing preoccupation of quantification exemplified by the emphasis on numbers enrolled, grades achieved, rankings of universities . . . which are presumed to correspond to differences in qualities of performance"; *predictability* exists in the growth of standardized courses with comparable syllabuses; and *control* abounds in "the regulation of teaching, learning and assessment through the introduction of centralized timetable, appraisal, and evaluation and grading procedures." The result, Furedi argues, is conformity and uniformity.

British scholars maintain that such practices as student outcomes assessment are ruining universities. Viewing their new system as a gestalt, some British scholars claim that the very act of thinking has become segmented. Rather than actively and creatively thinking while teaching, teaching in the classroom and lecture hall is divided into a series of potentially isolated acts performed sequentially on an academic assembly line that militates against intellectual creativity. Sometimes these acts are performed by separate workers or by teams. A department rather than an individual may set a "module's [course's] aims and objectives" and desired outcomes. An individual may prepare a course's PowerPoint slides (leading to legal questions about the ownership of both the intellectual content and the illustrative material associated with a course). Other individuals working for a textbook publisher may design exam questions. Yet another team may assess whether a course's outcomes have been achieved. The result, British sociologist Mary Evans (2004) writes, is "killing thinking."

Although British academics such as Furedi and Evans seem to detest contemporary British assessment practices, such strong opinions may not count for much in a market culture that favors mining data. What may be more significant is that McDonaldization transcends the marketing and auditing of higher education. It implies the imposition of a new form of government, an accountability regime.

IDEOLOGICAL INSTITUTIONS AND THE ACCOUNTABILITY REGIME

The escalation of the market logic that has characterized higher education since the 1970s is reminiscent of how the market logic and its demand for accountability have encroached on other organizational fields. Many of these fields concern ideas and ideology. Indeed, the literature in the sociology of organizations suggests that organizational fields involving ideas and ideology are more likely to experience a demand for accountability than are other organizational fields. As Hannan and Freeman (1989: 74) explain in a classic text, four conditions make the pressure for accountability particularly intense: (1) the production of "symbolic or information-loaded products, such as education"; (2) "substantial risk, as in medical care"; (3) "long-term relations between the organization and its employees or clients"; and (4) and "ostensible political purposes." Several of these conditions apply to universities. Their ostensible product is education. Faculty are long-term employees and alumni, long-term clients. Also, the emphasis on how the research university should contribute to workforce development and to industry suggests that higher education also has a political purpose. Finally, Hannan and Freeman suggest that the demand for accountability increases when resources become scarcer, as has been happening in higher education since the 1970s.

As Hannan and Freeman (1989) noted, market logic and its demand for accountability have also encroached on other organizational fields that deal in ideas and ideology. Such organizations are particularly vulnerable, because they are a bulwark of the social organization of any society. Although their structure may result from tensions between conflicting institutions and social forces, much as Starr (2004) suggests is true of the American mass media, they nonetheless provide justification for existing social arrangements, even as they recall past structures and presage those that are emerging (see Williams 1977). Education provides a guide not only to what a society believes its citizens must know, but also to ways of interpreting that knowledge. Every society has a significant moral investment in its ideological institutions.

The recent rich scholarship on these institutions discusses bookstores (Miller 2006), higher-education publishing (Thornton 2004; Thompson 2005), the media (Howard 2005; Turow 2006), even business schools (Khurana 2007). Thus, Miller (2006) tells the story of how independent bookstores lost ground to chains that stressed mass marketing, their owners learned to display books that were more likely to sell, and the owners modified key aspects of these stores to attract non-elite customers. Thornton (2004) explains how the market logic turned the acquisition of books for higher-education publishing from the use of personal networks to an emphasis on the creation of markets by international conglomerates. She also tracks how that key change affected both career paths in publishing and the governance of publishing firms, including an emphasis on accountability. Turow (2006) emphasizes how companies produce economy, effectiveness, and efficiency in their online marketing campaigns by designing a niche for everyone and placing everyone in their niche. Howard (2005) extends that argument to political campaigns and the "creation" of social movements.

Broadly speaking, all of these fields deal in "symbolic or information-loaded products." They are associated with the transmission of the ideological fare that supports a social system. But ideological fare is more than a buttress. Social structure and cultural factors, such as ideological fare, are inextricably linked. Each draws upon and changes the other. Indeed, the connection between ideologies and other social phenomena is so strong that it seems safe to suggest that a change in ideology generally indicates that a change in the structure of society either is occurring or has occurred. More is going on than the "de-churching" of higher education. The state is becoming more interventionist. It is increasingly sticking its auditing and accountability techniques into other institutions' business. Health care provides a case in point.

The health care industry obviously meets one of Hannan and Freeman's (1989) criteria, for they specified that accountability is associated with organizations that deal in "substantial risk, as in medical care." Scott and his associates (2000) emphasize the role of the state, as it imposed its power on professionals to centralize key aspects of health care and then ceded their power to corporate actors. These authors provide periodization of the transformation of health care in the late twentieth century. Their instructive discussion divides late twentieth-century medical care into three periods: *the era of professional dominance* (1945–65), when "professional bodies supported by the state dominated the arena"; *the era of federal involvement* (1965–82), when through Medicaid and Medicare, "the federal government became a major player in healthcare services"; and *the era of managerial control and market mechanisms* (1983–present), when "government policies shifted toward deregulation and a reliance on market forces, and large corporate groups entered the field" (21, 22). In an argument that also applies to the higher-education industry, Scott et al. (2000: 341, 342) suggest that *perceived crises*, such as a perceived *funding* crisis and a perceived crisis in *quality*, prompt state intervention. They add that the expansion of federal regulations prompt an "interventionist regime."

As in the health care industry, an interventionist regime is demanding accountability and is decentering the professionals who once dominated higher education. Starting in the 1970s, American higher education experienced a funding crisis. By the 1990s, universities throughout the world were gearing up to compete with American universities in the global marketplace. They wanted to keep their students home (to eliminate their "brain drain"), to attract dollars by inviting American students for a "year abroad," and to serve their states by building the corporate ties that had proved so attractive to American research universities after the passage of the Bayh-Dole Act of 1980. Government officials began to perceive a crisis in competition and so a crisis in quality, as, for instance, European universities worked to coordinate their offerings with one another and began to attract some Asian students, who a decade earlier might have sought an education in the United States.

The "system of professions" responds to such realignments, including the movement of capital within nations and from one nation to another (Abbott 1988; cf. Larson 1977). In the nineteenth century, British capitalists auditing their investments in the American train system prompted the rise of accountancy in the nineteenth-century United States. In the late twentieth century, states seeking to expand "workforce development" and "corporate competitiveness" encouraged universities to adopt a market logic, to account for their activities, and to abide by the consequences. Accreditation provides another example. It had once been voluntary. Now, since the federal government will only lend monies to students attending accredited institutions, accreditation is essentially mandatory. As both the federal government and the states have pushed for an accountability regime, they have also encouraged rationalization, centralization, the expansion of the staff, and the decentering of the professoriate. The state has been claiming power over institutions that once "volunteered" to work with it.[22]

The sheer power of the state matters. So does the power of the corporations with whom both states and universities are allied. This triumvirate of state, corporation, and university are intertwined in what Etzkowitz and his colleagues (1998) call "the triple helix" that transforms knowledge into capital. They use that term to emphasize the complex interactions among these institutions and to stress that innovations in which they are involved do not evolve in a linear fashion. Etzkowitz (2003: 293) argues that not only do the state and corporations change universities, but universities also have an impact on the corporate world. For instance, as "firms raise their technological level, they move closer to an academic model, engaging in higher levels of training and in sharing of knowledge. Government acts as a public entrepreneur and venture capitalist in addition to its traditional regulatory role in setting the rules of the game."

However, the power of the emerging accountability regime in which the state, the corporate world, and the universities participate does not explain why so few professors at Wannabe University have resisted their own decentering. To be sure, the imposition of the accountability regime has been gradual. It has applied criteria familiar to the professoriate. But why have so few professors even noticed what is going on?

10

The Logic of Compliance

Both organizations and individuals use "logics" to comprehend, justify, and (re)produce the social world as they understand it and so also to constitute their place within it. Logics take their meaning within a social context.[1]

To understand the need for universities to prepare undergraduates for the labor market, one must understand the problems that labor faces in a globalized capitalist economy. One must also accept specific notions of competition within both social and economic relations. Within universities, these notions of competition may drive some professors to try to distinguish themselves by becoming a local, nation, or international "star" (Solomon 2008). To them, the desire to stand out may seem a logical (or commonsensical) pursuit. They may say, "Everyone knows" how terrific it is to be a star. But "everyone" does not "know" the same thing. What one person or group identifies as common sense, another may deem to be irrational. For instance, instead of trying to distinguish themselves in competition with others, the Zuni try to "go with the tide."[2]

Logics may occur together even when they appear to contradict one another. Seemingly antithetical logics may compete, complement one another, or merely coexist. For instance, in the U.S. health care system, the market ethos and professional ethos are found together, although doctors no longer enjoy as much autonomy as they did in the mid-1900s and health care organizations may circumscribe physicians' options and even define the conditions of their work (Scott et al. 2000).[3]

Today universities invoke professional, market, and service logics. In universities, the market logic has not obliterated either the professional logic or the public service logic. Because logics may be used situationally, a manager may invoke one logic in a situation, but another in a different situation. Sometimes all three logics coexist in an uneasy tension and may be used to justify a decision. Indeed, each logic may be used to justify the same decision, for people may simultaneously interpret a phenomenon in terms of past, present, and emerging understandings of how the world does and should work.

International study is a case in point. It exemplifies what for some decades now Americans have called a "win-win" situation. An American university may invoke a service logic to encourage undergraduates to spend a year studying abroad, much as Wannabe's revised 2008 academic plan does, when it says that it "promotes civic involvement and cultural competence in a diverse and global environment." But international study may also aid corporate employers. If up to 30 percent of Wannabe University undergraduates were to study abroad, as that plan proposes, corporate America would benefit. The 2008 academic plan recognizes several ways that corporations and individuals would benefit. The American corporations that might eventually hire these students might become more competitive in a global and "internationalized economy," as might the United States. The students might also become more competitive within the American workforce, since they would be better "prepare[d] . . . for work and personal success as participants in an internationalized economy and an increasingly diverse society," as that 2008 document put it. At the same time, by sending its students abroad, the university might enhance its market position with potential applicants.

Also, under some conditions the university might benefit economically, although one high-level administrator believes that the university would encourage its students to study abroad and foreign students to attend Wan U even if there were no economic payoff. Currently very few international students are Wan U undergraduates. (In 2005 the director of athletics suggested that most of them were on sports teams.) If 30 percent of Wan U students study abroad and a comparable number of international students do not replace them to occupy their seats in classes, the university may not need to hire and tenure as many professors. After all, one can achieve a low student-faculty ratio by either hiring professors or sending undergraduates abroad.

As noted, there are many possibilities for how institutional logics interact with one another; because different groups with varying amounts of power, authority, or influence pledge allegiance to dissimilar logics. One group may be ambivalent about the logic that it embraces, much as Wannabe's provosts and presidents have been so ambivalent about "diversity and multiculturalism" that they could not establish a consistent organizational policy. It is also possible that one group might invoke an institutional logic in order to minimize conflict.

I believe that the central administrators involved in academic decisions recognized the importance of market logic to their jobs, but also believed they were devoted to "core academic values" (the professional logic) such as freedom of inquiry and a belief in how the humanities and the arts enrich people's lives. They might not have even realized that these logics conflicted. In early 2008, they seemed genuinely surprised when scientists criticized a preliminary version of the academic plan for subjugating the humanities and fine arts to "workforce development." In response, the next version of the plan mentioned the humanities and the fine arts in the context of "cultural enrichment," a logic that had been central to American research universities since the nineteenth century (Keohane 2006). Perhaps the central administration's claim to espouse this now-traditional logic helped the professoriate to ignore how the process of transforming Wannabe University also involved a devotion to a market ethos, the escalation of an accountability regime, and the decentering of the professoriate.

COMPETING LOGICS

We have seen that Wannabe University's top administrators make no bones about their commitment to the market logic. Their commitment to that ethos permeates the 2008 academic plan, but seems less central to the plans that some of the colleges and schools had drafted a few years earlier. I am going to pay particular attention to two plans, the 2008 draft university plan and the 2006 plan of the College of Liberal Arts and Sciences. Although the college's plan was undertaken and finished at the behest of Provost Wesley, who had also hoped to have completed the university's plan by 2006, the college plan was eventually to be revised to achieve consistency with the university's document once the board of trustees adopted it.

While the 2008 university academic plan invokes service and enrichment, it also stresses "the importance of collaborating with the State and with partners in the private sector to develop new products, processes, and entrepreneurial opportunities, and thus to foster economic growth and opportunity. . . ." As the central administrators see it, Wan U's strategic emphasis on the use of practical knowledge to alleviate daily problems, which President Whitmore and President Daniels had advocated in their inaugural addresses, is both politically and fiscally wise. By joining forces with both the state and local corporations, Wannabe University helps them and, even more important, helps itself. (Both heaven and capitalism "help him who helps himself.") By allying itself with the interests of the state and its corporations, the university reminds both the governor and the legislature that funding the university ultimately helps the state. Not only does it help to prevent the state's "brain drain," but also it helps to generate corporate income and so more jobs and more taxes. Also, if and when the university were to generate significant earnings by working with corporations, it might be able to address its own real and imagined budgetary shortages. Real shortages include the need to hire full-time faculty since the expansion of the student population in the 1990s. Students, faculty, and administrators were so aware of that shortage that "we must hire more full-time faculty" had become a Wannabe mantra. Imagined budgetary shortages included the specter of the state's economic rescissions that had afflicted Wannabe University in the 1990s and could appear again.[4] The market logic has amassed some accomplishments, including the transformation of students into consumers, of education into a commodity, of research into a revenue stream, as well as the imposition of centralized authority on academic matters. But professors still insist on the importance of "free inquiry." They give more than lip service to that concept, as seen in the logics embraced by the College of Liberal Arts and Sciences.

The 2006 strategic plan of Wannabe University's College of Liberal Arts and Sciences invoked conflicting logics. It consistently expressed a belief that applied research should be "responsive to the needs of communities and businesses." However, the college also insisted that "in the liberal arts, knowledge arises from the ongoing questioning of conventional beliefs about society and nature, which leads to the never-ending development and refinement of arguments and to the novel syntheses of existing ideas via new perspectives and information." Indeed, the college's plan stresses a traditional understanding of the importance of the arts and sciences.[5] As mentioned, when the college's faculty spoke at one of the provost's faculty and staff forums on the 2008 strategic plan, even the scientists were fervent in their insistence that the arts and humanities are essential to the mission of a research university and are not about workforce development.[6]

Some professors pointed to Dean Todd Alden's accomplishments in the humanities. He had established an Institute for the Humanities, which offered intellectual fare to the entire university. He consistently supported academic programs that never might be expected to become a revenue stream, such as the Department of Philosophy. Although his own research had not been humanist, he read novels and had collected art. Dean Alden seemed to value knowledge for its own sake. As a physicist put it, "He is one of us." The last batch of associate deans whom Dean Alden had appointed included scholars. One was a distinguished professor; another amassed federal grants; a third had won awards for his distinguished publications. Yet Dean Alden also cared about market forces. Rejecting the tenure of scientists who had not brought in grants or contracts, he had "hung tough" when he insisted that Wan U must maintain standards. When Provost Wesley spoke at Todd Alden's retirement party, he praised him for increasing his college's endowment. Nonetheless, if some Wannabe professors did not want to notice that their university was increasingly embracing a market logic, they could point to the urbane Dean Alden.

Other logics also discouraged some professors from noticing that change had occurred. One was the national orientation inherent in their profession. Educated at research universities often by professors who defined themselves by their work, encouraged to present their scholarship at professional meetings, financially rewarded for their scholarly achievements, some professors simply didn't care much about local affairs. Since they were caught up in their own research and their own lives, Wannabe University seemed to be merely their employer. It provided the context in which they did their important work, but it did not define the parameters of their lives. To be sure, these men and women understood that they had to have a job, but they played out their "careers" on a broader panorama, the national and international "invisible colleges" of their scholarly endeavors. Relatively few of them went to key meetings, such as the faculty forums on teaching (discussed in chapter 6), the provost's 2006 discussions of the academic plan with members of the several schools and colleges (perhaps 15 percent of the CLAS faculty attended their meeting with the provost), and the provost's 2008 discussion with the university faculty about the then-current draft of the academic plan (perhaps 150 of the roughly 1,000 professors with offices on the Ashton campus). Even fewer of them seemed to read the minutes of the University Senate and the monthly e-mail sent by its Executive Committee. (The head of the 2007–2009 Senate Executive Committee wished that faculty who were not in the Senate had contacted him about Senate matters; he felt he had encouraged them to do so.) As Lewis (1996) emphasizes, some professors viewed colleagues who participated in shared governance and frequented interminable meetings as "failed academics" (non-publishers). At Wan U some professors held this view, even though distinguished professors and accomplished grant-getters served in the University Senate and were on the Graduate Faculty Council. For instance, after attending the meetings of the Graduate Faculty Council as a favor to his department head, one professor, who had won prestigious awards in his specialty, criticized the other participants. He muttered: "They take themselves so seriously." However, this economist took his research so seriously that he rarely if ever participated in university affairs and so might not have known which of the other departmental representatives at the Graduate Faculty Council were thought to be distinguished in their own fields. One person from a politically engaged family who was also active in

campus affairs might have been referring to him when she said, "The problem at this university is like the problem in this country. Everyone thinks
that someone else will do the work to fix it."

Another reason that professors might not have noticed change was their
acceptance of measurement and so their acceptance of auditing and accountability. Like other members of contemporary society, they had come
to accept the ubiquity of counting and ranking—what sociologists call
"commensuration." As Espeland and Stevens (1994: 314) explain, commensuration is "the transformation of different qualities into a common
metric. . . . Whether it takes the form of rankings, ratios, or elusive prices,
whether it is used to inform consumers and judge competitors, assuage a
guilty conscience, or represent disparate forms of value, commensuration
is crucial to how we categorize and make sense of the world" (cf. Espeland
and Sauder 2007). The earliest application of commensuration to higher
education probably occurred in 1792, when British universities began to
grade students. Today, though, as the British sociologist Mary Evans (2004:
33) points out, in England "testing has become something of a national pas-
time (for those of course for whom it is not already a professional career) in
that schools, universities and the culture itself participate in the support,
creation, and transmission of tests about all aspects of human life. We test
and monitor our weight, our health, our ability to parent and to form lasting relationships." Like the British professors of whom Evans wrote, American professors are accustomed to giving accounts of their activities. In the
course of their daily life, they may fill out so many forms, that, like other
Americans, they may not think twice when reminded that their activities
constitute data (Howard 2006; cf. Turow 2006). In the United States, popular media invite us to test ourselves against television contestants such as
those on *Jeopardy!* and also to vote to place contestants in ranks that will
have a significant impact on their lives (*American Idol*, based on the British
show *Pop Idol*). The online news media, including the online version of the
State Capital Record, invite "users" to participate in opinion polls and to
rank the usefulness of news stories.

Testing, categorizing, and ranking have become so commonplace that
even very bright and observant people might not notice that these activities
are consequential. For instance, at a spring 2008 meeting of the Faculty
Standards Committee, Jeanne Sharpe suggested that assessment is "just"
organizing data into categories, putting "different things in different bas-
kets." She seemed stunned when a committee member reminded her that
even routine audits, such as the annual self-audits (1040 forms) submitted
to the Internal Revenue Service, may be read as a set of instructions about

how to behave. (Donate to charity by December 31; contribute to your re-tirement by April 16.) Embarrassed yet willing to admit her own errors, she volunteered, "I said something foolish."

Indeed, so many people take it so much for granted that one needs to "mine data" (or at the very least "consult" them) in order to make "respon-sible decisions" that it seems downright naive to suggest that significant decisions be made without analyzing data. An actor who eschews data may seem especially foolish when the data may be easily expressed as quantifi-able variables. "How else would you judge the quality of academic contribu-tions?" an American academic asked, when told that the British Research Assessment Exercise graded faculty publications as good, of national im-portance, or of international importance. *And that is just the point. Auditing quality is so ubiquitous that it is common sense.* Professors grade students to make them accountable. Administrators order faculties to devise ways to grade professors so that they will be accountable. Regional accreditation agencies grade colleges and universities in ways that are consequential. In all of these exercises, an administrator is supposed to follow the sort of pro-fessional guidelines recommended at business schools: Gather data, prefer-ably quantitative data, to analyze the likely outcome of an action and so to facilitate the decision about whether to take that action.[7] The context in which the Wannabe University administration and the professors explained these decisions made explicit their understanding that the methods of col-lecting and analyzing the data, including the definition of categories, sig-nificantly affect their decisions about how to act. And that, both groups appeared to believe, is "how it should be." As Mary Douglas observed (1992; quoted in Power 1997: 1), today "accountability and account-giving are part of what it means to be a rational individual."[8]

MAINTAINING LEGITIMACY

When change occurs in a gradual way, people may not even notice that something is different. In chapter 5, we saw that the central administration was introducing some changes slowly. Some structural factors also made it relatively easy for the administration to maintain legitimacy. One of these was the composition of the University Senate. Another was the "headship system." A third was the faculty itself.

THE SENATE

The University Senate is one leg of "shared governance." At most American colleges and universities, this body is a faculty senate. In the spirit of reform, during the Vietnam era Wan U broadened participation and redefined its

faculty senate as a university senate, which included administrative officers (deans), faculty members, professional staff (such as a librarian, the
registrar, a nurse), and undergraduate and graduate students. Numerically,
the faculty dominates the Senate; it holds 72 of the 91 seats.[9] In addition,
14 central administrators serve ex officio and regularly attend meetings.
In 2007–2008, three of the elected faculty senators were Asian American;
two elected senators had Latino names; historically there have been elected
African American senators. Everyone else was white.

Although the chairperson of the University's Senate Executive Committee in the academic years 2006–2008 frequently stated how fortunate this
elected body was to enjoy shared governance, the administration seems to
share more governance than the faculty. In the academic year 2007–2008,
five of the nine non-student members of the elected Senate Executive Committee either served or had once served Wan U in some administrative
capacity—either in a dean's office (two), in the provost's office (one), or
as head or associate head of a significant unit or department (one). (One
member was a student.) Also, the Senate deemed two key ex officio members so important that it informally broke its own bylaws to hear them.
Those bylaws specified an order of business: consideration of the minutes,
report from the Executive Committee, and next report from other committees. However, every meeting started with consideration of the minutes, a
report from the president or provost, and then the report from the Executive Committee.

Sometimes the presence of "administrative officers" (deans) and "ex officio members" (central administrators) seemed to stifle debate. At least,
relatively few elected senators spoke up at Senate meetings. One faculty
senator thought it was difficult to speak for the first time and that the longer a senator put off speaking, the harder it got to stand and say one's piece.
Others did not want to participate in controversial debates. "I am not a
person who favors confrontation," one respected senator said, when he rose
to question a presidential plan. Like many professors, he preferred to work
with the administration. Indeed, some professors felt that cooperating with
the administration was the only way to achieve one's goals. Thus, one professor said of a task force on which she served: "We know that they [the
administration] are trying to use us. We're not naive. But we all agree that
half a loaf is better than none." A member of another task force countered
criticism that he had sold out by exclaiming, "At least we're trying to do
something."

There were also other reasons for remaining silent at Senate meetings.
Some senators realized that the longer the meeting, the hungrier they would
get, since the meetings started at 4:00 in the afternoon. Still others found

meetings a formality. "The real business of the Senate occurs in its committees," a faculty member on the Executive Committee said. "Real business"
is also transacted at the Executive Committee's routine meetings with the
president and provost and also with groups of administrators. After the head
of a Senate committee talks about her committee's activities with the "Senate exec," the exec might choose to broach the topic with the president or
provost. It might recommend a structural or policy change; the central administrator might (or might not) accept the recommendation. How the various partners in these discussions view one another affects the outcome.

The composition of the University Senate seemed to encourage the central administration to see it as a tool to facilitate changes that the administrators favored. In his blog, President Daniels wrote, "A good feature of
our Senate is its inclusion of professional staff, graduate and undergraduate students in its membership. As Wan U matures and moves to greater
integration of academic programs—including graduate and undergraduate instruction, research, and community outreach—this forward-looking
structure of our Senate is well-suited to be an important contributor to discussions and initiatives in the coming year."

Senior faculty members with experience at major research universities
felt that the inclusion of administrators as ex officio and elected members
of the Senate muted dissent. "What's wrong with our Senate is who's in it.
Maybe the Senate would stand up for the faculty more, if it were a faculty
senate," one senior professor offered. "Most first-rate research institutions
[like the one where I used to teach] have a faculty senate." However, as
members of the Executive Committee saw it, the composition of the Senate and the Executive Committee could be an aid when seeking solutions
to problems. "I work with these people every day," one Executive Committee member said of central administrators. This person knew them well
enough to feel they respected her opinion. Needing a powerful ally on the
board of trustees, another member of the Executive Committee said, "Contacting [that trustee] is a good suggestion. I know him. I've presented before him and his committee twice." Some members of the Executive Committee seemed to feel that the mix of faculty and administrators increased
their credibility and so their ability to work informally for the good of all.
Some faculty wished for a senate that put the professoriate first.

DEPARTMENTAL STRUCTURE

The structure of Wan U's academic departments might also have discouraged faculty from speaking out. Instead of having elected chairpersons leading academic departments, Wannabe University has a "strong head system."
The terms "chairperson" and "headship" are meaningful. The title "chair-

person" implies collegial professionalism (Wolverton and Gmelch 2002); the title "head," bureaucratic hierarchy. I asked two ex-administrators about this distinction. Each had served as a department head and in the offices of deans and provosts. One who claimed to be process-oriented explained that a "head has authority, even power." He added, "I believe in a system of chairmen [sic]. That connotes colleagues acting together democratically. But we have a headship system here." The other, either more product-oriented or a politically sensitive fellow, disagreed. "There's really no difference between how you behave as a chair or as a head. It depends on the institution. In some institutional contexts, you have to share. In others you don't. When I was a head at Wan U, I shared information I might not have shared as the chair of my previous department [at another university]. I had to share at Wan U because my department had all these people running around with copies of our bylaws." What counts is that both men had a vision of working with colleagues.

Some departments had bylaws that encouraged heads to share responsibilities with "his" or "her" professors; some did not. In other departments, heads might choose to share. But the department head who viewed himself as working *for* his colleagues was rare indeed. At a reception, I was speaking with Chet Muller when an assistant professor in his department joined us; she reminded me that I knew her parents and had known her when she was young. "You work for Chet Muller now," I said. Muller corrected me, "No, I work for her." When I related this incident to several professors, they essentially said, "That's why he's such a good head; I wish my head thought like that." The department heads made recommendations for promotion and tenure; they were legally responsible for decisions about course loads, merit raises, and office assignments. They did not have to consult their senior faculty about their decisions. They could choose to tell their professors what had been discussed in the dean's meetings with department heads, but they did not have to do so. Indeed, heads might make seemingly significant decisions without consulting either their faculty or their department's elected Executive Committee. Although the contract between the faculty union, a chapter of the American Association of University Professors, and the administration contained a method to depose a department head, it was virtually impossible to do so; deans routinely backed department heads. Old-timers could think of only one instance in the past twenty-five years, when professors managed to convince a dean to recall a department head. However, that seeming high level of professorial and deaconal support did not indicate contentment and happiness.

Earlier, I noted that in 2003 members of several departments in the College of Liberal Arts and Sciences were squabbling. In two departments in the humanities, faculty in opposing camps were barely talking to one another. In several social science departments, professors were sending one another rude e-mails. One senior professor noted that his young colleagues, especially those who were untenured, wondered about the consequences of the discord for their careers. In the School of Engineering, younger and older professors expressed conflicting priorities. People in the School of Business were celebrating the arrival of a new dean; most had disliked the old dean; some had detested him so much that they called around the country to alert colleagues whenever they heard that he had applied for another deanship. In 2003 not many professors at Wannabe University emitted the glow of happy campers. I suspect they were becoming inert.

CREEPING LEGITIMACY, CREEPING PRESSURE

The gradual institutionalization of the administration's legitimacy over academic matters has helped to feed professorial inertia. In an e-mail, an informant explained: "It's like the proverbial frog in the pot. If you drop the sucker in boiling water, he will jump out; but if you increase the heat slowly enough, he eventually finds himself boiled. The administration and feds and state are increasing the heat under our pot fairly slowly." The analogy is apt. It recalls the comment of the University of Michigan's ex-president James Duderstadt (2000): a university president faces the task of keeping the frogs from jumping out of the wheelbarrow—of leaving for a job at another university. Although many Wannabe University professors are accomplished scholars, they are probably not as likely as University of Michigan professors to be offered a job or to receive "feelers from other universities." Even if they quickly notice that the pot is getting hotter, they may have no place to jump. Others may not want to jump. They may choose to endure the heat for personal or family reasons. For instance, their children may want to graduate from high school with their friends from elementary school.

Presidents and provosts increased the pressure on deans.[10] Deans increased the pressure on department heads. Fewer and fewer department heads stood up to the deans. "I don't want to say anything about this matter to the dean," a department head told a colleague. "I have other important matters to discuss with him, things I think we need more. I don't want to use up my credit." Deans had once adjudicated between the collegiality of departments and the bureaucracy of the central administration (Wolverton and Gmelch 2002). By 2003 department heads mediated between deans and colleagues.

Also by 2003 some faculty had slowly learned to accept decreasing professorial power and others were learning to do so. Having the right to make certain types of decisions included having the responsibility to attend meetings and to complete more committee assignments. To many, doing more of anything, let alone everything, seemed at the very least an unacceptable demand and at the very most a detestable chore. Especially after the central administration increased the student-teacher ratio, demands on faculty increased. (Recall in the 1990s, the central administration increased the undergraduate population, an unusually large number of professors retired as part of a "golden handshake," and the administration did not hire enough faculty to replace them—let alone expand the faculty to take into account the expanded undergraduate enrollment.) As discussed in chapter 8, the pressure to do more—teach more undergraduates, spend more time advising undergraduates, get more grants, publish more books and articles, graduate more Ph.D.'s, sponsor more postdocs—was taking its toll. Although when asked, both Provost Johnson and Provost Wesley had agreed that one person "can't do everything," each man seemed to harbor a secret belief that too many professors were slacking off—or so it seemed to faculty.

Under pressure to complete tasks, few people volunteered to assume more tasks. Perhaps that pressure explains why so few older professors in the College of Liberal Arts and Sciences complained when Dean Todd Alden held only one college meeting a year. Before Dean Alden's arrival in 1996, that college's deans had convened several meetings a year. They were "bravura affairs," one old-timer recalled. "Everyone went. . . . Why? We discussed the curriculum and everyone wanted to make sure that their department's ox would not be gored." Dean Alden called annual meetings to approve some curriculum changes and to approve the granting of degrees, as mandated by the bylaws. In 2008 roughly sixty of the six hundred professors attended, many of them members of the large curriculum committee. "Now," the same old-timer offered, "the dean doesn't have to call a meeting to make some kinds of changes. He just does it." The older professors don't seem to care. Once upon a time, an older professor advised, a provost might have said, "That's an academic decision; a department should decide it." He added that nowadays the provost isn't about to cede authority. Rather, provosts and their staffs are busy taking on more and more.

Adjusting to the decisions of the deans, the central administrators, and their department heads, younger professors don't know that business was ever conducted in another way. They didn't realize that a tradition of shared governance meant that some sorts of decisions were reserved for the departments, not the central administration, and that those decisions were to be reached democratically. As older professors retired and the university became more centralized, the young assistant and associate professors lost access to "institutional memory." They did not know the way it once had been.[11]

WEAK SOCIAL CONTROL MECHANISMS

As deans and central administrators take on more and more, professors are left with less and less. Careful not to contradict their bureaucratic superiors in public, acting as though they were members of a mechanistic bureaucracy, most professors watch their p's and q's. Almost all behave as though administrators could fire them or, at the very least, make their working conditions most unpleasant.

Every now and then, a professor gets out of line. A few professors do so with some regularity. He accuses all of his colleagues of lying. She screams at people in department meetings. He has a temper tantrum in the dean's office or the computer center. He has a grant to do research that "buys off" his teaching, so he moves a thousand miles away and shows up at Wan U five times a year. Professors tell one another that if the Accuser or the Screamer or the Researcher-Missing-in-Action worked in a corporation, he or she might have been fired years ago. "My son's corporation would never put up with that." However, academics can get away with ignoring some of the rules, especially if they are bringing in money.[12]

So can central administrators. Both professors and administrators talk about a provost who was hired to do a specific task—say, write an academic plan—but took three years to do so. They comment about the administrator who couldn't fire anyone. They tell one another about the administrator who couldn't balance a budget. Or the one who didn't read the executive summaries placed on his desk. They talk about an administrator who was told that his contract would not be renewed after his current five-year contract was up, and some of them whisper about waiting for someone's five-year contract to be up.

However, no one talks about administrators being fired for not doing their jobs. Though their careers follow a corporate path, they appear to have a professional exemption from corporate practice. Although vice provosts may proclaim, "We serve at the pleasure of the president," and note that they can be returned to their academic departments, no one expects the corporate president or provost to return from whence he came, the presidency, provostship, or deanship of another university. Nor do professors expect them to return to teaching; some presidents and provosts haven't taught in years. Rather, some professors who have served as administrators advise that it is difficult to fire the corporate presidents and provosts. They have complex five-year contracts.

Resentment mounts as the accountability regime increasingly sets the conditions of professors' work lives. A few older and well-published professors are now saying publicly, even at University Senate committee meetings, "I know who's watching me, but who's watching them?" One criticizes, "It's all about revenue and rankings, the market." Another says that the people in his wife's corporation "don't have five-year contracts like that. It's simple: If you don't make a profit, if you mess up too big, you leave." To be fair, of the last seven provosts and presidents, at least four were either fired or encouraged to resign near the end of their five-year term. Nonetheless, to the faculty, the central administrators seem to be emulating aspects of the market ethos—but not the one that says if you don't do your job well, you get fired. Professors seem to feel that the market logic goes just so far.

WHAT'S UP AT WAN U?

The original European universities were the institutional children of the Catholic Church. Harvard and Yale were founded to train Protestant clergy. A variety of churches, but churches nonetheless, founded a host of local liberal arts colleges in the early nineteenth century. Today other forces are also participating in the development of higher education. Making higher education subordinate to other non-church institutions, through centralization, rationalization, and corporatization, these forces have been engaging in the de-sanctification of universities. The classic professions—medicine, law, academia—are being transformed as the state eases the way for market forces. New institutional logics, pervasive auditing, and an accountability regime have fed an emphasis on workforce and capital development. Together they announce that knowledge is simply not to be valued in and of itself.

Perhaps knowledge never was valued for itself. Just as today's public universities are becoming subordinated to the state, those first European and American colleges were subordinated to religious institutions. Similarly, the Morrill Act, which established the land-grant universities, was not intended to promote pure knowledge, but rather to serve the states. It is difficult, if not impossible, to locate the fount of pure knowledge. An absolutely unreliable source says that it was once housed in the Seven Cities of Cibola, but it may now be found between the Building for Undergraduate Education and the Wan U Art Museum.

As for Wannabe University, it will prosper. Reshaping the university by cutting programs and investing wisely, its corporate administrators will probably manage to "grow its faculty" and perhaps even to reduce the student-faculty ratio, though not the size of lecture classes. Nor are they likely to check the growth of its staff. "Old-timers" in the professoriate recall the moment in the 1990s when the central administration ordered department heads and deans to cease and desist their practice of giving every professor a "merit raise." If every professor receives such a raise, the then-provost declared, the raises are not based on merit. These professors no longer express anger or surprise that in the same year everyone working in Top Hall received a raise. (Apparently, they were all meritorious.) Increasingly, professors began to understand that the central administrators and many deans are corporate administrators who come, try to place their stamp on the organization, and go. They also realize that the corporate administrators genuinely want public research universities to survive, even as many professors wish that the new administrators would find different ways for the university to endure and to serve the state.

In 2008 the corporatization of Wannabe University is proceeding apace. New deans with initial loyalty to Provost Wesley are arriving. With one exception, the announcements for the new deans have discussed their administrative experience before mentioning their scholarly quality. For example:

> [At his current job, the new dean] is responsible for budgets and recruitment and retention of faculty. He has overseen innovations in teaching. . . .
>
> He is a co-investigator on a National Science Foundation grant that is designed to increase the number of minority students seeking degrees in technical fields such as math, science, and engineering.
>
> He also has worked toward increasing faculty diversity, introducing measures to broaden hiring searches and to support the appointment of women in science and technical fields.
>
> [His disciplinary] research is in . . .

That announcement seemed particularly noteworthy since some professors interpreted the new dean's experience with issues of diversity as the final death knell to the Office of Multiculturalism and International Affairs. The new dean was qualified to have his college absorb components of the old office.

The 2008 academic plan will be approved by the board of trustees. The last time a full academic plan was presented to the board, trustees criticized it for being too vague. "These statements apply to a lot of fields," one had objected. "I can't tell what you intend to do, how you're going to invest . . ." This time the academic plan is much more specific. It names academic fields in which the university should invest. It offers a plan to identify disciplines where the university should divest. In theory at least, the plan should eliminate organizational ambivalence. In practice, it probably will not.

The pressure to get grants will not abate. Grants will probably be part of the productivity measure used to decide which graduate programs will fold. E-mails from the vice provost for research and dean of the graduate school to the faculty Listserv will continue to announce seminars where one may learn how to patent one's discoveries and profit from one's research. (That job has been redefined so the next occupant will be the vice president for research and dean of the graduate school; he will have more direct responsibility over more units. At a public meeting, President Daniels announced that this arrangement is "how it's done at the top research universities.") The *Wannabe Weekly* will continue to spotlight professorial inventions and to hint at the possibility of striking it big, maybe even buying a McMansion on the same street as some of the professors who had previously patented their findings.

The provost's office will continue to pressure the faculty to improve its teaching. The Institute for Teaching and Learning will offer suggestions to old professors and new professors, graduate assistants, and maybe even the staff teaching the first-year experience courses, should any of them wish to drop by the institute to take a short seminar. The institute is even going to offer for-credit courses on teaching to graduate students. The central administration will continue to mount experiments in the Building for Undergraduate Education, where the institute is located. "When they want to do something with teaching, they try it there first," a former dean said. "They're [the staff are] easier to fire than we [professors] are." (In spring 2008, middle managers in the BUE wondered when Provost Wesley would leave and whether Jeanne Sharpe would depart too. Her big mistake, a few of them said, was to be so loyal to the provost.)

President, provosts, and deans will continue to be corporate administrators. To behave ethically, they will continue *not* to volunteer information; the less one says, the less likely one will tell a lie, and lying is not ethical. To protect their units, they will continue to tuck bits and pieces of their budgets in out-of-the-way places. The trick is to protect oneself, while seeming transparent. They understand that, as used today, the concept of transparency is an outgrowth of audits. As Strathern (2000: 292) puts it, "Now audit endorses transparency as one of its own aims. . . . Auditing thus reinforces the requirement that administrators in all kinds of professions become more managerial and accountable." Some administrators will continue to make supportive statements about topics that make them feel ambivalent, such as diversity; Wan U will increasingly invest in international education. Wan U's administrators just don't have the confidence *not to conform* by following current best practices on a matter that everyone has agreed is as important as preparing students (and the state) for the global economy. Few people discuss that old service hacksaw "doing what's right." Besides, more international students can compensate for the demographic decrease of high school graduates in the region.

Wan U will remain a conformist university doing what must be done to elbow its way up the rankings, to survive in and to serve the neo-liberal state. It will increasingly impose an accountability regime. As the decades pass, working at a university will become more and more like working in the corporate world, although professors are quick to point out that they still have more freedoms than their counterparts in corporations.[13] Here and there, my expectations will prove wrong. Perhaps the Senate group pushing for a renewed emphasis on multiculturalism and diversity will succeed. Its members can always invoke the logic that Mike Sugarman used when he was head of the Wan U Board of Trustees: Teaching students to work with people who are not like them (and by extension to operate in a multicultural world) is good for business. And as President Daniels and Provost Wesley remind, diversity is a key component of the new academic plan.

President Rick Daniels is a scholar, the first scholar with a position of power in the central administration in almost two decades. He shares many faculty values. Yet professors insist that "his stock has fallen" since the second faculty forum on the 2008 academic plan, when his words and attitude made it clear that he likes to get his own way. At least one respected professor has publicly announced that he does "not trust Rick Daniels." (Trust is, of course, a prerequisite for people to work constructively together. "You don't have to like each other," a canny administrator once told me. "But you do have to be able to trust that the people you are dealing with will keep their word.") This professor notes that Daniels was not willing to listen to faculty when he was positive that his preferred course of action was clearly the "best practice." Nonetheless, Rick Daniels presents himself as being much more open to students than was his predecessor, James Whitmore, as each man demonstrated in their inaugural address.

Each president had inserted a little bit of himself in a seemingly off-the-cuff remark during his address. The contrasting comments bespeak contrasting styles. Standing tall and formal, James Whitmore had quoted Clark Kerr's famous comment, "I have sometimes thought of [the university] as a series of individual faculty entrepreneurs held together by a common grievance over parking." Rick Daniels greeted his wife, brothers and sisters, son and daughter. Smiling warmly, he noted grandchildren arrayed before him. He wiggled his fingers at them and said, "You are being very, very good, clapping to the music."

Some professors enjoyed President Daniels's obvious fondness for young people, including undergraduates. Others found it undignified. Though not a scholar, James Whitmore was more presidential, they said. Nonetheless, Rick Daniels will do what has to be done to invest the state's monies wisely and to assuage both taxpayer and legislative resentment of never-ending raises in tuition. He will "mine data," cut and chop, and make "business-like" decisions. He will present himself as someone who cares about the students, not just what they learn, but also how they live during their years at Wannabe University—though it's also his job to care about breaking even. Rick Daniels seems to enjoy getting to know people, although professors have not been quick to strike up friendships with him.

As the accountability regime matures, that may be as good as it gets. James Whitmore was right: Wannabe University is being transformed.

Acknowledgments

"I can't wait to read the acknowledgments," my editor Doug Mitchell said after he had read a very early draft of some chapters for this book. I thank him for his faith in this project, but I am sorry to disappoint, for I can mention very few of the people who helped me. I can't even thank my informants still working at Wannabe University, for I did what I could to protect them from being implicated in my collection of data. I had a general policy of not interviewing my friends. I also made it a point to let people know about my research so they could watch what they said to me and around me in order *not* to serve as informants. I can't even thank by name the professors and administrators who nonetheless spoke with me and who consented to be interviewed, for to do so is to broadcast the identity of this pseudonymous university. Nonetheless, I do thank explicitly the professors and staff of Wannabe University who put up with my presence even when they realized that I was writing a book in which they might appear.

I also thank several people who work or worked at Wannabe who read chapters for me. I asked them if I had described certain practices and processes with sufficient accuracy, and they were good enough to tell me when I had or had not. Frequently, they confined their remarks to "That's not how it works" or "That's not what happened," and so alerted me to the need to look again. Sometimes they noted, "You took some license here. But that's okay; that's how it works." I appreciated such statements, for I felt as though these readers were acknowledging some of the ethical dilemmas in which I sometimes found myself as I tried to disguise who had said what.

I am fortunate to work with Claudio Benzecry, Bandana Purkayastha, and Clint Sanders, three of the outstanding University of Connecticut sociologists who do qualitative work. They were kind enough to discuss ethical issues and principles of participant observation with me. Mark Abrahamson was generous in sharing his expertise on the sociology of organizations, as were several other sociologists whom I called when I realized that I just hadn't read enough. I appreciate the help of Paul DiMaggio, Steven Brint, and Calvin Morrill, who recommended some really useful books and articles. I am very grateful to Howard Becker and Walter W. Powell, who offered terrific critiques of both an early version and the penultimate version of this manuscript. Erin DeWitt, my copy editor, was a joy to work with. I am particularly glad that I have good friends who ask insightful questions. Barrie Thorne, Caroline Persell, Mark Abrahamson, and Richard Rockwell read an early draft of early chapters and shared ideas that made me think.

I started this book in 2003 and finished it in 2008. Before I began collecting these data, I had not tackled a very large research project for over a decade. I would like to thank the people who lost their temper and so prompted me to lose mine. As a result, I began to ask questions about what was happening to higher education today. I hope that my answers are useful to other professors at other colleges and universities, and that they, too, can recognize the changing world in which we live.

Notes

CHAPTER 1

1 Stevens (2007) discusses the flow of applications at a prestigious, private liberal arts college. Although the chase after better rankings clearly concerns status, Stevens also emphasizes the re-production of social class. The title of his ethnography, *Creating a Class*, simultaneously refers to the admissions process through which the college creates a freshman class and the reproduction of social class. Stevens describes how the college's admissions procedures and the stratification of public and private high schools articulate to make the admission of white upper-class and upper-middle-class students more likely than the admission of other sorts of students. For an account of the history of admissions to exclusive colleges, see Karabel (2005). Staff in the Wan U bursar's office feel that the families of today's Wan U students are wealthier than those of twenty years ago.

2 The vice president for student affairs "pays close attention to the residence and dining halls, which make money," an administrator who reported to him said. "Without those programs," according to another administrator, "I wouldn't be here. They pay for what I do."

3 In sociology, "transformation" has a more technical meaning. Scott et al. (2000: 24, 25) point out that "profound institutional change" is (1) multilevel and (2) discontinuous, (3) involves new rules and governance mechanisms, (4) new logics, (5) new actors, (6) new meanings, (7) new relations among actors, modified population boundaries and modified field boundaries.

4 I am gong to write as though all colleges and universities are nonprofits. There are, however, roughly eight hundred for-profit higher-educational institutions (Ruch 2001: 61).

5 These examples are merely illustrative. At Wannabe University, as at some corporate headquar-ters, many services performed by hourly employees are outsourced to save money.

6 Thus, it seemed quite appropriate when in 2007 Wannabe University installed the former town manager of a city with over sixty thousand residents as vice president and chief operating officer.

7 Some sociologists speak of a "market logic" rather than a "market ethos." Friedland and Alford (1991: 243) explain that institutions are "both supraorganizational patterns of activity by which in-dividuals and organizations produce and reproduce their material subsistence and organize time and space. They are also symbolic systems, ways of ordering reality, thereby rendering experience of time and space meaningful." Accordingly, the institutions and individuals define and consti-tute logics. Friedland and Alford identify the capitalist market, a macro-societal phenomenon, as a key institutional logic (232). Although the terms "ethos" and "logic" have different connota-tions, I shall use them as though they are interchangeable.

According to Charles Smith (2004), since markets are by definition a social arrangement for determining value, higher education has been involved in markets for some time. As he puts it, markets are "mechanisms for establishing a consensual definition of goods and services under conditions of ambiguity" (71). Thus, because they are designed to achieve consensus about often-controversial policies, one can discuss faculty promotion and tenure committees and curriculum committees as markets. To Smith, the most important difference between today's universities and those of a hundred years ago is the degree of managerial (or administrative) centralization.

8 According to the "new institutionalism," professional associations pay a significant role in organizations' response to internal and external exigencies. Through association with one another, Powell and DiMaggio (1991) report, professionals exchange information about solutions to problems that their organizations face.

9 Wilson (2007) reports that some small colleges are adding football to attract more male students. As a result, they are increasing their enrollment and also earning more money. However, in *Unpaid Professionals*, Andrew Zimbalist (1999) argues that the athletic departments of universities rarely break even and notes that his generalization is difficult to prove, because of variation in how athletics departments report their budgets.

10 Members of the board and the board's minutes referred to its head as "chairman" rather than "chair." I will follow their practice.

11 According to Martin and Samuels (2004) in the *Chronicle of Higher Education*, "College presidents leave their positions more frequently today than ever before. In the previous generation, the typical term of office might have been a decade or more. But the average length of service for higher education's chief executives has shortened significantly. By 1990 the average term had been reduced in some institutional categories to little more than five years. Various sources project that in a given year, one-fourth to one-third of the accredited colleges and universities in the United States are either preparing for or engaged in presidential searches."

12 Espeland and Stevens (1998) provide a fine introduction to sociological approaches to ranking and measurement. From the point of view of the sociology of culture, what's involved here is a competition for distinction (see Bourdieu 1984) and celebrity (see Gamson 1994). However, in the context of higher education, the claim of a university or college to be ranked high among its peers may also involve the reproduction of social class (see Stevens 2007).

13 Espeland and Sauder (2007) analyze how *U.S. News & World Report*'s ranking of law schools influence admissions to law schools. In essence, they reify the schools' status and affect admissions.

14 One irony is that several decades ago, Harvard was itself a quasi-wannabe, its president James Conant working to transform it from a regional Brahmin university to a national meritocratic university (Keller and Keller 2007: xiii, 49).

15 In a process in which some administrators at Wan U hoped to participate, some of the supposed "best" of the research universities imitate other institutions rather than to strike out on their own (on Harvard, see Bradley 2005; cf. Keller and Keller 2007; on Elon University, see Keller 2004). Kraatz (1998) suggests that institutions imitate colleges and universities in their networks rather than those that are elite.

16 The term "accountability regime" is becoming common in the literatures about education and management. I first encountered it in Shore and Wright (2000) and Giri (2000: 187). Smith (2004) uses the term to discuss deprofessionalization. See chapter 2.

17 In chapter 2, I consider theories about the contribution of education to national wealth.

18 The secretary of education's Commission on the Future of Higher Education made a similar statement in its 2006 report: "The benefits of obtaining post-secondary education are significant not only to the individual but to the nation as well." The report "A Test of Leadership: Charting the Future of U.S. Higher Education" (prepublication copy) is available at http://www.ed.gov/about/bdscomm/list/hiedfuture/reports/pre-pub-report.pdf.

19 These days any discussion of college athletics involves a discussion of revenue streams and the problems that members of profitable teams face. Some of these issues involve women students and students from underrepresented minorities. My university's institutional review board did not grant permission to study students.

20 Rose Laub Coser first told me about the relationship between power and jokes. See Coser (1960). Cf. Holmes, Schnurr, and Marru (2007).

21 Members of this committee include the provost, the chief financial officer, the chief operating officer, the vice president for student affairs, and two deans.

22 The Wannabe website includes news reports mentioning the university that have been published anywhere in the world. However, it never includes stories about scandals at Wan U.

23 Relationships among the vice presidents and directors also emphasize the importance of spin. Among the direct reports (people who report directly to the president) at the president's Wednesday morning meeting are the director of the Division of Athletics and the director of University Relations. Both are very powerful. "You know [the director of athletics]?" an associate dean once asked me and seemed impressed when I answered that I did. But sometimes the director of the Division of Athletics seems to defer to the director of University Relations, who also acts as a lobbyist for Wan U. At least, I have heard him make a point of demonstrating how well he knows the director of University Relations. "I'll discuss that with [the director of University Relations] at our Wednesday meeting," the director of the Division of Athletics told the University Senate. "I have to meet with [him] anyway," he said to an executive committee. Indeed, once during a meeting, the director of the Division of Athletics used his Blackberry to speed-dial the director of University Relations. Spin matters.

CHAPTER 2

1 Although mission statements were originally associated with business plans, these days a variety of organizations have them. In the Ashton area, these organizations include the university, the town, the local hospital, an interdenominational charity, churches, and a synagogue. The regional organizations that accredit universities and colleges require mission statements. See, for example, Standard One of the New England Association of Schools and Colleges, Commission on Institutions of Higher Education: "The institution's mission and purposes are appropriate to higher education, consistent with its charter or other operating authority, and implemented in a manner that complies with the Standards of the Commission on Institutions of Higher Education. The institution's mission gives direction to its activities and provides a basis for the assessment and enhancement of the institution's effectiveness." Downloaded from http://www.neasc.org/cihe/stancihe.htm, February 13, 2008.

2 See Gumport (2002). She compares ideologies about service in three state universities and notes how "serving" local corporate interests contributed to SUNY Stony Brook's increasing involvement in, and profit from, research. Here Gumport is defining service much as she says that Stony Brook did—service to corporate interests. This is a version of the old GM motto: What's good for General Motors is good for the country—only now what's good for the state's industries is good for the state. On Stony Brook, cf. Gelber (2001).

3 Most American research universities have a faculty senate. However during the Vietnam War, inspired by the call for participatory democracy and also by campus unrest, the Wannabe Faculty Senate was reorganized as the University Senate with seats reserved for professors, students, middle managers, and even deans. The president or provost delivered a monthly report to the Senate. They and the vice provosts attended as observers, as did some middle managers when they thought that items on the month's agenda were germane to their responsibilities.

4 As argued by Duderstadt (2000) and Eckel and Kezar (2003).

5 A central administrator made this comment at a 2007 forum on improving the quality of the faculty's teaching. He was merely articulating how the administration had run the university for over a decade. On educators' use of the concept culture, see Kuh and Whitt (1988).

6 I consulted two histories of Wannabe University, which must remain uncited.

7 Cited in reports to the University Senate.

8 Data in this paragraph were calculated from the NCAA website, the Wannabe U website, and the state website with data about the Ashton public schools. Information about coaches at other

schools was taken from field notes at meetings of the Wan U Athletic Committee and also from the *State Capital Record*.

9   A program review is an in-depth analysis of a department's academic quality accomplished by nationally prominent scholars in the field. Although there is some variation from one college or university to the next, the basic process is set. The department (its head, chair, or a committee) prepares a self-study that outlines its graduate and undergraduate programs along specified lines; the dean (or provost) sends the self-study to an invited committee of nationally known professors, who also receive a list of questions of interest to the administration. These nationally recognized scholars visit the department for two days; they interview all of its members and also meet with key administrators. They then file a report to which the department may respond.

10 Mainstream approaches are more likely to receive large grants from national sources.

11 Note that like corporations, universities now collect proprietary data to assess their market position. The main reason that admitted students enrolled elsewhere was finances.

12 In chapter 6, I discuss how the quality of universities is measured.

13 A standardized score takes into account the range of scores, departure from the mean, and number of departments being measured.

14 A published report implies that a powerful politician had to convince President Ned Oakes to lobby for funds designed to help improve Wannabe University's national standing.

15 Zelda F. Gamson (1998: 103) notes that "higher education is a mammoth industry. There are thirty-six hundred colleges and universities in this country with one million faculty members and fifteen million students. The property owned by colleges and universities has been estimated to be worth over $200 billion, total expenditures to be $175 billion, and annual university research and development expenditures to be about $20 billion."

16 SUNY Stony Brook is one university that rose pretty rapidly. See Gelber (2001) and Gumport (2002). So did Brandeis University, in part by hiring leading scholars accused of leftist leanings during the McCarthy era.

17 In 2005 and again in 2008, there were attempts to change the unusual structure of Wan U's programs to combat racist and sexist practices. Wan U had a higher retention rate of underrepresented minorities than most comparable universities. See chapter 8.

18 "They erected parking garages where I went to graduate school," one professor said. "Watch what happens next. They're going to start charging an arm and a leg for parking." In the academic year 2006–2007, resident students paid an annual fee of $102, student commuters $80 to $300 depending on the location where they chose to park, and faculty and staff up to $600. Ehrenberg (2000) puts the cost of maintaining a parking space at over $600 in the late 1990s.

19 Scholars who stress the impact of globalization on institutions of higher education are using a variant of this theory. See, e.g., Slaughter and Leslie (1999) and Slaughter and Rhoades (2004).

20 A third solution, eliminate tenure, is much more difficult to accomplish. However, many institutions of higher education have instituted a variation of eliminating tenure, the post-tenure review. This practice is discussed in chapter 9.

21 Some theorists such as Williams (1977) would reject this dichotomization.

22 The idiom stresses how much our very language favors training for practical affairs over education for intellectual growth.

23 For instance, when the top administrators and trustees of Wannabe University sought an agreement with a Middle Eastern country, a legislator complained because that country would not admit Israelis. Very much wanting the contract, the administrators sought help from Jewish organizations that were willing to argue that the agreement would help Israel and so help Jews. No one asked whether the Jewish students at Wannabe University would feel at ease in that Middle Eastern country.

24 The classic analysis of how universities changed at the beginning of the twentieth century is still Veblen's *Higher Education in America* (1918).

25 Thus Slaughter and Leslie (1999: 37) maintain, "As supply-side economics and debt-reduction policies were instituted, entitlement programs, particularly Social Security, Medicare, and primary and secondary education, expanded enormously. . . . This combination of policies . . .

had powerful consequences for postsecondary education. . . . None of the nations treats higher education as an entitlement program. . . . [L]ess public money was available for postsecondary education, and what new money was available was concentrated in technoscience and market-related fields in what amounted to a higher education version of supply-side economics."

26 I am emphasizing the Latin derivation of educate—*ex ducere*—to lead.

27 See, e.g., Lewis (2006), a severe criticism of how Harvard College has strayed from its earlier ideals.

28 The British literature argues that when Great Britain increased the proportion of "post-graduates" obtaining some form of higher education, relevant agencies turned from an emphasis on education to an emphasis on training. See especially Evans (2004) and the various essays in Hayes and Wynyard (2006). I discuss British versions of accountability in chapter 9. Some sociologists and economists place this observation in the context of a grand narrative. According to Slaughter and Leslie (1999: 30), in the world characterized by new forms of international economic competition, "post-secondary education was directed toward national 'wealth creation' and away from its traditional concern with the liberal education of undergraduates."

29 The classic text is Starr (1982); cf. Scott et al. (2000).

30 This doctor says his family has gone from "piecework" to "piecework" in three generations. His grandmother did piecework for the garment industry and now he does piecework, too. Computers obviously facilitate such assessments.

31 Echoing Strathern (1997, 2000) and Power (1994), Smith calls this sort of deprofessionalization a "regime of accountability" or "accountability regime."

32 Traditional sociological discussions of accounts, such as Scott and Lyman (1968), do not place the concept in the context of long-term social change. As they use it, the term frequently means "a story of or version of an event."

33 But see Gawley (2008).

34 Trow (1998) analyzes accountability from the point of view of university administrators, including how universities adapt to survive. He distinguishes between internal and external accountability.

35 As we will see in chapter 8, this feat is accomplished when professionals accede to demands for benchmarking and other forms of measuring their worth. Social scientists generalize that cultures socialize individuals. The notion of an audit culture and its coercive accountability regime works somewhat differently. Individuals (departments, institutions) must change themselves to make themselves auditable.

36 Rumors, which I cannot verify, claim two such instances have occurred within the memory of many professors.

CHAPTER 3

1 The dean of the College of Liberal Arts and Sciences was reputed to shudder at the term "signature," usually associated with "signature products." Supposedly he preferred the term "overarching program" to refer to interdisciplinary programs that spanned colleges. The dean was said to have "academic values."

2 Weisbuch (2007). Robert Weisbuch is president of Drew University.

3 Gumport and Syndman (2006) argue that this change in educational ideology has been associated with the rise of academic management, academic consumerism, and the repositioning of academic fields. However, they do not ask what prompted these three trends. Friedland and Alford (1991: 243) identify the capitalist market, a macro-societal phenomenon, as a key institutional logic (232). Institutional logics with quite different emphases can coexist. (See chapter 10.)

4 Strictly speaking, Wannabe University gathers "*metrics*" that serve as "performance indicators." "Benchmarking" implies observing the practices others use to reproduce their success. Now and again, a manager might be sent to observe others' practices, but by and large, administrators hired consultants, went to conferences, and tracked others "performances" with "metrics" developed for that purpose. Since the administrators at Wan U use the term "best practices," I shall too. But it is a misnomer (see Birnbaum 2001: 76ff.).

5 Some of these items duplicate measures used by *U.S. News & World Report*. For instance, the undergraduate educational experience is measured by three items: average verbal and math SAT scores, the student-faculty ratio, and six-year graduate rate. The metric for national reputation is the university's score on that year's edition of *U.S. News & World Report*'s "America's Best Colleges."

6 That change parallels the development of television programming in the last decades of the twentieth century. First, both sought to appeal "to a general audience." Then both became more specialized. Television's development was intended to maintain viewers whose eyeballs, as Gitlin (1983) once put it, could be sold to advertisers.

7 The faculty and staff page includes a link to one's time card.

8 Sometimes the branding process seems a joke. At least one high-level administrator was embarrassed by another's attempt to introduce a "unified statement" that would represent the university on its website. That administrator learned of the "unified statement" secondhand. Someone told someone who told the administrator that at a meeting concerned with aspects of teaching, branding had been discussed. A middle manager passed around a copy of a proposed "unified statement." (It was not called a slogan.) Rather like the unified statement "LEARN!" being used by another university, Wan U's statement would encapsulate its attitude toward education. To capture the spirit of the "unified statement," I will pretend that Wannabe University is nicknamed "U State." Under that condition, the proposed unified statement reads in part: "U State starts with YOU." Middle managers had explained that if a conversation was proceeding awkwardly when a professor was speaking with a student, to get things going the professor could always say, "U State starts with You." That slogan was a rare exception to Wan U's otherwise sophisticated branding. It was never officially introduced.

9 The *Chronicle of Higher Education* (Hoover 2006) notes that especially at private universities, "branding" is increasingly a responsibility of those in charge of "enrollment management." At Wan U, the director of admissions reports to the vice provost for enrollment management.

10 As DiMaggio and Powell (1991) point out, conformity (and branding) may be coercive. If our competition has built a better fitness center, we need one too, or we cannot compete.

11 The 2006 "Report of the Secretary of Education's Commission on the Future of Higher Education" also discusses higher education as a mature industry.

12 During the 1980s, admissions offices began to evolve into offices of enrollment management. A good ethnography of admissions practices is Stevens (2007).

13 Keller (1983) recommended a managerial solution: Universities should use strategic planning. However, rather than comparing universities to corporations, he quoted Clark Kerr's comparison of universities to public utilities. Kerr had said, "The greatest change in governance now going on is not the rise of student power or faculty power but the rise of public power. The governance of higher education is less and less by higher education. . . . The 'ivory tower' of yore is now becoming a regulated public utility" (cited in Keller 1983: 24, 25).

14 Obviously the criteria the magazine used are relevant. See chapter 6.

15 At a meeting of the Senate's Growth and Development Committee, several professors suggested expensive solutions to nighttime accidents involving pedestrians. After the meeting, one professor said, "At the very least, you can get more powerful lightbulbs." Wannabe's chief operating officer said, "That is the first practical suggestion I've heard." The essays in Bowen and Shapiro (1998) give a sense of administrators as practical people.

16 At a meeting, the director of athletics referred to the university's patent on its logos and mascot, how his department licensed those items, and the significant income his department (which he called "the university") derives.

17 For instance, federal grants generally cost medical schools money. As the head of the Wan U Board of Trustees explained at one routine board meeting, medical research is so expensive that a medical school may spend $1.25 for every $1.00 in federal monies that it receives. Also, foundations, such as the Ford Foundation, generally do not provide indirect costs.

18 The classic scandal involves a university that allegedly built a shopping center with the indirect

costs that it accumulated from research grants. Other people say the university used the monies for furniture not associated with the grant.

19 The secretary of education's Commission on the Future of Higher Education might have had the claims of these researchers in mind, when its 2006 report suggested: "The benefits of obtaining post-secondary education are significant not only to the individual but to the nation as well." Universities help to increase the nation's wealth.

20 When reporting to Provost Tyler Johnson, one vice provost for research offered to fund a grant writer whom several social sciences would share, if each department wrote a mission statement. The vice provost explained that some "cutting edge" social science required funding and the university should position itself in those fields. Eventually Provost Gerald Wesley was to require that every academic and administrative department write a mission statement.

21 One dean successfully folded a "soft" natural science. Supposedly another lost his job when he sought to meld two science departments into one unit and created intense faculty unrest.

22 A central administrator thought that the emphasis on nanotechnology was unwise. He noted that, according to the 1996 study of the National Research Council, the relevant science departments of a neighboring state university were "better" than those of Wannabe University. Also, the federal government had just integrated the neighbor's nanotechnology research into a regional consortium. Wan U was not in the consortium.

23 A vice provost had negotiated down the fine, which had originally been larger, because it covered another offense as well.

24 Some years later at the dean's retirement party, the provost praised him for increasing the endowment of his college.

25 The name is itself telling: since it establishes a dichotomy between human and non-human resources, it implicitly reduces humans to objects (resources).

CHAPTER 4

1 Titles of some high-placed central administrators changed several times as the trustees worked to determine which structure best suited their goals for Wannabe University.

2 Contemporary sociologists invoke "institutional logics" to discuss transitions from one sort of administrator to another. Thus, Thornton and Ocasio (1999; cf. Thornton 2004) discuss how one group of editors replaced another, when higher-education publishing changed from an editorial to a market focus. Gumport (2002) and Gumport and Snydman (2006) point out that higher education is also changing from one logic to another. Both logics coexist.

3 This description is indebted to Simmel's (1950) discussion of the "stranger who comes today and stays tomorrow." Provosts leave; associate vice provosts may stay.

4 Wan U's administrators seem to experience more upward mobility than its professors. On the whole, from graduate school until the job from which they retire, professors tend to show downward mobility—a common finding in the sociology of science (Cole and Cole 1973).

5 There was one significant exception. However, the search committee found that neither the local candidate nor the national candidates were qualified for the job. In an e-mail, the provost advised the entire faculty that a local professor would do the job for the next two years, while the job was redefined and another national search undertaken.

6 There are two views of this dean as micromanager. A supposed friend of this dean jokes that the dean is such a micromanager that he even reads the curriculum vitae of every professor in the college to keep track of how individuals and departments are performing. An associate dean whom the dean mocked publicly praises the dean for this practice, saying he takes care to know about the work of the college's faculty. I assume that this dean's judgment of others' character is not his greatest strength. Some but not all deans manage to get their way without mounting threats.

7 Informants tended to agree on the identity of bullies. By and large, people in specific structural positions were more likely to be called bullies than people with less power.

8   To translate this statement: The *Science Citation Index* counts how many times a particular publication is cited in specific journals that have been identified as important. (Most of these journals are American, creating some potential biases.) The entries are available in multiple forms. One method of classification is by author. Since the *Index* is computerized, it is possible to calculate how many times the publications of each scientist are listed as being cited. Supposedly, the greater the number of citations to a person's work, the better the scientist. So, this administrator is announcing that his work is of very high quality—better than the publications of all but three other people associated with Wan U.

9   On rare occasions, Wan U recruits senior faculty, such as department heads. Arriving at their new job from more prestigious universities, some of them have talked about how much better their former department is than "you are." Often such praise for past colleagues usually means that no one has tried to integrate the new person into the department culture. I said words to this effect to a central administrator: "You certainly speak better of your last place than of this place." S/he replied, "They haven't been very nice to me here."

10 However, some professors in that department had achieved significant recognition in the state and also nationally.

11 Recall Rose Laub Coser's (1960) observation that people who have power maintain a monopoly on making jokes. In operating rooms, she reported, the chief surgeon makes the jokes and the nurses and interns laugh appreciatively.

12 One former president had also done a bad job reading reports. According to some subordinates, if one wanted the president to have some information, one had to tell certain people who regularly briefed him. Subordinates claimed that he never read past the executive summary that introduced complex reports.

13 I never attended a private meeting of the trustees. However, some Senate meetings and Senate committee meetings also fit this description. People tried to work out their disagreements before the meeting so as not to embarrass one another or place one another on the spot. Professors also follow normative guidelines when a committee meeting involves genuine debate or the sharing of private information. The minute-taker lifts his hands from the keyboard of his laptop. If a speaker turns to the minute-taker while making a sensitive point, the minute-taker might say, "I've stopped taking notes."

CHAPTER 5

1   These parties also broadcast who is currently in favor. For instance, just before Gerald Wesley arrived at Wan U, the *State Capital Record* had roundly and extensively criticized a powerful Wan U administrator. Few people at the reception for Gerald Wesley greeted this man, although just weeks before they had gladly gone over to shake his hand, their faces lit by large and friendly smiles.

2   According to two central administrators, they also try to influence trustees' actions so that they will follow what the top central administrators believe to be the correct path of action. Because he was politically accomplished in a hierarchical bureaucratic tradition, Chairman Bill Hardway was difficult to influence, they agreed.

3   When two deans found out that I was writing this book, they phoned a friend of mine to ask what I had learned. The more information I gathered, the more I found myself involved in potential information exchanges.

4   Or course, philosophic issues and practical problems are related. To address the practical problem of diversifying the faculty, a central administrator proposed the establishment of formal plans. Provost Johnson did not want schools and colleges to establish plans to diversify their faculty and staff. He felt such plans smacked of the worst aspects of affirmative action. Provost Wesley okayed the creation of such plans. See the chapter and discussions in Bowen and Shapiro (1998); cf. Keohane (2006).

5   The central administration had decided to "grow the enrollment" after commissioning a study on research productivity. The consultants recommended both a larger student body and a larger

faculty. More students generate more tuition (within limits dependent on the costs of educating, housing, and feeding them). More faculty would give researchers more colleagues to stimulate their work.

6   As a trustee said to me at a reception, "Why wouldn't he want to help a company build student-housing near campus that the university would not have to pay for?"

7   There is an exception to this generalization, as there are to most generalizations. In an interview, one dean rhetorically asked, "What kind of university do we want this to be?"

8   Within eighteen months of Wesley's arrival, President Whitmore tendered his resignation. Someone who believed that Wesley had aligned himself with Bill Hardway volunteered that he was right to have done so, reasoning that a weakened Whitmore could not have protected Wesley's job. On the other hand, Wesley publicly praised Whitmore as a "wonderful mentor to me."

9   On college budgets as tubs, see Kirp et al. (2003) and Keller and Keller (2007).

10 By 2008 Provost Wesley seemed to have perfected this technique. A special task force recommended shortening the number of weeks in summer sessions, because residential life staff did not have sufficient time to clean rooms before one shift of students moved out and the next moved in. Even before that change, some faculty had complained that teaching summer school created difficult learning situations, because undergraduate classes lasted three hours and fifteen minutes. Most of the members of this task force were either middle managers (generally from the Building for Undergraduate Education), associate deans, or department heads. One senior faculty member complained to me that such decisions were educational, not administrative matters.

11 Several years earlier, Wan U had "restructured" the central administration.

12 Legitimacy is a central concern of the new institutionalism.

13 Respectable Research University did not have a School of Human Development and Family Studies; it had a department.

14 One professor recalls the vote: "At the meeting, I was sitting across the table from Elsa Paris. I am friendly with Elsa and John Paris. [Elsa taught in the School of Human Development and Family Studies and John in the College of Liberal Arts and Sciences.] I voted to fold the schools, and later John, a moral fellow, asked me why I had done so. I remember explaining to him that I was worried that if we didn't find a way to save money that the university would begin to let go untenured professors. But my vote was irrelevant. The motion [to fold the two schools] was defeated." He continued, "It was one of the few times that the Senate stood up to the administration."

15 An informant said: "The [then-]chairman of the board of trustees told me that he had ordered [then-president Ned Oakes] to fire [Samuel] Darning that week or he would fire Ned next week."

16 The term "stakeholders" arrived in academe from corporate settings. It is also a legal term. The term has become increasingly common at Wannabe University and, I suspect, at other educational institutions as well. By emphasizing that people in certain roles have "something at stake," the term seems to connote that those people's interest in a matter is akin to an investment.

17 This provost also justified his decision in terms of revenue streams. According to the *Wannabe Weekly*, he argued that "the new arrangement, administering the four schools as one division, could create other benefits, such as enabling the Wan U Foundation to better use its staff to support the new, larger health care division. Currently, he said, the four schools are too small for the foundation to staff each school independently with a constituent fund-raiser."

18 In 2008, when at a public meeting about the newest Wan U academic plan, a professor asked Provost Wesley about the reorganization of his vice provosts. Wesley replied, "Some years ago, there was a controversy when I reorganized three schools. I don't need an academic plan to [decide the responsibilities of my vice provosts]."

19 There is a serious intellectual question here: Do the most important scholarly advances emerge from the mainstream or from mavericks? So far as I know, no department was reviewed twice under this regime. Instead, Provost Wesley was to form a task force to review program reviews.

20 Morrill (1995) describes this kind of organization of white-collar work as a mechanistic bureaucracy. His key example is a bank.

21 On the consequences of improper bureaucratic behavior, see Morrill (1995).

22 The provost appoints some members of a deaconal review committee, including the dean (of another school) who chairs it. Groups of departments also elect members to the review committee.

23 Wannabe University provosts have left for the presidencies of other universities before the president constituted a review committee. Some administrators felt that one provost would not have been reappointed, but that he had "certainly landed on his feet."

24 This man was suing both the provost and the president for firing him. The dean of the College of Liberal Arts and Sciences is said to have engaged in similar behaviors. However, that college is so large that is would be almost impossible to organize the faculty in its many departments, research centers, and institutes. Instead, one department might strategize about how to take advantage of another's misfortunes.

25 So that they could share their concerns when the provost was not present, the deans had breakfast together once a month in a nearby city.

26 Speaking at this dean's retirement party roughly fourteen months later, Provost Wesley praised him for "coming to visit me" when "he had a disagreement with a policy. . . . rather than banging on the table."

27 There had been talk of recording students' local addresses in 1997, when Wan U adopted the computer program PeopleSoft. In the intervening years, there had been so much turnover at the top of the Division of Student Affairs that many staffers did not know about an earlier attempt (and failure) to incorporate local addresses in student records.

28 A well-known passage in sociological literature on organizations points out that subordinates do not always obey orders. In it, Scott (1992: 65) describes Philip Selznick's view of how organizations are not always rational: "Selznick's image corresponds . . . to Alice's efforts at croquet with equipment and competition provided by the Queens of Hearts. Alice swings her flamingo mallet but the bird may duck his head before the hedgehog ball is struck; just so the manager issues his directives but they may be neither understood nor followed by his subordinates."

29 A distinguished scientist who had been receiving a stream of large grants for decades asked permission to speak at the committee meeting. He said: "In my [specialty], more and more people are getting jobs at medical schools, because they permit research incentive awards [RIA's]. That's changing the field. Also, these RIA's mean that fewer people can get research grants; it's become even more competitive. More people are applying for an RIA, which increases the total budget, but the funding agencies aren't receiving more monies. So when some people get these now-larger grants, fewer people can receive grants. Nationally, the amount of research that can be done diminishes." This professor added, "I don't think that RIA's are ethical."

30 Their reasons were practical, not ideological. Not only did the group discuss the experiences of other universities; it also spoke to the economics of the situation: "Up to this point, a major incentive for PIs [principal investigators] at Wan U to request grant support for graduate students has been that the expense was reasonable when balanced against the amount of time committed to a project by a graduate student. Charging tuition to grants will put this amount over the threshold of reasonable PI behavior. A PI wishing to maximize his or her output from a particular award would be foolish (and perhaps even negligent) to request support for a graduate student, contributing twenty hours per week on a project, over a technical assistant or postdoctoral fellow, contributing forty hours per week, given their respective annual costs . . . ; the hourly labor cost for a graduate student would be $30, compared to $20 for a technician or $21 for a postdoc. The resultant predictable decline in number of graduate students would have a negative impact on Wan U's national standing given that the number of Ph.D. degrees conferred annually is an important measure of a university's research productivity as indicated by most major indices (e.g., Lombardi, NRC, etc.). However, we also note that this decline would reduce the amount of funds the administration would capture from tuition charges."

31 Unfortunately, he mentioned his department's success in front of a high-ranking member of the central administration, causing someone else to joke, "Your department is going to have to do it for real now."

32 Two years later, after that provost launched his academic plan, a different group of men said, "I don't think we have to do a good job [fulfilling the central administration's mandate]. I don't think this administration is going to last very long."

CHAPTER 6

1 On the difference between student-centered learning and teacher-centered learning, see, e.g., Kuh et al. (2005) and the essays in O'Banion (1997).

2 The theme of a December 2007 reception held for three key politicians was that a university is about education, and by instructing students, the university serves the state. One concrete example that several speakers invoked was that a highly regarded state university prevents "brain drain." With humor, one speaker noted that once the best state high school graduates had decamped for the University of Michigan, but that he had recently met several graduates of Michigan high schools who were being graduated from Wan U.

3 The terms in quotations refer to statements made by committee members at four forums held by the Provost's Task Force on Teaching, Learning, and Assessment to discuss their report to the provost. The chairs of the task force were the vice provost for education and instruction and the associate dean of the School of Education. Almost half of the committee members were professors, many of whom had won teaching awards. An informant explained that the other members were department heads, heads of institutes, and associate deans recruited to the committee to encourage professors to "buy into" the committee's concerns.

4 Abbott (1981, 1988) suggested that professions are organized around a core of abstract knowledge. According to Sandefur's study of lawyers (2001: 400), prestige within a profession accrues to "work that approaches the center or core of the profession." The core knowledge of academic professions is *not* how to teach. It is an organized series of ideas and findings about the profession's subject matter (organelles or stratification systems or string theory), including the methods for generating more knowledge.

5 The School of Education is, of course, a partial exception, since research about teaching is nearer to its "core concerns." See Sandefur (2001) and Abbott (1988).

6 Some professors believe that colleagues who serve on university committees, including the University Senate, are failed researchers. As a social scientist said, "They're on those committees because they don't publish—except for Joan, who's really bright." However, both scientists with a history of steady funded research, scientists with board of trustees chairs, and professors who have won prestigious awards have represented faculty on the Senate and have also become associate deans. This social scientist's comment captures the faculty emphasis on research.

7 People who have been elected to membership on the University Senate's Executive Committee are another exception, even if their careers have been stalled at the rank of associate professor.

8 Thus, one professor recalled that he had published more than others in his graduate school cohort and was the only one to garner a job in a research university. His colleagues had gotten jobs in liberal arts colleges.

9 The *U.S. News & World Report* rankings have been rightly criticized both theoretically and methodologically. See, e.g., Gater (2002) and Monks and Ehrenberg (1999). The key variable predicting a university's ranking is students' SAT scores. The better the students' scores, the higher the university's ranking. Student scores are also correlated with social class (Geiger 2002). On multi-colinearity, see Chang and Osborne (2005).

10 A term such as "yield rate" emphasizes how much higher education has become a business. Another example of a yield rate might be how many shirts can be cut from a length of cloth.

11 Out-of-state applicants also tend to have higher grade-point averages and higher median SAT scores than in-state applicants.

12 On the relationship between admissions offices and guidance counselors, see Stevens (2007).

13 Data gathered for the Wannabe vice provost for enrollment indicate that students who voluntarily or involuntarily leave after their first year are less likely than other students to have done well in

this one-credit course. However, other factors are also probably at work. According to Geiger (2002) and as discussed in chapter 8, family income is the best predictor of both retention and graduation rates.

14   For fall 2006, Wan U admitted roughly 5,000 transfer and first-year students to matriculate at its campuses, so its 2005–2006 admissions costs would have been roughly $3.4 million. That year, it spent roughly $790 million on academic, research, and student services as well as operating, support, and physical plant services.

15   One Wan U central administrator liked to drop casually the information that he had worked at an "AAU university" and then to add equally casually that Wannabe University was not even a member.

16   A dean made this comment when a professor moved from Wan U to the best department in his field and received a hefty raise to do so. He also made this comment when a professor left for an endowed chair at a more highly ranked public university.

17   At issue was the nature of graduate committees on which these professors had served. Although they had served on the committees for master's theses, they had not served on dissertation committees. However, if all of that department's students were defined as potential doctoral candidates, these two professors qualified for consideration in the NRC review. Since they both had good publication records, the dean and department head wanted them to be included in the official version of the department's doctoral faculty.

18   Not only are the salaries of such professors quite high, but it is very expensive to set up a scientist's lab. As of 2007, the most the College of Liberal Arts and Sciences had paid to establish a lab for a new professor was $500,000, and that sum is probably not competitive with top-notch private research universities. At least one other Wan U college has spent more on a laboratory. In 2007–08, a midwestern university lured a CLAS scientist with a hefty raise and a million-dollar laboratory.

19   Kirp et al. (2003) discuss how the job "dean of admissions" became subservient to the corporate title "vice president" or "vice provost for enrollment management."

20   CLAS was the largest college and had the largest budget, an ex-administrator pointed out. It was therefore one of the likeliest sources of monies for other schools.

21   One year there were so few seats for sophomores in some required courses that only sophomores could receive permission to enroll. The next year, to forestall that problem, only first-year students would be given those special permissions and sophomores were out of luck. Professors and graduate instructors reported being besieged by students demanding (not requesting) help because they could not get registered in enough courses to qualify as full-time students and to keep their room in the dormitory.

22   Students are more likely to cut classes of over 80 students than classes with 30 students. They fear that the professor of a small class may notice their absence, but figure that the instructor of a large class might not even know their name.

23   Many did get jobs elsewhere, however the training components did not work out as planned. Fellows complained that the courses on teaching were boring. Also, so few faculty members attended the organizational meeting for fellows and mentors, that this portion of the program was discontinued.

24   These informants illustrated the difficulties that women in the administration faced, even as they bemoaned the "macho" environment in which both they and the women worked. Punning, one said that the work environment was so "macho" that several women in very important jobs had become "macha." This administrator seemed to identify himself as a feminist and said he could not understand why there were so few successful women administrators at Wan U.

25   Even as they noted a potentially difficult climate for women in Top Hall, administrators credited Mary Matthews's ambition for her departure. Some of the statements that managers made about both her and a (female) successor seemed to confirm how difficult it was for women to serve in the Wannabe administration.

26   I heard this comment with some frequency. More than once, the person making this statement

had left Wannabe University under a cloud. Nonetheless, I suspect that there is some truth to the accusation.

27   The staff unions have approved this teaching. Some newly hired middle managers even have such teaching written into their appointment letter. Some courses had such names as "the psychology of . . . ," "the economics of . . . ," "the biology of . . . ," although the instructors of these one-credit courses were not faculty members in those departments.

28   As her subordinates reminded me, Sharpe was incredibly loyal to her boss. She always deferred to him in public. As discussed in chapter 9, ultimately many professors blamed Sharpe for her boss's policies. As all administrators do, Sharpe made some errors. Unlike many, she usually owned up to them. However, both faculty and administrators were happy to blame Sharpe when they did not like the policies of the central administration. See Fisher (2007) on the problem of academic women in positions of authority.

29   Upper-division courses are open to juniors and seniors. The University Senate has authority to approve lower-division courses, including which courses receive general-education credit.

30   The matter spent almost a year in committee before going to the University Senate. Because the provost was in charge of interdisciplinary courses, Sharpe continued to appoint committee members, but at least one of the colleges had to approve an academic course for a student to receive credit. Courses not sponsored by the colleges, such as the first-year experience class sponsored by the provost's office or senior-year experience sponsored by the vice provost for student affairs, were not subject to approval by the colleges.

CHAPTER 7

1   A central administrator reminded me that sometimes subordinates wrote e-mails and other memos for the provost and president. This memo concludes by quoting a contemporary poet; stylistically it appears to have been written by a subordinate known for superb writing and editing skills.

2   His wife, an expert in programming, was also involved in the project. I do not know whether professors regarded her with implicit sexism or whether they extended to her the disdain they felt for assessment. But despite her expertise and education, even feminist faculty referred to her as "the provost's wife" rather than by her name.

3   Nonetheless, some administrators placed some credence in them. According to an informant, at a orientation session for new faculty, the head of the Institute for Teaching and Learning supposedly said that they had high standards to meet, since 80 percent of Wannabe's faculty scores at least eight (out of ten) on the university's SETI. Since the discussion of SETIs revolved around a professional literature, DiMaggio and Powell (1991: 67) would call them an influence on "normative isomorphism."

4   Vice Provost Sharpe was replying to an e-mail. I had asked her, "Is the term 'student-centered learning' counterproductive when talking to faculty?"

5   At Wannabe University (and throughout academia), the Institute for Teaching and Learning offers instructors training in digital technologies and pedagogy, including such matters as how best to write a syllabus, rewrite an exam, train graduate assistants to grade papers, and even where to stand in a large lecture hall so as to engage the students. The advice can be quite detailed. One author advises walking around a large lecture hall to maintain eye contact with each student. He suggests standing still before one wants to make an important point. However, he advises not to stop walking in the middle of an important point.

6   Student evaluation forms used at Wannabe University asked students to rate their professors from one to ten on a variety of characteristics. Because the social science literature suggests that informants have difficult making such fine distinctions and is also critical of other characteristics of the existing form, the task force asked that a committee be appointed to revise the form. The statement assumes there is a difference between an 8.2 and an 8.5 and reifies it. It also exemplifies the tendency of administrators to assume that statistics have concrete social

meanings. See Espeland and Stevens (1998) on commensuration; Espeland and Sauder (2007); Birnbaum (2001).

7   Speaking of his priorities to a meeting of the faculty of the College of Liberal Arts and Sciences in 2006, Provost Wesley emphasized his intention to give funding priority to such units as the School of Nursing and the School of Education, whose graduates could alleviate shortages in the state's labor force.

8   This reasoning is incorrect if one feels that the faculty who teach undergraduate courses are "overqualified" for that job, because graduate students could be expected to have mastered the material enough to teach undergraduates.

9   Note that the word "productivity," commonly used to describe (and quantify) how much research a professor has published and how many grants she has received, might also be applied to the manufacture of widgets.

10   When such books as *What the Best Teachers Do* (Bain 2004) discuss engaging students, they stress the match between a way of teaching and the material to be taught.

11   A professor skilled with computers teased out the information that this version was the eleventh draft prepared by Wan U's new president. For more about him, see chapters 8 and 9.

12   "The committee that advises the U.S. Department of Education on accreditation has recommended that the government suspend recognition of the American Academy for Liberal Education for accrediting any new institutions or programs until it comes into compliance with federal requirements. The National Advisory Committee on Institutional Quality and Integrity, which polices the bodies that accredit higher-education institutions and programs, took the action last month at a scheduled review of several accrediting agencies. The committee acted after determining that the academy had not adequately demonstrated that it requires the institutions it accredits to assess what their students have learned" (Bollag 2006a).

13   When in early 2008 Provost Wesley presented a few items in the new academic plan to the board of trustees and then to the University Senate, all items were expressed in goals, objectives, and metrics. Another set of corporate terms also regularly cropped up at meetings with administrators and at meetings of the board of trustees: people spoke of encouraging "stakeholders" to "buy into" programs and policies that support change and so to promote a new "campus culture." Harvey (2005) notes that such business (or "entrepreneurial") language is part and parcel of neo-liberalism.

14   This quotation is also an example of "spin" (see Frankfurt 2005). I spoke with several members of the Senate who said they had never heard this explanation of course renumbering. Nor could I find such a discussion in the Senate minutes. The professors with whom I spoke, including those doing the course numbering in their departments, said that some quirks in the PeopleSoft computer program that managed enrollment required a four-number system. Others noted that in some departments, the current three-number system had reached its capacity; more combinations were necessary, and a new three-number system would not solve the problem because the registrar's office would not be able to tell the old system from the new. A four-number system was akin to adding a "1" before an area code when dialing a long-distance number. It permitted more combinations. When I showed a senior professor the quotation about leading professors, he immediately said that the explanation for course numbering given to the Regional Accreditation Agency was an example of vacuous leadership. No one specified the likely source of funds to teach Capstone courses, which usually have relatively small enrollments.

15   For an analysis of everyday life as a consumption process, see Bauman (2007).

16   A colleague reminded me that Weber (1958) similarly conflates intellectual activity and student life in his essay "Science as a Vocation."

17   The website appears to confuse its responsibilities for helping the faculty with the faculty's responsibility for planning a course. The website insisted: "Because our motto is 'I.D. before I.T.,' we do not design for a specific mode of delivery. Rather, *the courses we design* can be delivered, with minor adjustment, at any point of the face-to-face to pure distance continuum" (emphasis added).

18   This teacher of large classes also scored well on student evaluations. He explained, "I try to use

a variety of media—current songs, cartoons, videos, graphs—to convey what I want from the students. . . . I'm trying to speak to their experiences, not to make them think I care. I don't know how they do it over in the sciences, but I'm trying to show them that what I teach has a lot to do with their life. . . . Having kids helps me know what they're into."

19   In the academic year 2006–2007, I attended several meetings about the shortage of counselors at Student Health Services. A new head of that unit was hired in fall 2007. In spring, the student newspaper revealed a continued shortage of counselors, including long waits to get appointments even if one thought one needed medication. Until 2007, all of the counselors had been white. Wan U had an out-of-date fitness center and an out-of-date infirmary. So far as I know, the fitness center was scheduled for replacement before the infirmary.

CHAPTER 8

1   There has been no public discussion of why President Whitmore resigned from his job. In public, all he said was: "It's time." According to informed sources, the board of trustees had given James Whitmore a deadline by which to resign. The chairman of the board headed the search committee for a new president.

2   A dean reminded me that presidents also operate under constraints. The size of President Daniels's merit raise depends on how well he has met the goals set by the board of trustees.

3   Recall the middle manager who defensively asked me, "What's wrong with that?"

4   According to a usually accurate source, the wife of the acting provost had made a critical comment at a party after the first time her husband had not been appointed the "permanent" provost. That comment supposedly influenced his eligibility for the provost's job after his second stint as an acting provost. "Parties matter," my source said. The same source claims that President Whitmore had nonetheless told the acting provost that he would receive the job if Gerald Wesley turned it down.

5   At a public meeting, the head of an interdisciplinary program suggested that the term "outreach" implied the superiority of the university over the people whom it was helping. She suggested that the term "public engagement" implied equality. Provost Wesley did not embrace this point in his response, although he did decide to name that new administrator the vice provost for public engagement.

6   The comment sounds cynical, but it was made as a professional observation, not as a criticism. The professor did not mean to be cynical, just to say how organizations work.

7   Others praised President Whitmore for that fund-raising.

8   An unwillingness to speak truth to power also occurs without rapid administrative turnover. Some faculty claimed that a powerful central administration had a tendency to get even. They called him "vindictive." Soon after President Daniels arrived, I overheard one of his colleagues explain that the new president was trying to decrease, if not eradicate, administrative intimidation by modeling the following notion: "We are all professionals here. If you make a mistake, apologize and let's get on with it. . . . Let's all get back to work."

9   As requested by the board of trustees, President Whitmore hired a consulting firm to recommend a new management plan. One middle manager echoed the ideas of neo-institutionalism by suggesting that consultants roam the country, making similar recommendations to the universities that hired them. Eventually, he joked, all those universities would look the same. Then, the consultants would change the template so that the process of organizational restructuring could begin all over again.

The consulting firm suggested that Wan U "restructure the overall academic affairs management" and the financial management to centralize aspects of accounting, hiring, and technology and to "implement multiple sharing strategies" among its campuses. Restructuring would avoid duplication among and within campuses and would "maximize . . . synergies." Doing so would conserve fiscal, "information technology and human resources." As recommended, President Whitmore appointed a chief operating officer, who assumed some responsibilities that had been assigned to the provost and some responsibilities assigned the top managers on other Wan U campuses. The consultant had also suggested renaming specific job titles to those used by many other research universities. As the administration brought job descriptions and titles more in line with the consultant's recommendations, the board made appropriate adjustments in the university bylaws and in bureaucratic procedures and responsibilities.

The board and the administration did not accept every recommendation. The consulting firm had proposed that Wan U use Lombardi measures to benchmark its progress up the ranks of research universities. Publicly at least, Wan U continued to cite the *U.S. News & World Report* rankings.

10 Provost Johnson did not sympathize. Instead he stated that he had recently been talking to a star player on the football team who had experienced a similar problem. Between classes, studying, training, and games, he didn't have time to see his friends, so he had created a solution. Now he studied with his friends. The provost did not say whether he expected the professor to bring his children to committee meetings.

11 A department head who had been invited to colloquia concerning the humanities and fine arts made a similar point at the public meeting about the academic plan: she could not recognize her group's input.

12 One department head in the humanities affirmed the rumor that he had not been told that his discipline was to house a "signature program" until the plan was published. Members of the board of an interdisciplinary program had a similar problem. Meeting with Provost Wesley, they discussed being deemed a signature program and asked how they were to accomplish all that "his plan" required when they had only three faculty members, whom they shared with other departments.

13 This statement was made about a year before Provost Wesley issued his academic plan. Muller had been in office for well over a decade. His attitude toward his leadership defined him as an "old-fashioned department head" (see chapter 4). Speaking with me, he identified his job as serving his colleagues, not exercising power over them.

14 Departments that are known to apply strict criteria and to refuse tenure to colleagues are said to have a powerful argument for receiving a replacement for the person whom they fired. Supposedly deans and central administrators dislike "softies" (who always vote to approve tenure and so leave it to the dean to fire people). Often professors like to show off that they are "macho" by arguing for the application of "strict standards" for tenure and promotion. There are other considerations as well. Everyone at the meeting of the Senate committee knew that if a department head fights for a junior member and loses badly, he may have used up his poker chips and might not be able to do anything for the next person whose tenure or promotion might be coded as problematic. Conversely, being tough on tenure might help a department amass "chips," including the "right" to retain an academic line and hire on it. Like playing poker, judging tenure cases seems to be a macho activity.

15 Other sorts of problems also arise, when an individual is jointly appointed to a disciplinary department and an interdisciplinary program. Several people with joint appointments reviewed those arrangements with me, and I saw how other cases were handled when I observed some tenure decisions. At Wan U, tenure is granted within the department, not the program. The department might want the assistant professor to publish their research in leading disciplinary journals and may discount scholarship published in interdisciplinary journals with which they are not familiar. When these individuals are to be considered for tenure, the department might ask colleagues in the discipline to serve as referees, but not professors who do work in the interdisciplinary specialty. Some of the distinctions between disciplinary and interdisciplinary research are finely honed; but, for instance, research in the sociology of gender does not necessarily contribute to gender studies.

16 Christine Zozula coined this concept in her master's thesis on a city court with dual and conflicting goals: to treat offenders therapeutically and to express allegiance to "broken windows theory"; that is, the belief that minor offenses necessarily lead to major offenses (Zozula 2008; cf. Merton and Barber 1976).

17 Organizational theorists might disagree. For instance, Gumport and Syndman (2006: 463) say

that "higher education is both a public and a private good." They view identification as public as being "inherent in the very identification of a college of university as an institution of higher education," and identification as private as inherent in the cost and return to those who have attended such an institution.

18   This "overrepresentation of Asian Americans" is currently quite common in academe. See, for instance, "Diversity," *U.S. News & World Report America's Best Colleges*, 2008 ed., p. 39. I do not mean to imply that Asian Americans do not face discrimination. For instance, some professors claim that admissions officers may hold Asian Americans to higher standards.

19   There are significant variations within the Asian American group. According to some faculty, some of these variations correspond to parents' social class and others to parents' or grandparents' nation of origin. Data about applicants are not readily accessible, and I did not use the Freedom of Information Act to gather information. As several members of the Senate who have worked to increase the enrollment of underrepresented minorities reminded me, "Victor is a good guy." One added that he had worked with Steibel on a program to increase the "seamless flow" of qualified students from community colleges and said that Steibel "understands."

20   There is also organizational ambivalence in the hiring and tenuring of faculty. Here's a summary of what many professors of color claim: In the social sciences, arts, and humanities, scholarship germane to inequality is more likely to appear in specialized than general journals. However, often one qualification for tenure is publishing in the leading general journals in a field. Inasmuch as African American social scientists are more interested in issues of inequality and racism than are other social scientists, they are less likely to have their work published in the "leading journals" and so less likely to be "qualified" for tenure. Professors with joint appointments in a multicultural institute, say women's studies or Asian American studies, are also in a precarious position. They receive their tenure in a discipline, such as sociology or English and American literature. But the disciplinary professors voting on their tenure and promotion may not value the interdisciplinary journals in which they publish their work.

21   In the order of their founding they are the African American Cultural Center, the Puerto Rican/ Latin American Cultural Center, the Women's Center, the Women's Studies Program, the Institute for African-American Studies, the Asian American Cultural Center, the Asian American Studies Institute, the Institute for Puerto Rican and Latino Studies, and the Rainbow Center. Most of the academic lines involved joint appointments, for some academic departments were willing to hire someone on a "free" line subsidized by Vice Provost Wilson and (usually) the dean of CLAS, but might not have hired a woman or a person of color if left to their own devices. Especially when universities are financial strapped, it is harder to get academic departments to accept such arrangements, since they have figured out that there is no such thing as a free lunch.

22   Some months later, an associate dean told me that these programs should be in CLAS, because "we pay for them"; that is, pay for half of the professors' salaries.

23   Special tables were also reserved for special groups, such as reporters, the university's vice presidents (including the provost), and its vice provosts. When a former middle manager met me at a meeting, I pointed out who sat where. My companion whispered to me, "A place for everyone and everyone in their place."

24   A white woman served as the board's secretary and also headed its Committee on Student Life. It reported after the committees that "really mattered": Academic Affairs, Financial Affairs, Audit and Compliance, and Building and Grounds.

25   I suspect that people who worked in the BUE felt that they fulfilled their tasks better than other people did, for Sharpe was not the only person to make that error. A faculty member who served as a part-time administrator had observed to me how much the programs in BUE were contributing to the retention rate; he did not mention the older and more extensive programs in the cultural centers. Judging from how some administrators behaved, it was also customary to take credit when one could—unless, of course, a bureaucratic superior had good reason to do so.

26   In fall 2008, the provost announced that the office was to be dismantled in 2009. Details gradually emerged. Some international studies programs were to be placed under the purview of a new vice provost. The cultural centers were to report to a chief diversity officer, who reported to the

president. A task force appointed by the provost was to recommend how the academic programs on diversity and inequality were to be administered.

27   "Goal 3E: Diversity and Internationalization: Expand Our Understanding of Cultural Differences through Scholarship, Creative Activities, and Research"; "Goal 2D: Infuse Diversity throughout the Curriculum." At a meeting with faculty about the plan, the president asked whether diversity should be integrated in the proposal or have its own section. After those who sent e-mails recommended a separate section, a section was devoted to diversity in the final draft.

28   http://store.acenet.edu/, last downloaded June 12, 2008.

29   An administrator asked me, "Don't you think there's real merit in hiring women and minorities?" He was a member of a racialized ethnicity. The question had shocked me; except for the people who worked in the Office of Multiculturalism and International Affairs, I had never heard that question from an administrator at Wan U.

CHAPTER 9

1   At a subsequent meeting of the Senate, a resolution established a task force to review the question of charging graduate tuition to grants. President Daniels said he would be happy to work with the task force.

2   Daniels did not specify which rankings he was discussing.

3   On for-profit colleges and universities, see Ruch (2001).

4   In a classic bit of humor, March and Sutton (1997; cited in Khurana 2007: 307) use the term "priests of research purity" to refer to researchers whose loyalty is to their discipline, not their organization.

5   Universities tend to be either optimistic or disingenuous about which activities actually turn a profit. For instance, in May 2008 the NCAA announced: "Just 17 of the more than 300 athletics programs in all of Division I—about 5 percent—earned a net profit between 2004 and 2006, with ticket sales and private donations accounting for more than half of all revenue. Sixteen of those profitable sports programs—a number that may exceed some expectations—were from the elite Division I-A, or what is now called the Football Bowl Subdivision, where the median amount of college support was 24 percent of the costs of sports programs" (Kelderman 2008).

6   This cycle is a version of what Robert K. Merton and Harriet Zuckerman called "the Matthew Effect" (Merton1968).

7   One said, "We should be tougher. We should hire people who will get grants within their first three years and get tougher on tenure. We need people who will get NIH grants. [These tend to be larger than NSF grants and permit professors to charge the tuition of graduate student research assistants to the grant.] Too many people get tenure."

8   A scientist checked the president's figures and claimed that Daniels had engaged in an academic sin, "fudging the data." I rechecked. The president's interpretation of the data was valid. The incident indicates how much the faculty's attitude toward Rick Daniels had changed after the second forum on the 2008 academic plan.

9   The head of the board of trustees might advise a president to resign, if that president had taken a risk that did not work out.

10   The faculty tended to believe that both presidential and provostial views have an impact. Consider a hypothetical possibility. A canny department head might worry about how the central administration would respond to a request for additional monies from a department engaged in what the president might identify as extravagant practices, such as wasting faculty time and energy on unfunded graduate students. To be sure, because he sat atop the bureaucratic hierarchy, the president might never hear that the department was wasting its time and effort on such weak graduate students. But the dean of the graduate school would know about the profligacy. Wanting to please his bureaucratic superiors, he might invoke the president's views in a way that "harmed" the profligate department.

11   The suggestion involves a shift in power. Wan U's vice provost for undergraduate enrollment management reports to the provost. Normally, a vice president reports to the president.

12   Note that the measures used to indicate quality potentially discriminate against underrepresented minorities. African Americans and Latinos are more likely to attend unranked colleges than whites, and so their admission to a graduate program may hamper a graduate department's identification as a "good" program.

13   The vice provost for research discussed these indicators with the Senate, presenting these data for a very good program and a very weak program. When he was asked the source of the data, he answered, "They are Lombardi data." That response stifled challenges to that section of his presentation.

14   The provosts' realization is reminiscent of the *Chronicle*'s 2003 statement about wannabe universities. Not every wannabe can increase its ranking, because the universities standing higher on the ladder are getting better too.

15   But see Lewis (1997), who favors tighter controls over the professoriate.

16   A central ruling forced departments to disband those accounts.

17   All of these quotes are from the website of the Quality Assurance Agency, http://www.qaa.ac.uk/ and were downloaded the week of May 5, 2008. Trow (1998) provides an account of the British system. He points out that it is the most extreme accountability system in Europe and is based on a basic mistrust of the academy.

18   The team examines such documents as a self-evaluation; program handbooks; curricular documents, module, or unit guides; program annual monitoring reports; summaries and/or analyses of student questionnaire data and follow-up actions; external examiners'/verifiers' reports for the previous three years; student intake and progression data for the previous three years. The team may also request minutes of relevant meetings, including examination/verification or assessment boards; summary of equipment and other resources; practical or work-placement handbooks; program approval; validation and revalidation documents; student destinations (further study and employment statistics); subject staff list and short profiles (indicating main teaching and research interests and any administrative responsibilities of lecturers, and responsibilities of other staff). The team also needs to see a sample of student work, including work relevant to the "achievement of intended learning outcomes" and "a representative sample of student work that demonstrates use of the full range of assessment methods used in both formative and summative assessments." This list was adapted from www.qaa.ac.uk/reviews/academicReview/ acrevhbook2004/HandbookAcademicReview.pdf (downloaded April 2008).

19   The audit teams should be able to determine "the range and appropriateness of teaching methods employed in relation to curriculum content and programme aims; how staff draw upon their research, scholarship, consultancy or professional activity to inform their teaching; the ways in which participation by students is encouraged and how learning is facilitated; how the materials provided support learning and how students' independent learning is encouraged; student workloads; how quality of teaching is maintained and enhanced through staff development, peer review of teaching, integration of part-time and visiting staff, effective team teaching and induction and mentoring of new staff." www.qaa.ac.uk/reviews/academicReview/acrevhbook2004/ HandbookAcademicReview.pdf (accessed May 5, 2008).

20   These quality assurance audits can also articulate with the "Bologna process," which European Institutions of Higher Education are developing. That process facilitates the enrollment of a student at different institutions of higher education for specific courses.

21   Rules specify both the conditions under which an individual may be exempted from the Research Assessment Exercise and the calculation of group productivity, including calculations when some professors were exempted from the exercise.

22   In very different theoretical languages, authors are discussing how the nation-state is claiming more power and shifting it to market forces. Scott et al. (2000) adapt the term "interventionist regime" from Mary Ruggie's (1996) book on health policy in the United States, Britain, and Canada. The British scholar Richard Gombrich (2000) writes of "dirigisme." That term refers to the power of a centralized state (indeed, to the power of the pre-revolutionary French king) to impose its will on the rest of society. It seems an apt term to characterize the centralized imposition of national authority on British higher education. Other theorists remind that no matter how

important professors believe universities to be, higher education is a subordinate institution. Thus, Brint and Karabel (1991: 36) paraphrase Karl Marx's famous remarks in *The Eighteenth of Brumaire*, when they speak about the development of community colleges, whose emphasis on service seems to have been adopted by research universities: "organizations may make their own history, but they do not make it just as they please." Dorothy Smith (2004) makes much the same point about the implication of ruling relations in the corporatization of universities and deprofessionalization of the professoriate. She also cites David Harvey (2005), who uses the term "neo-liberalism" to indicate how in such seemingly disparate nations as the United States, the United Kingdom, and China, a rationalized state has indeed become interventionist as it centralizes power and authority over subordinate institutions.

CHAPTER 10

1 For an especially good discussion of the context of logics, see especially Friedland and Alford (1991).
2 Carmelita Sanchez, the first woman to serve as lieutenant governor of the Zuni, credited her achievement with learning to go with the tide (Bowannie 2005: 9).
3 The critic Raymond Williams makes much the same point about what he terms *structures of feeling*, "affective elements of consciousness and relationships, not feeling against thought, but thought as felt and feeling as thought" (1977: 132). He argues that emergent, residential, and dominant structures of feeling are all "part of the undeniable experiences of the present."
4 Indeed, in May 2008 the governor announced a significant deficit; the threat of possible rescissions sent a shiver through the faculty and the administration. In mid-September President Daniels requested that all departments make a 3.5 percent cut in their budget. Student aid was exempt from this rescission.
5 That mission statement declares: "CLAS faculty and students review and critically assess the foundations of human knowledge. They are dedicated to the traditional values of the liberal arts and sciences, which include both intellectual independence and the capacity to integrate insights from the humanities and the natural, physical, and social sciences. By nurturing in its members a sense of curiosity and providing experiences in discovery and collaboration, the College of Liberal Arts and Sciences prepares faculty and students to be leaders in their communities and workplaces, and to become lifelong learners. . . . [Its professors] are involved primarily in basic research, but many are also engaged in applied research that is responsive to the needs of communities and businesses, consistent with Wannabe University's overarching land-grant mission. . . ."
6 The first 2007 draft of the plan mainly mentioned the arts and humanities in the section devoted to workforce development.
7 On the explosion of statistical analyses at "leading" business schools, see Khurana (2007).
8 Power continues, "It is through the giving and monitoring of accounts that we and others provide of ourselves, and of our actions, that the fabric of normal human exchange is sustained. These accounts only become objects of explicit checking in situations of doubt, conflict, mistrust and danger" (1). Cf. Trow (1998).
9 The membership also includes three administrative officers (deans), nine professional staff members, five undergraduate students, and two graduate students.
10 Toward the end of my observation period, the deans were meeting regularly for breakfast in the state capital. There they discussed campus matters without the provost and vice provosts who attended the Council of Deans.
11 Although the faculty rarely mentions it, much institutional memory also resides in the minds of departmental and college secretaries. After one of the deans left, his secretary asked to be transferred. The new acting dean noted that the secretary had taken the unit's institutional memory with her.
12 Arguing that the professoriate should be held more accountable, Michael Lewis (1997) provides

tales of what he terms faculty "malpractice"; cf. Trow (1998) on reasons for accountability in academe.

13 Stanley Aronowitz (1998) writes: "I am one of a shrinking minority of the professoriate who have what may be the last good job in America. . . . I pretty much control my paid work time. I work hard but it's mostly self-directed. I don't experience leisure as time out of work because the lines are blurred" (205). He also notes, "Academic labor, like most labor, is rapidly becoming decomposed and recomposed. The full-professor, like the spotted owl, is becoming an endangered species. . . When professors retire or die, their lines frequently follow them," and they are replaced with contingent labor (216).

References

Abbott, Andrew D. 1981. "Status and Status Strain in the Professions." *American Journal of Sociology* 86: 819–35.

———. 1988. *The System of Professions: An Essay on the Division of Expert Labor*. Chicago: University of Chicago Press.

Arnone, Michael. 2003. "The Wannabes." *Chronicle of Higher Education* 49 (17) (January 3): A18.

Aronowitz, Stanley. 1998. "The Last Good Job in America." In *Chalk Lines: The Politics of Work in the Managed University*, ed. Randy Martin, 202–21. Durham, NC: Duke University Press.

———. 2001. *The Knowledge Factory: Dismantling the Corporate University and Creating True Higher Learning*. Boston: Beacon Press.

Attewell, Paul, and David E. Lavin. 2007. "Distorted Statistics on Graduation Rates." *Chronicle of Higher Education* 53 (44) (July 6): B16.

Attewell, Paul, David E. Lavin, Domina Thurston, and Tania Levey. 2007. *Passing the Torch: Does Higher Education for the Disadvantaged Pay Off across Generations?* New York: Russell Sage Foundation Books.

Bain, Ken. 2004. *What the Best Teachers Do*. Cambridge, MA: Harvard University Press.

Barrow, Clyde W. 1990. *Universities and the Capitalist State*. Madison: University of Wisconsin Press.

Bauman, Zygmunt. 2007. *Liquid Modernity*. Cambridge, UK: Polity Press.

Berdahl, Robert O., and T. R. McConnell. 1999. "Autonomy and Accountability." In *American Higher Education in the Twenty-first Century*, ed. Philip G. Altbach, Robert O. Berdahl, and Patricia J. Gumport, 70–88. Baltimore: Johns Hopkins University Press.

Berger, Peter, and Thomas Luckmann. 1967. *The Social Construction of Reality*. New York: Doubleday Anchor.

Birnbaum, Robert. 1989. "Presidential Succession and Institutional Functioning in Higher Education." *Journal of Higher Education* 60 (1): 123–35.

———. 2001. *Management Fads in Higher Education*. San Francisco: Jossey-Bass.

Bollag, Burton. 2006a. "Conservative Colleges Accreditor Criticized." *Chronicle of Higher Education*, January 6: A37.

———. 2006b. "Spellings Wants to Use Accreditation as a Cudgel." *Chronicle of Higher Education*, November 24: A1.

Bourdieu, Pierre. 1984. *Distinction*. Cambridge, MA: Harvard University Press.

Bowannie, Mary. 2005. "Carmelita Sanchez: Zuni's First Woman Lt. Governor." *The Spirit of Zuni* (magazine).

Bowen, William G., Sarah A. Levin, James Shulman, and Colin Campbell. 2003. *Reclaiming the Game: College Sports and Educational Values*. Princeton, NJ: Princeton University Press.

Bowen, William G., and Harold T. Shapiro, eds. 1998. *Universities and Their Leadership*. Princeton, NJ: Princeton University Press.

Bradley, Richard. 2005. *Harvard Rules: The Struggle for the Soul of the World's Most Powerful University*. New York. HarperCollins.

Brint, Steven G. 1994. *In an Age of Experts*. Princeton, NJ: Princeton University Press.

———. 2002. "The Rise of the Practical Arts." In *The Future of the City of Intellect*, ed. Steven G. Brint, 231–59. Stanford, CA: Stanford University Press.

Brint, Steven G., and Jerome Karabel. 1989. *The Diverted Dream*. New York: Oxford University Press.

———. 1991. "Institutional Origins and Transformations: The Case of American Community Colleges." In *The New Institutionalism in Organizational Analysis*, ed. Water W. Powell and Paul J. DiMaggio, 337–60. Chicago: University of Chicago Press.

Brubacher, John S., and Willis Rudy. 2002. *Higher Education in Transition: A History of American Colleges and Universities*. New Brunswick, NJ: Transaction.

Bucher, Rue, and Joan Stelling. 1977. *Becoming Professional*. Beverley Hills, CA: Sage.

Chang, Gordon C., and J. R. Osborne. 2005. "Spectacular Colleges and Spectacular Rankings." *Journal of Consumer Culture* 5 (3): 338–64.

Clark, Burton R. 1983. *The Higher Education System: Academic Organization in Cross-National Perspective*. Berkeley: University of California Press.

———. 1993. "Faculty: Differentiation and Dispersion." In *Higher Learn-*

ing in America, 1800–2000, ed. Arthur Levine, 163–78. Baltimore: Johns Hopkins University Press.

———. 1998. *Creating Entrepreneurial Universities.* New York: Oxford Pergamon Elsevier Science.

———. 2004. *Sustaining Change in Universities: Continuities in Case Studies and Concepts.* New York: Open University Press.

Cole, Jonathan, and Stephen Cole. 1973. *Social Stratification in Science.* Chicago: University of Chicago Press.

Coser, Lewis A. 1974. *Greedy Organizations.* New York: Free Press.

Coser, Rose Laub. 1960. "Laughter among Colleagues." *Psychiatry* 23: 81–95.

Crane, Diana. 1988. *Invisible Colleges.* Chicago: University of Chicago Press.

Daniels, Arlene Kaplan. 1988. *Invisible Careers: Women Civic Leaders from the Volunteer World.* Chicago: Chicago University Press.

DiMaggio, Paul, and Walter W. Powell. 1991. "The Iron Cage Revisited." In *The New Institutionalism in Organizational Analysis*, ed. Walter W. Powell and Paul J. DiMaggio, 63–82. Chicago: University of Chicago Press.

Douglas, Mary. 1992. "The Normative Debate and the Origins of Culture." In *Risk and Blame: Essays in Cultural Theory*, 125–48. London: Routledge.

Duderstadt, James J. 2000. *A University for the Twenty-first Century.* Ann Arbor: University of Michigan Press.

Eckel, Peter, Barbara Hill, and Madeleine Green. 1998. "On Change: On the Road to Transformation: Managed Change." Downloaded from acenet.edu, May 2003.

Eckel, Peter, and Adrianna Kezar. 2003. *Taking the Reins: Institutional Transformation in Higher Education.* Westport, CT: Praeger.

Ehrenberg, Ronald G. 2000. *Tuition Rising: Why College Costs So Much.* Cambridge, MA: Harvard University Press.

Espeland, Wendy, and Michael Sauder. 2007. "Rankings and Reactivity: How Public Measures Recreate Social Worlds." *American Journal of Sociology* 113 (1): 1–40.

Espeland, Wendy, and Mitchell Stevens. 1998. "Commensuration as a Social Process." *Annual Review of Sociology* 24 (1): 313–43.

Etzkowitz, Henry. 2003. "Innovation in Innovation: The Triple Helix of University-Industry-Government Relations." *Social Science Information* 42 (3): 293–337.

Etzkowitz, Henry, Andrew Webster, and Peter Healey. 1998. *Capitalizing Knowledge: New Intersections of Industry and Academia.* Albany: State University of New York Press.

Evans, Mary. 2004. *Killing Thinking: The Death of the Universities*. London: Continuum.

Fecher, R. J., ed. 1985. *Applying Corporate Management Strategies*. New Directions for Higher Education, no. 50. San Francisco: Jossey-Bass.

Fisher, Ginny. 2007. "'You Need Tits to Get on around Here': Gender and Sexuality in the Entrepreneurial University of the 21st Century." *Ethnography* 8 (4): 503–17.

Fishman, Mark. 1980. *Manufacturing the News*. Austin: University of Texas Press.

Fogg, Piper. 2002. "Chancellor Says Transformation; Biologists, Mumbo-Jumbo." *Chronicle of Higher Education*, November 1: A10.

———. 2004. "For These Professors Practice Is Perfect." *Chronicle of Higher Education*, April 16: A12.

Frankfurt, Harry G. 2005. *On Bullshit*. Princeton, NJ: Princeton University Press.

Freidson, Eliot. 2001. *Professionalism: The Third Logic*. Chicago: University of Chicago Press.

Friedland, Roger, and Robert R. Alford. 1991. "Bringing Society Back In: Symbols, Practices and Institutional Contradictions." In *The New Institutionalism in Organizational Analysis*, ed. Walter W. Powell and Paul J. DiMaggio, 232–61. Chicago: University of Chicago Press.

Furedi, Frank. 2002. "The Bureaucratization of the British University." In *The McDonaldization of Higher Education*, ed. Dennis Hayes and Robin Wynyard, 33–39. Oxford: Greenwood.

Gamson, Joshua. 1994. *Claims to Fame*. Berkeley: University of California Press.

Gamson, Zelda F. 1998. "The Stratification of the Academy." In *Chalk Lines: The Politics of Work in the Managed University*, ed. Randy Martin, 103–11. Durham, NC: Duke University Press.

Gans, Herbert. 1979. *Deciding What's News*. New York: Random House.

Garfinkel, Harold. 1967. *Studies in Ethnomethodology*. Englewood Cliffs, NJ: Prentice-Hall.

Gater, Denise S. 2002. "A Review of Measures Used in *U.S. News and World Report's* 'America's Best Colleges.'" University of Florida: TheCenter. Downloaded from http://mup.asu.edu/Gater0702.pdf, June 13, 2008.

Gawley, Tim. 2008. "University Administrators as Information." *Symbolic Interactionism* 31 (2): 183–204.

Geiger, Roger. 2002. "The Competition for High Ability Students: Universities in a Key Marketplace." In *The Future of the City of Intellect*, ed. Steven Brint, 82–106. Stanford, CA: Stanford University Press.

———. 2004. *Knowledge and Money: Research Universities and the Paradox of the Marketplace*. Stanford, CA: Stanford University Press.

Gelber, Sidney. 2001. *Politics and Public Higher Education in New York State: Stony Brook—A Case History*. New York: Peter Lang.

Giri, Ananta. 2000. "Audited Accountability and the Imperative of Responsibility: Beyond the Primacy of the Political." In *Audit Cultures: Anthropological Studies in Audit, Ethics, Accountability and the Academy*, ed. Marilyn Strathern, 173–95. New York: Routledge.

Gitlin, Todd. 1980. *The Whole World Is Watching*. Berkeley: University of California Press.

———. 1983. *Inside Prime Time*. New York: Pantheon Books.

Gittelman, Sol. 2004. *An Entrepreneurial University: The Transformation of Tufts University 1976–2002*. Lebanon. NH: Tufts University Press of the University Press of New England.

Gladieux, Laurence E., and Jacqueline E. King. 1999. "The Federal Government and Higher Education." In *American Higher Education in the Twenty-first Century*, ed. Philip G. Altbach, Robert O. Berdahl, and Patricia J. Gumport, 151–82. Baltimore: Johns Hopkins University Press.

Goldberger, Marvin L., Brendan A. Maher, and Pamela Ebert Flattau, eds. 1995. *Research-Doctorate Programs in the United States: Continuity and Change*. Washington, DC: National Academy Press.

Gombrich, Richard F. 2000. "British Higher Education Policy in the Last Twenty Years: The Murder of a Profession." Lecture on January 7 in Tokyo at the Graduate Institute of Policy Studies (GRIPS). http://indology/info/papers/Gombrich/uk-higher-education.pdf. Downloaded May 21, 2008.

Gordon, David M. 1996. *Fat and Mean: The Corporate Squeeze of Working Americans and the Myth of Managerial "Downsizing."* New York: Free Press.

Gouldner, Alvin. 1957. "Cosmopolitans and Locals: Toward an Analysis of Latent Social Roles." *Administrative Science Quarterly* 2: 281–306.

Gumport, Patricia J. 2002. "Universities and Knowledge: Restructuring the City of Intellect." In *The Future of the City of Intellect*, ed. Steven Brint, 47–81. Stanford, CA: Stanford University Press.

Gumport, Patricia J., and Stuart K. Snydman. 2006. "Higher Education: Evolving Forms, Emerging Markets." In *The Non-Profit Sector: A Research Handbook*, ed. Walter W. Powell and Richard Steinberg, 462–84. 2nd ed. New Haven, CT: Yale University Press.

Hannan, Michael T., and John Freeman. 1977. "The Population Ecology of Organizations." *American Journal of Sociology* 82: 929–64.

———. 1989. *Organizational Ecology*. Cambridge, MA: Harvard University Press.

Harvey, David. 2005. *A Brief History of Neo-Liberalism*. New York: Oxford University Press.

Hayes, Dennis, and Robin Wynyard, eds. 2006. *The McDonaldization of Higher Education*. Oxford: Greenwood.

Hill, Barbara, Madeleine Green, and Peter Eckel. N.d. "What Governing Boards Need to Do and Know about Institutional Change." Downloaded from www.acenet.edu. Accessed May 2003.

Hochschild, Arlie Russell. 1997. *The Time Bind*. New York: Metropolitan Books.

Holmes, Janet, Stephanie Schnurr, and Meredith Marru. 2007. "Leadership and Communication: Discursive Evidence of a Workplace Culture Change." *Discourse and Communication* 1 (4): 433–51.

Hoover, Eric. 2006. "Enrollment Managers Reveal Top Worries." *Chronicle of Higher Education*, September 1: A65.

Howard, Philip N. 2005. *New Media Campaigns and the Managed Citizen*. New York: Cambridge University Press.

Hughes, Everett Cherrington. 1958. *Men and Their Work*. Glencoe, IL: Free Press.

Jackall, Robert. 1988. *Moral Mazes: The World of Corporate Managers*. New York: Oxford.

Karabel, Jerome. 2005. *The Chosen: The Hidden History of Admission and Exclusion at Harvard, Yale, and Princeton*. New York: Houghton Mifflin.

Kelderman, Eric. 2008. "Colleges Foot a Large Share of Athletic Expenses, New NCAA Data Show." *Chronicle of Higher Education*, May 23: A15.

Keller, George. 1983. *Academic Strategy: The Management Revolution in American Higher Education*. Baltimore: Johns Hopkins University Press.

———. 2001. "Governance: The Remarkable Ambiguity." In *In Defense of Higher Education*, ed. Philip G. Altbach, Patricia J. Gumport, and D. Bruce Johnson, 304–22. Baltimore: Johns Hopkins University Press.

———. 2004. *Transforming a College*. Baltimore: Johns Hopkins University Press.

Keller, Morton, and Phyllis Keller. 2007. *Making Harvard Modern*. New York: Oxford University Press.

Keohane, Nannerl. 2006. *Higher Ground: Ethics and Leadership in the Modern University*. Durham, NC: Duke University Press.

Keup, J., A. Walker, H. Astin, and J. Lindholm. 2001. "Organizational Culture and Institutional Transformation." ERIC Digest, no. ED 464521.

Khurana, Rakeesh. 2002. *Searching for a Corporate Savior: The Irrational Quest for a Charismatic CEO*. Princeton, NJ: Princeton University Press.

———. 2007. *From Higher Aims to Hired Hands: The Social Transformation of American Business Schools and the Unfulfilled Promise of Management as a Profession.* Princeton, NJ: Princeton University Press.

Kirp, David, Elizabeth Popp Berman, Jeffrey T. Holman, and Patrick Roberts. 2003. *Shakespeare, Einstein, and the Bottom Line: The Marketing of Higher Education.* Berkeley: University of California Press.

Kraatz, Matthew S. 1998. "Learning by Association? Interorganizational Networks and Adaptation to Environmental Change." *Academy of Management Journal* 41 (6): 621–43.

Kraatz, Matthew S., and Edward Zajac. 1996. "Exploring the Limits of the New Institutionalism." *American Sociological Review* 61: 812–36.

Krier, Dan, and William G. Staples. 1993. "Seen but Unseen: Part-Time Faculty and Institutional Surveillance and Control." *American Sociologist* 24 (3–4): 119–34.

Kuh, George D., Jillian Kinzie, John Schuh, Elizabeth Whitt, and associates. 2005. *Student Success in College; Creating Conditions that Matter.* San Francisco: Jossey-Bass.

Kuh, George D., and Elizabeth J. Whitt. 1988. *The Invisible Tapestry: Culture in American Colleges and Universities.* ASHE-ERIC Higher Education Research Report, no. 1. Washington, DC: Association for the Study of Higher Education.

LaPidus, Jules B. 2001. "Graduate Education and Research." In *In Defense of American Higher Education,* ed. Philip Altbach, Patricia Gumport, and D. Bruce Johnstone, 249–76. Baltimore: Johns Hopkins University Press.

Larson, Magali Sarfatti. 1977. *The Rise of Professionalism.* Berkeley: University of California Press.

Lawrence, G. B., and A. L. Service. 1977. *Quantitative Approaches to Higher Education Management.* ERIC/Higher Education Research Report, no. 4. Washington, DC: American Association for Higher Education.

Levine, Arthur. 2001. "Higher Education as a Mature Industry." In *In Defense of American Higher Education,* ed. Philip Altbach, Patricia Gumport, and D. Bruce Johnstone, 38–58. Baltimore: Johns Hopkins University Press.

Lewis, Harry R. 2006. *Excellence without a Soul: How a Great University Forgot Education.* New York: Public Affairs.

Lewis, Lionel. 1975. *Scaling the Ivory Tower: Merit and Its Limits on Academic Careers.* Baltimore: Johns Hopkins University Press.

———. 1996. *Marginal Worth: Teaching and the Academic Labor Market.* New Brunswick, NJ: Transaction.

Lewis, Michael. 1997. *Poisoning the Ivy.* Armonk, NY: M. E. Sharpe.

Lewis, Michael J. 2003. "Forget Classrooms: How Big Is the Atrium in the New Student Center?" *Chronicle of Higher Education*, July 11: B7.

Lohmann, Susanne. 2004. "Darwinian Medicine for the University." In *Governing Academia*, ed. Ronald G. Ehrenberg, 71–89. Ithaca, NY: Cornell University Press.

Long, J. Scott, and Mary Frank Fox. 1995. "Scientific Careers: Universalism and Particularism." *Annual Review of Sociology* 21: 45–71.

MacTaggart, Terrence, ed. 2007. *Academic Turnarounds: Restoring Vitality to Challenged American Colleges and Universities.* Westport: Praeger.

March, James G., and Robert Sutton. 1997. "Organizational Performance as a Dependent Variable." *Organizational Science* 8 (6).

Martin, James, and James E. Samuels. 2004. "When Showing a President the Door, Open It Carefully." *Chronicle of Higher Education*, December 10: B15.

McGuinness, Amis C., Jr. 1999. "The States and Higher Education." In *American Higher Education in the Twenty-first Century*, ed. Philip G. Altbach, Robert O. Berdahl, and Patricia J. Gumport, 183–215. Baltimore: Johns Hopkins University Press.

McManis, F. L., and W. C. Parker. 1978. *Implementing Management Information Systems in Colleges and Universities.* Littleton, CO: Ireland Educational Corporation.

Merton, Robert K., with Elinor Barber. 1976. "Sociological Ambivalence." In *Sociological Ambivalence and Other Essays*, ed. Robert K. Merton, 3–31. New York: Free Press.

Merton, Robert K. 1968. "The Matthew Effect in Science." In *The Sociology of Science*, ed. Robert K. Merton, 439–59. Chicago: University of Chicago Press, 1973.

Miller, Laura J. 2006. *Reluctant Capitalists: Bookselling and the Culture of Consumption.* Chicago: University of Chicago Press.

Monks, James, and Ronald G. Ehrenberg. 1999. "*U.S. News and World Report*'s College Rankings: Why Do They Matter?" *Change* 31 (6): 42–51.

Morrill, Calvin. 1995. *The Executive Way: Conflict Management in Organizations.* Chicago: University of Chicago Press.

Mowery, David, Richard Nelson, Bhaven Sampat, and Arvids Siedonis. 2004. *The Ivory Tower and Intellectual Innovation.* Stanford, CA: Stanford University Press.

Naples, Nancy. 1996. "A Feminist Revisiting of the 'Insider/Outsider' Debate." *Qualitative Sociology* 19 (1): 18–36.

O'Banion, Terry. 1997. *A Learning College for the 21st Century.* Phoenix: American Council on Education and the Oryx Press.

Olson, Christa L., Rhodri Evans, and Robert F. Schoenberg. 2007. *At Home in the World: Bridging the Gap between Internationalization and Multicultural Education.* Washington, DC: American Council on Education.

O'Neil, Robert M. 1999. "Academic Freedom: Past, Present and Future." In *American Higher Education in the Twenty-first Century*, ed. Philip Altbach, Robert Berdahl, and Patricia Gumport, 89–108. Baltimore: Johns Hopkins University Press.

Phillips, Damon J., and E. W. Zuckerman. 2001. "Middle-Status Conformity: Theoretical Restatement and Empirical Demonstration in Two Markets." *American Journal of Sociology* 107 (2): 379–429.

Phillips, Kevin. 2003. *Wealth and Democracy.* Bantam Dell.

Powell, Walter W., and Paul J. DiMaggio, eds. 1991. *The New Institutionalism in Organizational Analysis.* Chicago: University of Chicago Press.

Powell, Walter W., and Stine Grodal. 2005. "Networks of Innovators." In *The Oxford Handbook of Innovation*, ed. Jan Fagerberg, David Mowery, and Richard Nelson, 56–85. New York: Oxford University Press.

Power, Michael. 1994. *The Audit Explosion.* London: Demos.

————. 1997. *The Audit Society: Rituals of Verification.* New York: Oxford University Press.

Rhoades, Gary. 1998. *Managed Professionals: Unionized Faculty and Restructuring Academic Labor.* Albany: State University of New York Press.

Rhoades, Gary, and Barbara Sporn. 2002a. "New Models of Management and Shifting Modes and Costs of Production: Europe and the United States." *Tertiary Education and Management* 8 (1): 3–28.

————. 2002b. "Quality Assurance in Europe and the U.S.: Professional and Political Economic Framing of Higher Education Policy." *Higher Education* 43 (3): 355–90.

Ritzer, George. 1993. *The McDonaldization of Society.* Thousand Oaks, CA: Pine Forge Press.

————. 1998. *The McDonaldization Thesis.* Thousand Oaks, CA: Pine Forge Press.

————. 2000. *The McDonaldization of Society: New Century Edition.* Thousand Oaks, CA: Pine Forge Press.

Rourke, Francis E., and Glen Brooks. 1966. *The Managerial Revolution in Higher Education.* Baltimore: Johns Hopkins University Press.

Ruch, Richard S. 2001. *Higher Education, Inc.: The Rise of the For-Profit University.* Baltimore: Johns Hopkins University Press.

Ruggie, Mary. 1996. *Realignments in the Welfare State.* New York: Columbia University Press.

Sandefur, Rebecca L. 2001. "Work and Honor in the Law: Prestige and the Division of Lawyers' Labor." *American Sociological Review* 66 (3): 382–403.

Schmidt, Peter. 2002. "Governance of Alabama Universities under Attack." *Chronicle of Higher Education*, April 5: A20.

Scott, Marvin B., and Stanford Lyman. 1968. "Accounts." *American Sociological Review* 33 (1): 46–62.

Scott, W. Richard. 1981. *Organizations*. Englewood Cliffs, NJ: Prentice Hall.

Scott, W. Richard, Martin Reuf, Peter J. Mendel, and Carol B. Caronna. 2000. *Institutional Change and Healthcare Organizations: From Professional Dominance to Managed Care*. Chicago: University of Chicago Press.

Selingo, Jeffrey. 2006. "College Presidents and Governing Boards Must Strengthen Bonds, Report Says." *Chronicle of Higher Education*, September 29: A34.

Shore, Chris, and Susan Wright. 2000. "Coercive Accountability: The Rise of Audit Culture in Higher Education." In *Audit Cultures: Anthropological Studies in Audit, Ethics, Accountability and the Academy*, ed. Marilyn Strathern, 57–89. New York: Routledge.

Shulman, James, and William G. Bowen. 2002. *The Game of Life: College Sports and Educational Values*. Princeton, NJ: Princeton University Press.

Simmel, Georg. 1950. *The Sociology of Georg Simmel*. Compiled and translated by Kurt Wolff. Glencoe, IL: Free Press.

———. 1972. *Georg Simmel on Individuality and Social Forms*. Ed. Donald N. Levine. Chicago: University of Chicago Press.

Slaughter, Sheila, and Larry L. Leslie. 1999. *Academic Capitalism: Politics, Policies and the Entrepreneurial University*. Baltimore: Johns Hopkins University Press.

Slaughter, Sheila, and Gary Rhoades. 2004. *Academic Capitalism and the New Economy: Markets, State, and Higher Education*. Baltimore: Johns Hopkins University Press.

Smith, Charles W. 2000. *Market Values in American Higher Education*. Lanham, MD: Rowman and Littlefield.

———. 2004. "Globalization, Higher Education and Markets." In *Globalization and Higher Education*, ed. Jaishee K. Odin and Peter T. Manicus, 69–81. Honolulu: University of Hawaii Press.

Smith, Dorothy E. 2004. "Despoiling Professional Autonomy: A Woman's Perspective." In *Inside Corporate U: Women in the Academy Speak Out*, ed. Marilee Reimer, 31–42. Toronto: Sumach Press.

———. 2005. *Institutional Ethnography: A Sociology for People*. Toronto: Alta Mira Press.

Solomon, Catherine Richards. 2008. "Personal Responsibility in Professional Work: The 'Star' as Ideological Code." In *People at Work: Life, Power and Social Inclusion in the New Economy*, ed. Marjorie DeVault, 180–203. New York: New York University Press.

Starr, Paul. 1982. *The Social Transformation of American Medicine*. New York: Basic Books.

———. 2004. *The Creation of the Media*. New York: Basic Books.

Stevens, Mitchell. 2007. *Creating a Class: College Admissions and the Education of Elites*. Cambridge, MA: Harvard University Press.

Stinchcombe, Arthur. 1965. "Social Structure and Organizations." In *Handbook of Organizations*, ed. James G. March, 142–93. Chicago: Rand McNally.

Strathern, Marilyn. 1997. "'Improving Ratings': Audit in the British University System." *European Review* 5 (3): 305–21.

———, ed. 2000. *Audit Cultures. Anthropological Studies in Accountability, Ethics and the Academy* [EASA series in Social Anthropology]. London: Routledge.

Thompson, James B. 2005. *Books in the Digital Age*. Cambridge: Polity Press.

Thompson, James D. 1967. *Organizations in Action*. New York: McGraw Hill.

Thornton, Patricia H. 2004. *Markets from Culture: Institutional Logics and Organizational Decisions in Higher Education Publishing*. Stanford, CA: Stanford University Press.

Thornton, Patricia H., and William Ocasio. 1999. "Institutional Logics and the Historical Contingency of Power in Organizations." *American Journal of Sociology* 105 (3): 801–43.

Trow, Martin. 1998. "On the Accountability of Higher Education in the United States." Downloaded from http://igs.berkeley.edu/publications/working_papers/99-8.pdf, June 1, 2009.

———. 2003. "Leadership and Academic Reform: Biology at Berkeley." In *The Search for Excellence*, ed. J. Rogers Hollingsworth, Ellen Jane Hollingsworth, and Jerald Hage. New York: Cambridge University Press.

Tuchman, Gaye. 1978. *Making News: A Study in the Construction of Reality*. Glencoe, IL: Free Press.

Turow, Joseph. 2006. *Niche Envy: Marketing Discrimination in the Digital Age*. Cambridge, MA: MIT Press.

U.S. News and World Report. 2008. "America's Best Colleges."

Veblen, Thorstein. 1918/1957. *Higher Learning in America: A Memorandum on the Conduct of Universities by Businessmen*. New York: Sagamore Press.

Washburn, Jennifer. 2005. *University, Inc.: The Corporate Corruption of Higher Education*. New York: Basic Books.

Weber, Max. 1958. *The Protestant Ethic and the Spirit of Capitalism*. New York: HarperCollins.

Weisbuch, Robert. 2007. "Branding Isn't a Dirty Word." *Chronicle of Higher Education*, January 26: C3.

Williams, Raymond. 1977. *Marxism and Literature*. Oxford: Oxford University Press.

Wilson, J. A., ed. 1981. *Management Science: Applications to Academic Administration*. San Francisco: Jossey-Bass.

Wilson, Robin. 2002. "Bickering Decimates a Department." *Chronicle of Higher Education*, October 18: A12.

———. 2007. "The New Gender Divide." *Chronicle of Higher Education*, January 26: A36.

Wolverton, Mimi, and Walter H. Gmelch. 2002. *College Deans: Leading from Within*. Westport, CT: Oryx Press.

Zimbalist, Andrew. 1999. *Unpaid Professionals*. Princeton, NJ: Princeton University Press.

Zozula, Christine. 2008. "Broken Windows, Broken People: Interaction in a Quality of Life Court." MA thesis, University of Connecticut.

Zusman, Ami. 1999. "Issues Facing Higher Education in the Twenty-first Century." In *American Higher Education in the Twenty-first Century*, ed. Philip G. Altbach, Robert O. Berdahl, and Patricia J. Gumport, 109–48. Baltimore: Johns Hopkins University Press.

Index

Abbott, Andrew D., 43
academic branding. *See* branding
academic conformity. *See* conformity
academic departments: decreasing power of
    department heads, 79–80; departmental
    "receivership," 16, 32; departmental reviews,
    22, 100–101; departmental structure, 200–202;
    limitations on eclectic, 31–32; merit reports,
    182–83; self-study, 181; "strong head system,"
    200–202
academic freedom, 156–57
academic "lines," 82–83, 107, 123
academic professions, status system of, 142
accountability regime, 12, 21, 208, 214n16,
    217n31; and audit culture, 45; vs. centralized
    British system in 1990s, 23–24, 184–87; and
    conditions of faculty work lives, 204–5; and
    de-churching of universities, 45; four condi-
    tions for, 188–89; and ideological institutions,
    188–91; individual, 182; as panopticon, 45. *See
    also* student outcomes assessment
accountability vs. auditing, 178–79
accounting, incursions on activities of other
    workers, 44
accreditation, 142–45, 191
Accreditation Board for Engineering and Technol-
    ogy (ABET), 145–46
adaptation theory, 37–38
adjunct professors, 68
administrators, Wannabe University: as corporate
    administrators, 206; difficulties of women,
    17, 224nn24–25; disdain for professoriate,
    6; emphasis on immediacy and short-term
    effects, 90; inferiority complex, 71; national
    searches for, 78; past experiences as templates

for decision-making, 83; and professional
    organizations, 83–85; salaries, 70, 71; self-
    identification as "cosmopolitan," 71–72;
    view of other administrators, 82–83; view
    of own activities as essence of university, 6;
    view of Wannabe as good career stepping-
    stone, 69–71. *See also* central administration,
    Wannabe University; deans, Wannabe Uni-
    versity; outside administrators (professional
    managers); presidents, Wannabe University;
    provosts, Wannabe University
admissions "yield rate," 10, 118, 223n10
advising program, 127, 128
African American middle managers, on issues of
    race and racism, 17, 168–69
African American students, underrepresentation
    at Wannabe, 165–66
African American studies, 171
Alden, Todd (dean of College of Arts and
    Sciences), 103, 203; accomplishments in the
    humanities, 195–96; appointment, 121–22;
    elimination of programs, 181–82; introduction
    of "postdoctoral teaching fellow" or "faculty
    in residence," 125; and Women's Studies
    Program, 167
Alford, Robert R., 213n7, 217n3
Allon, Natalie, 186
American Association of University Professors,
    96; and post-tenure review, 163, 183; and
    tenured professors, 37
American Council on Education, 171
American Sociological Association, 85
American universities: built-in conflict, 7;
    celebration of top rankings, 9–10; decentral-
    ized structures, 5; knowledge subordinated

American universities (*continued*)
    to needs for profit and recognition, 11; radical
    disbursement of authority, 5; as wannabes, 10.
    See also research universities
ancillary income, 13
architecture, 53
Aronowitz, Stanley, 233n13
Ashton (home of Wannabe University), 1;
    establishment of downtown "area" to attract
    students, 34; intersection with Wannabe
    University, 76–77; location, 70; vision state-
    ment, 152
Asian Americans: largest minority at Wannabe in
    1994, 28, 229n19; proportion of state popula-
    tion, 165, 229n18
Association of American Universities (AAU), 153;
    membership in, 119–20
Attewell, Paul, 55
audit culture, 21, 44–45, 144–45; as accountabil-
    ity regime, 12; changes in research universities
    as result of, 21–22; and individual self-
    auditing, 61; negation of faculty's professional
    expertise, 145
auditing: vs. accountability, 178–79; as form of
    surveillance, 12
auxiliary income, 7, 13, 57

Barrow, Clyde W., 40–41
Bayh-Dole Act (University and Small Business
    Patent Procedures Act of 1980), 58–59, 61, 190
benchmarking, 50, 177, 217n4, 227n35
Bensman, Joseph, 16
"best practices," 187, 208, 217n4; adapted to
    improve revenues, 176; and benchmarking,
    50; brought back by administrators from
    conferences and seminars, 8; and middle-
    status conformity, 7, 22, 47, 48, 53, 100, 141,
    154, 177, 207
biochemistry, 59
biomedical research, 59
biotechnology, 59
Birnbaum, Robert, 50, 109
Board of Trustees Distinguished Professor, 62
"Bologna process," 231n20
bookstores, 189
brain drain, 12–13, 35, 190, 194, 223n2
branding, 50–51; advertising of university during
    televised sporting events, 52–53; architecture,
    53; as "best practice," 48–49; *Chronicle of
    Higher Education* on, 218n9; as conformity, 49;
    and imitation, 141; as joke, 218n8; selling the
    brand, 52–53; website as branding, 51–52
Brint, Steven G., 75, 149, 175, 231n22

British higher education: accountability regime,
    184–87; British Quality Assurance Agency, 184,
    185; and rationalization, 40, 185–86; Research
    Assessment Exercise, 186, 187, 198, 231n21
British Higher Education Funding Council, 184
budget process, 64, 102, 183
Building and Grounds Committee, 95
Building for Undergraduate Education (BUE), 30,
    127–28, 207, 229n25
bureaucratization, 4
Bush, George W., 146, 187

Cambridge University, Great Britain, 40
capitalism, and increased surveillance of "liberal
    professions," 42–43
Center for Entrepreneurship, 173
Center for Regenerative Biology, 61
Center for Science and Technology Commercial-
    ization, 64–65
central administration, Wannabe University, 6–7,
    22; ambivalence toward diversity, 164–72;
    avoidance of negative publicity, 46, 89; bench-
    marking, 50–51; commitment to market logic,
    194; competition with other institutions, 6–7;
    conflation of education and lifestyle, 23; corpo-
    ratization of education, 22; costly attempts to
    make money, 1996–2007, 56–57; "disincen-
    tives" for too little research, 63–64; focus on
    improving national rankings, 23, 118–21, 127;
    hiring of contingent faculty, 125; importance
    of spin, 20, 215n23, 226n14; importance of
    teaching and learning to reputational rankings,
    112–13, 117–18; increase in enrollment without
    increases in faculty size, 122–24; incursions
    into academic affairs, 176, 193–94; mainte-
    nance of legitimacy through University Senate,
    198–200; pressure on faculty to audit them-
    selves, 61; primary goals of attracting students
    and fostering economic development, 12–15;
    professional responsibilities policy, 163–64,
    182, 183; quest for out-of-state students, 27–28;
    search for new "revenue streams" and "key
    revenue drivers," 7, 8, 22; stem-cell research
    and nanotechnology as investment priorities,
    61; structural confusion, 163–64; and student
    outcomes assessment, 106–7; and transforma-
    tion of university, 1–4, 33; 2008 draft strategic
    plan, 194–95, 206, 226n13; "upgrading" of
    research profile, 140; view of accountability
    regime as form of protection, 33; view of news
    reports as form of audit, 45–46; weak social
    control mechanisms, 204–5. *See also* organiza-
    tional culture, Wannabe University

centralization, politics of, 4, 22, 88–92, 205; and accountability regime, 92; enabled through professional managers, 79–80; gradual institutionalization of legitimacy, 105–7

Chronicle of Higher Education: on accreditation agencies, 143; on branding, 218n9; on college president turnover, 214n11; discussion of problems when boards engage in micromanagement, 85; identification of wannabe universities, 15, 60, 70; report on student unions, 53; and universities' goal of top rankings, 10

Clark, Burton, 5, 6, 7, 8, 95

class size: effect on pedagogy, 124–25; enrollment strains on, 122–23, 224n21

"coercive accountability," 12, 180

collaboration, 159

College of Continuing Studies, downgraded to division, 97

College of Liberal Arts and Sciences: committee of liaisons, 147; Courses and Curriculum Committee, 130; increase in funded research, 64; increase in student body and strain on courses, 122–23; 2006 strategic plan, 194, 195–96

commensuration, 118, 197, 225n6

Commission on the Future of Higher Education, 142, 214n18, 219n19

commodification, 4, 41; of knowledge and job preparation, 11; of research, 174–78; and student outcomes assessment, 149

"community of learners," 113

compliance, logic of, 192–94

computer technologies, 59

Conant, James, 214n14

conformity, 218n10; and advertising, 49; association of middle status with, 36; as dialectic between imitation and individuation, 49; and management fads, 49, 50–51; motivation for, 36; process of, 37; of Wannabe student body, 49; and web pages, 49. *See also* middle-status conformist, Wannabe University as

consulting firms (headhunters), 69

contingent faculty labor, exploitation of, 125

continuous quality improvement, 50

continuous quality management, 144

corporatization, 22, 49, 59, 205, 206

Coser, Rose Laub, 215n20, 220n11

Council of Deans, 96, 102, 103, 104, 232n10

Daniels, Richard (Rick) (president, 2007–), 21, 207; awareness of links among research, revenues, and graduate education, 175; and data mining about graduate students, 177–81; and diversity planning, 172; and elimination of programs, 181; faculty attitudes toward, 173, 230n8; management style, 208–9; and Office of Institutional Research, 180; search for new revenue streams, 173; task of strengthening university, 152–53; on University Senate composition, 200

Darning, Samuel (provost under President Oakes), attempt to fold schools, 98–99, 129

data, as agent of change, 179–81

data-based management, 179

"data mining," 23, 177–81, 198

dean of admissions, 224n19

deans, Wannabe University: activities limited to own school, 94; creative accounting, 183; dean of graduate school and NRC rankings, 120–21; decreased authority to run their colleges, 102–5; massive turnover in, 93; reaction to Wesley's academic plan, 104; reappointment based on grant activity, 64; School of Human Development of Family Studies, 99–100; support of department heads, 201; typical day of, 76; view of selves as mediators between administration and departments, 103. *See also* Alden, Todd (dean of College of Arts and Sciences)

de-churching of universities, 41–42, 190

departments. *See* academic departments

deprofessionalization, 42–47

DiMaggio, Paul, 38, 89, 214n8, 218n10

disciplinary associations, merging of concerns with professional managers, 85

distinguished teaching professorships, 62, 137

diversity, organizational ambivalence, 164–72, 193, 229n20

Division of Student Affairs, Office of Off-Campus Services, 106

donors, response to negative publicity about university, 46

Douglas, Mary, 198

Duderstadt, James: *A University for the Twenty-first Century*, 73, 202

Duke University: "Professors of the Practice," 30; profit from biological and technological research, 59

dysfunctional departments, 18

Eckel, Peter, 4–5, 159

education vs. training, 41

elite private universities, 10

"elite status," reference to social class, 10

Eminent Scientists Program, 173

"empire-builder," 128

employment patterns, increase in contingent labor force, 38

entrepreneurial activities, 13
Espeland, Wendy, 118, 197
Etzkowitz, Henry, 59, 191
European universities, 205
Evans, Mary, 40, 186, 188, 197
"excess capacity," 122–23
external auditors, 43
external politics, 88, 89
external reviews, 23, 31–32, 181–82

faculty "entrepreneurs," 25
faculty grants and contracts: charging of tuition
    of graduate assistants to, 108–9, 177, 222n30,
    230n11; direct costs, 57; indirect costs, 57–58,
    63; productivity measure of graduate program
    quality, 206. See also funded research
faculty in residence, 125
faculty members, Wannabe University: and the
    audit culture, 61–65, 197; criticism of admin-
    istrators and trustees who make changes
    without faculty input, 81–82; cumulative
    pressures of administrative discontinuity,
    154–61, 162–63, 203; disincentives for too little
    research, 63–64; downward mobility, 219n4;
    forms for application for promotion and
    tenure, 106; increase in number of part-time
    instructors, 68; lack of input into administra-
    tive initiatives, 78, 159–61; less than 6 percent
    people of color in 1994, 28; loss of collegiality,
    95; methods of opposing centralization,
    107–10; non-monetary and monetary rewards
    for research accomplishments, 61–63; opposi-
    tion to Provost Darning, 98–99; professional
    inertia caused by administration's power
    over academic affairs, 128, 202–5; reaction to
    distinguished professorships, 62; on regional
    campuses, 94–95; resistance to inclusion of
    research assistants' tuition in grants, 108–9;
    ritual compliance, 109–10; self-protection
    strategies, 155–57; some agreement with
    administrative initiatives, 110–11; some resis-
    tance to change, 26, 31; tensions with BUE
    programs, 127–28, 129; and tenure review
    cases, 162, 228n14; and "transformation" of
    the university, 3, 26; use of Senate or Gradu-
    ate Faculty Council to oppose centralization,
    108–9; view of administrators, 89–90; view of
    teaching role, 113–14, 116–17
faculty research, 174–75; commodification of,
    58–59, 174–78; disincentives for too little,
    63–64; external recognition of, 116; importance
    of to promotion and tenure, 115–16; incentives
    for, 61–63; as measure of schools and deans,

64; relation to income and graduate educa-
    tion, 175–76; as service to the state, 174–75; vs.
    teaching, 113–17
faculty teaching assessment. See student out-
    comes assessment
federal government, indirect power over teaching
    through accreditation agencies, 142–45
federal patent policy, 58–59
"Finish in Four" program, 124
first-generation college students, 164
First-Year Experience Program, 30, 118, 127,
    128–29
fitness center, 53
Foucault, Michel, 40, 102; panopticon, 45
Freeman, John, 177, 188, 189, 190
Friedland, Roger, 213n7, 217n3
full-time non-tenure instructors, 125
funded research, 60–61; staffing requirements,
    64–65
Furedi, Frank, 187–88

Gamson, Zelda F., 216n15
Gawley, Tim, 183
Geiger, Roger, 11
General Education Oversight Committee
    (GEOC), 147
globalized capitalist economy, 192
Gmelch, Walter H., 76, 103, 202
Gombrich, Richard, 186, 231n22
graduate admissions, 178
Graduate Faculty Council, 111
graduate programs, development of metrics to
    measure quality, 179–81
Grodal, Stine, 59
Gumport, Patricia, 49, 217n3

Hannan, Michael T., 177, 188, 189, 190
Hardway, Bill (chairman of the board, 2003–
    2009), 175, 220n2; attempts to control media
    reports, 86–87; control of administration, 86,
    94, 98; on lines of authority, 101; reporting of
    Wilson to, 168
Harvard University: decentralized schools, 102;
    as quasi-wannabe, 214n14
Harvey, David, 226n13, 231n22
Hawthorne, Lloyd, 180
Healey, Peter, 59
health care industry, 190, 192
health maintenance organizations (HMOs), 42
higher education: de-churching of universities,
    41–42, 190; deprofessionalization, 42–47;
    funding crisis beginning in 1970s, 190; highly
    stratified, 10; industrialization of, 41; logics of,

192–93; reorganization of in late nineteenth century, 40–41

higher education, as changing industry: demographic transformation, 53–56; directed toward national wealth creation, 59; as growth industry in 1970s, 53–54; new view of as industry rather than social institution, 49; obsession with ranking and market ethos, 11; promotion of research by federal government, 54; and transformation of knowledge into capital, 59; trends, 53–56; universal education in 1980s, 53–56

higher-education publishing, 189

Higher Graduation Rate Program, 118

hiring letters, administrative review of, 163–64

history, Wannabe University: first national sports title, 29; largest employer in region, 33; latecomer to "reputational arms race," 29; reputation as "party school," 33–34; scandals reported in state media, 46–47; start as two-year agricultural school, 27; tuition, 21; university in 1996, 7, 27–35

Honors Program, 30, 125, 127

Howard, Philip N., 189

hyper-instrumental rationality, 185–86

ideological institutions, and accountability regime, 188–91

imitation: limit of, 141–42; and management fads, 50

individually designed major, 30, 125, 127

individuation, and management fads, 50

industrialization, 41

information dissemination: board attempts to control media reports, 19, 86–87; dedication to spin, 20

Institute for Student Success, 30, 127

Institute for Teaching and Learning, 114, 127, 207; Instructional Design Department website, 150; staffing, 30, 66, 138; stress on caring teaching techniques, 150; training in digital technologies, 225n5

institutional logics, 49, 185, 192–93, 219n2; competing, 194–98, 217n3. See also market ethos

institutional memory, 203, 232n11

"institutional transformation": in changing society, 39–40; in literature about higher education, 4–7; social-scientific explanation of long-term change, 40–41

instrumental rationality, 185–86

intellectual property, 7

Interdisciplinary Course and Curriculum Committee, 129

internal audits, 43, 182

internal control system, 144–45

internal politics, 88, 89

internal promotions, 67

internationalism, fashionable fad of 2005–2008, 171

international students, 207

international study, 193

introductory receptions, ceremonial and political, 88

isomorphism, 38

Jackall, Robert, 76

Jacobs, Jack (professor and department head), 79

Johnson, Tyler (provost under President Whitmore), 21, 92; accomplishments at the university, 155; attempt to fold schools, 99; departure for presidency of another university, 68, 88; emphasis on funded research, 154; failure to impose harmony among administrators, 126; introduction of "disincentives" for too little research, 63–64; introduction of "postdoctoral teaching fellow" or "faculty in residence," 125; introduction of "research incentive award," 62–63; investment in stem-cell research, 61; opposition to hiring goals for underrepresented groups, 170, 220n4; "Policy on Faculty Professional Responsibilities," 163, 183; struggle for power against deans, 93

Karabel, Jerome, 175, 231n22

Keller, George, 32–33, 218n13; Academic Strategy, 54–55

Keohane, Nannerl, 41, 173, 194

Kerr, Clark, 25, 208, 218n13

Kezar, Adrianna, 159

Kirp, David, 50, 224n19

knowledge, transformation into capital, 59, 191

land-grant colleges, 27, 205

Latino students, underrepresentation at Wannabe, 165–66

Lavin, David, 55

legal education, reorganization of, 41–42

legitimacy, 198–200, 221n12

Leslie, Larry L., 43, 59, 216n25

Lewis, Lionel, 115, 142, 196

Lewis, Michael, 232n11

Lombardi Program on Measuring University Performance of the University of Florida (TheCenter), 120

Long, Ralph (president of Respectable Research University), 93

long-term change, theories of, 40–41
Lynch, Peter (assistant to President Whitmore), 3, 47, 77; and undergraduate housing shortage, 90–91

Making News (Tuchman), 18
management, politics of, 82–87
management by objectives, 50
management fads, 49, 50–51
market ethos, transformation of educational values to business values, 7–8, 174, 189, 192, 194, 205, 213n7
Marx, Karl, 231n22
"master teachers," 30
"the Matthew Effect," 230n6
Matthews, Mary (former vice provost of education and instruction), 30, 116, 121; expansion of administration's involvement in teaching and learning, 127, 128, 154, 161; and Office of Undergraduate Education and Instruction, 112–13; turf wars with Steibel and Alden, 122, 125–26
McDonaldization, 186, 187
McLuhan, Marshall, 187
mechanistic bureaucracy, 94, 104, 156, 204, 221n20
medical education, reorganization of, 41–42
merit forms, 182–84, 186
merit raises, 64, 115, 205
methodology, 15–21
middle managers: mission to improve retention and graduation rates, 119; suggest procedures that have worked elsewhere, 153–54
middle status, association with conformity, 36
middle-status conformist, Wannabe University as, 22, 35–37, 208; architecture, 53; fitness center, 53; introduction of same "innovations" as other middle-status research universities, 36–37; management fads, 49, 50–51; "mission statements," 50; student union, 53
Miller, Laura J., 189
Mills, C. Wright, 91
mission statements, 20, 113, 215n1; and conformity, 50; for each department, 219n20; emphasis on importance of teaching by 2005, 136; failure to mention diversity in 2006, 168; lack of emphasis on teaching in mid-1990s, 117
modernity, and academic change, 40–41
Morrill, Calvin, 221n20
Morrill Act, 27, 174, 205
Muller, Chet (department head), 161, 162–63, 164, 201, 228n13
multiculturalism, 166; "good for business," 208; and tenure, 229n20. *See also* diversity

nanotechnology, 61, 219n22
Naples, Nancy, 76
National Academy of Engineering, 34, 121
National Academy of Sciences, 34, 77, 120, 121
National Advisory Committee on Institutional Quality and Integrity, 143
National Collegiate Athletic Association (NCAA): book of regulations, 8; Division IA schools and black athletes, 28
National Institutes of Health, 54, 83
National Research Council, 83, 120; rankings of quality of doctoral programs in U.S., 34, 224n17
National Science Foundation, 54
negative publicity, cost in money and power, 46
neo-liberalism, 141, 231n22; and decreased funds for higher education, 58–59
new institutionalism, 38–39, 82, 214n8, 221n12
new managerialism, 11, 22, 73, 83–85
news coverage, as expression of "relations of ruling," 19–20
news reports, validity of as data sources, 18–19
non-faculty professionals: increase in those engaged in "quality assurance," "development activities," and "incubation" of faculty ideas, 22, 66; numbers of full- and part-time at U.S. institutions, 1976–1995, 67; numbers of full- and part-time at Wannabe University, 1998–2007, 67; and shift in character of labor force, 66
North Carolina University at Chapel Hill, profit from biological and technological research, 59
North Central Association of Colleges and Schools, 143

Oakes, Ned (acting president, 1990; president, 1991–1996), 129; attempt to start research park, 60; change in board membership, 8; construction program, 8; emphasis on athletics, 26–27; identification of athletes as key to change, 8
Office of Institutional Research, 180
Office of Multiculturalism and Diversity, 166, 167
Office of Multiculturalism and International Affairs (renamed), 166, 206
Oklahoma State University, 70
open patents, 59
organizational change: and adaptation to "technical environment," 37; theories of, 37–39
organizational culture, Wannabe University, 95; administrative control of deans, departments, and colleges, 95, 102; differing emphasis of each succeeding provost, 161–62; emphasis

on long workday and workweek, 157–58; loci of academic power, 95; managerial styles, 159–60; as "mechanistic bureaucracy," 94, 104; neo-institutionalism, 38–39; and "new managerialism," 11

out-of-state yield rate, 118

outreach, 154, 227n5

outside administrators (professional managers), 72–73; attitudes toward authority, 79–80; conduct that professors perceive as bullying, 79–80; constraints upon, 75–76; as corporate beings, 75–76; enable centralization of authority and bureaucratic rule, 80; exclusion from some aspects of local culture, 76–77; faculty view of, 74–82; involvement with national organizations, 84; likelihood of moving from one organization to another, 78, 93; more likely than insiders to introduce radical change, 73–74; and power, 73–74, 75; publications of, 77–78

"outsider," as social-psychological or structural designation, 76

parking spaces, average price of maintaining, 39, 216n18

participant observation, 16, 17

part-time instructors, 125; increase in, 22; solution to budgetary constraints, 38

patents, 13, 174; and Bayh-Dole Act, 58–59, 61, 190; open, 59; on university logos and mascots, 218n16

peer evaluation, 134, 138–39, 146

people of color: on board of trustees, 169–70; isolation of at Wannabe University, 17–18; less than 6 percent on faculty in 1994, 28; middle managers on issues of race and racism, 168–69; underrepresentation as students at Wannabe, 165–66

PeopleSoft, 222n27, 226n14

pharmacology, 59

Phillips, Damon J., 36

"Points of Pride," 3–4, 150, 152

policies and procedures, objectified as relations of ruling, 20

"Policy on Faculty Professional Responsibilities," 163, 183

postdoctoral teaching fellow, 125

post-tenure review, 163, 183–84

Powell, Walter W., 38, 59, 89, 214n8, 218n10

Power, Michael, 11–12, 44–45, 144–45, 198, 217n31, 232n8

presidents, Wannabe University: appointment of internal search committees to hire provosts,

deans, and vice provosts, 69; departure for "better" research universities, 70; mostly professional presidents since 1980s, 69. See also Daniels, Richard (Rick) (president, 2007–); Oakes, Ned (president, 1990–1996); Whitmore, James (president, 1996–2007)

private research universities, top spots in U.S. News & World Report's "America's Best Colleges," 55

professional associations, role in "new managerialism," 83–84

professional logic, 192

professional managers. See non-faculty professionals; outside administrators

professional meetings, centrality to "new managerialism," 84–85

professional presidents, 69, 84

professional responsibilities policy, 163–64, 182, 183

professions, expansion of accounting and statistics within, 43

professoriate: conflicts between those in professional schools and those in liberal arts and sciences, 6; conflicts between younger and older, 26, 32, 162, 202; emphasis on scholarship, 115–16; as "managed professionals," 42; orientation toward discipline, 6; reaction to administrative emphasis on undergraduate education, 23; review of relationship with administration, 22; view of administrators as "managers," 6; view of own activities as essence of the university, 6

programmatic goals, 50

program reviews, 216n9; and intra-field conflicts, 31–32; suppression of dissent, 32

provosts, Wannabe University: departure for better jobs elsewhere, 69–70; differing emphases, 161–62. See also Darning, Samuel (provost under President Oakes); Johnson, Tyler (provost under President Whitmore); Tremaine, Mike (provost under President Whitmore); Wesley, Gerald (provost under President Whitmore)

public research universities. See research universities

public service logic, 192

pure knowledge, 205

"pure" university scientists, 174, 230n4

rationalization, 40, 185–86, 205

rationalized scheduling, 41

"recapturing indirect costs," 57–58

Regional Accreditation Agency (RAA), 23; and student outcomes assessment, 144 "relations of ruling": and faculty assessment program, 138; news coverage as expression of, 19–20

research. *See* faculty research

Research and Development Corporation, 65

Research Assessment Exercise, 186, 187, 198, 231n21

research incentive awards (RIAs), 62–63, 108, 222n29

research parks, 60

research professorships, 62

research revenue stream: cost of promoting, 65–68; doubled from 1997 through 2007, 64

research universities: combat for research funds and recognition in 1990s, 29; combination of four different ideals, 173–74; deans report to provost, 102; decline in state support, 55–56; education resembles training at community colleges, 175; efforts to attract traditional customer base, 55; embedded in corporate and global purposes and practices, 49, 59; faculty senates, 215n3; marketing of brands, 49; mission statements, 136; new administrative relationship to professoriate, 21; new emphasis on business, 21; new ways to increase "revenue streams," 49–50; northern, and local competition, 70–71; organizational ambivalence, 23; practical solutions to problems of twenty-first century, 56–57; and research parks, 60; stability of rankings in status hierarchy, 36; traditionally lower importance of teaching relative to research, 113, 114, 115

resource allocation, 57

Respectable Research University, 93

retirement receptions, 1–2

Rhoades, Gary, 10, 42, 59, 65, 66

Ritzer, George, 185, 186, 187

"the road to nowhere," 90–91, 91, 95

Rockwell, Norman, 42

Ruggie, Mary, 231n22

rules and regulations, 20

Sandburg, Carl, 105

Sauder, Michael, 118

scholarship about teaching and learning (SATL), 114–15

School of Allied Health, dissolving of, 97, 98

School of Business, expansion of, 123

School of Education, production of computer programs, 65

School of Engineering Center for Fuel Cell Research, 61

School of Human Development and Family Studies, dissolving of, 97, 98

School of Pharmacy, expansion of, 123

Science Citation Index, 220n8

Scott, W. Richard, 190

secondary audits, 44

self-study, 144–45

Selznick, Philip, 222n28

senior administrators, cost of replacement, 66–68

Senior-Year Experience, 129

shared governance, 26, 196, 203

Sharpe, Jean (vice provost for education and instruction), 131; on assessment, 197–98; co-chair of Task Force on Teaching, Learning, and Assessment, 132–33; and data-based management, 179; "good organizational reasons" for teaching assessment, 136, 137; incursions into faculty affairs, 129–30; Interdisciplinary Course and Curriculum Committee, 129–30; loyalty to provost, 75, 207; and retention of underrepresented minority groups, 170

Shore, Chris, 45

signature programs, 48, 217n1, 228n12

Simmel, Georg, 49, 219n3

Slaughter, Sheila, 43, 58–59, 216n25

Small Town in Mass Society (Vidich and Bensman), 16

Smith, Charles, 213n7

Smith, Dorothy E., 19–20, 42–43, 217n31, 231n22

Snydman, Stuart K., 217n3

social sciences, departments in "receivership," 31–32

Spellings, Margaret (secretary of education), 142, 149, 187

spin, importance of to central administration, 20, 215n23, 226n14

Sporn, Barbara, 65, 66

staff. *See* non-faculty professionals

staff, expansion of (non-faculty) professional. *See* non-faculty professionals

staffing requirements: for funded research, 64–65; Institute for Teaching and Learning, 30, 66, 138

stakeholders, 85, 99, 172, 221n16

Stanford University, profit from biological and technological research, 59

Starr, Paul, 189

State Capitol Record, 19, 46–47, 89; online version, 197

state funding, decrease in, 7–8

state legislators: ambitions for Wannabe University, 35; interest in higher education as preparation for workforce, 22, 189; response to negative publicity about Wannabe, 46

Steibel, Victor (vice provost for enrollment management), 121; "Finish in Four" program, 124; lack of resources for international education, 167; remarks on diversity, 165, 166; and retention of underrepresented minority groups, 170, 229n19; on retention rates and rankings, 119; survey of students who did not choose Wannabe, 34; turf wars with Matthews and Alden, 122

Stevens, Mitchell, 197, 213n1

Stinchcombe, Arthur, 141, 177

strategic plan, Wannabe University: claim that learning environment promotes research, 136; importance of diversity, 168

strategic planning, 50, 218n13

Strathern, Marilyn, 40, 207, 217n31

structural confusion, consequences of, 163–64

structural inertia, 177

student body, Wannabe University: almost entirely white in 1994, 28; conformity, 49; effect of expansion on advising and enrichment programs, 125; effect of expansion on class size, 122–23; expansion of, 1998–99, 27–28; most black men as athletes in 1994, 28; in 1996, 33

student-centered education, 149–51; conflation of learning with student life, 150; conflation of learning with style, 151

Student Evaluation of Teacher Instruments (SETIs), 132, 225n6

student outcomes assessment, 23, 132–41, 187; assembly-line analogy, 148; and distinguished teaching professorships, 137; faculty and departmental coercion, 146–47; faculty attitudes toward, 133–35, 137–40; federal accountability threat, 130, 131, 142–45, 148–49; meetings to discuss, 147; peer observations, 134, 138–39, 146; stress on new technologies, 134; teaching portfolios, 134–35, 146

student unions, 53, 149

Sugarman, Mike (chairman of the board, 1997–2003), 166, 168, 208

summative evaluations, 134, 146

surveillance, 41; audits as form of, 47; in British universities, 40

Taking the Reins (Eckel and Kezar), 32

Task Force on Teaching, Learning, and Assessment, 113–14, 115, 131–32; claim of observer objectivity in classroom observations, 138–39;

recommendations sent to University Senate for approval, 135; and "workforce development of faculty," 132, 134

teaching and learning: central control of, 129–30; stress on importance of in Wannabe bylaws, 114, 136–37. See also student outcomes assessment

teaching assistants, 68

teaching portfolios, 134–35, 146

"teaching professors," 30

teaching role, overlooked in promotion and tenure system, 113–14

teaching vs. research, 113–17

technology transfers, 7

television advertising, 52–53

Texas Technical University, 70

Thatcher, Margaret, 184

Thornton, Patricia H., 189

Thyme (professor), 138

"total quality management," 50

town-gown relations, 76–77

transparent procedures, as form of surveillance, 44

Tremaine, Mike (provost under President Whitmore): campaign to improve undergraduate teaching, 30, 154; emphasis on multiculturalism and diversity, 166; facilitation of funded research, 60; failure to impose harmony among administrators, 126; initiatives, 29–30, 155, 158; new hires to help improve national rankings, 121–22; positioning for future career steps, 126–27; program reviews, 30–31, 100; reorganization of administration, 27

"triple helix," 59, 191

trustees, board of, 2; African American members, 169–70; appointment of Whitmore, 8; changes in, 85–86; committee heads, 169; public meetings of as ceremonial, 87; as university professionals, 85–87

truth to power, willingness to speak, 155, 156, 157, 227n8

Turow, Joseph, 189

University of Michigan: senior administrators whom President Duderstadt thanks for help during his presidency, 74

University of South Carolina, 70

University of Utah, 70

University of Wisconsin, patenting of biological discoveries, 59

university receptions, 1–2

university research. See faculty research

University Senate: Executive Committee, 199; Faculty Standards Committee, 96, 108, 115, 135, 136–37, 187; and maintenance of legitimacy for central administration, 198–200; presence of administrators in, 199–200, 215n3; Scholastic Standards Committee, 135; and shared governance, 198–99; Student Welfare Committee, 149

U.S. Department of Education, and accreditation agencies, 143–45

U.S. News & World Report annual college rankings, 4, 7, 117, 218n5; association with "elite" status, 10; criticized both theoretically and methodologically, 223n9; efforts of colleges and universities to change practices to attain, 118; emphasis on teaching and learning, 119; indicators more easily manipulated by universities than other measures of quality, 119–21; influence on law school admissions, 214n13; research university reliance on, 23. *See also* commensuration

Veblen, Thorstein: *Higher Education in America*, 5, 216n24

vice president for student affairs, 213n2

Vidich, Arthur, 16

visiting professors, solution to budgetary constraints, 38

wannabe universities: competition for high ranking, 10–11; defined, 15

Wannabe University Foundation, 56

Wannabe University Research and Development Corporation, 64–65

Wannabe Weekly, 20, 30; listing of provosts' accomplishments, 19; published by Office of University Relations, 19; reports on commercial development of faculty research, 65, 207; on university's web philosophy, 20

Washburn, Jennifer, 50

Weber, Max, 11

website, Wannabe University, 19, 20; as branding, 51–52; no mention of education, 150; no mention of scandals at Wan U, 215n22; "parents'" website, 51–52

Webster, Andrew, 59

Wesley, Gerald (provost under President Whitmore), 61; "academic restructuring plan," 21, 22, 96–102, 158, 159–60; ambivalence toward diversity issues, 171–72; approval of hiring goals for underrepresented groups, 170, 220n4; on assessment, 131; concentration of power in central administration, 91–92, 94–97, 98, 101–2; "corporate outsider" and "professional manager," 98; elimination of programs, 102–5, 129, 181; emphasis on outreach, 154; and external accountability threat, 148–49; and external review process, 182; funding of assistant vice provost for assessment, 131; and graduate program quality, 176; and increased authority of "business side" over "academic side," 100; introduction of, 88, 92–94; loss of two-thirds of deans under, 102–5, 129; managerial style, 159–60; past jobs, 93–94; push to charge granting agency for graduate students' tuition, 109; task forces, 96; use of accountability regime to justify actions, 100. *See also* Task Force on Teaching, Learning, and Assessment

Western Association of Schools and Colleges, 142–45

Whitmore, James (president, 1996–2007): control of budget, 29; "corporate" vice provosts for research under, 60; diversity initiatives under, 166–72; emphasis on business, 25; emphasis on quantified accomplishments, 4; facilitation of funded research, 60; goals, 14–15; hiring of consulting firm, 227n9; hiring of staff to promote research, 64–66; on impact of increased enrollment, 123–24; introduction of Provost Wesley, 92; language of managerial literature about higher education, 4; management style, 208; as "professional president," 8–9; role in trustees' meeting in 2002 and 2005, 86; search for revenue streams associated with biology, 61; theme of university in "Top Twenty-five," 9, 152; and transformation of university, 1, 3, 5, 25, 152–53; turnover of provosts under, 154–55; and undergraduate housing shortage, 90–91; weekly meeting with vice presidents and directors, 20, 95

Wilson, Kevin (vice provost for multiculturalism), 166; reports to board of trustees, 169–70; staving off attempts to dismantle office, 170–72; warding off attacks on program, 167–68

Wolverton, Mimi, 76, 103, 202

Women's Center, 166

Women's Studies Program, 166, 167

workforce development, as purpose of higher education, 11, 22, 189, 191, 226n7

Writing Center, 30, 127

"zero base budgeting," 50

Zuckerman, E. W., 36